Just Another Maniac Monday

Jennie Marts

Copyright © 2014 by Jennie Marts
All rights reserved under International and Pan-American Copyright Conventions

By payment of required fees, you have been granted the *non-exclusive*, *non*-transferable right to access and read the text of this book. No part of this text may be reproduced, transmitted, downloaded, decompiled, reverse engineered, or stored in or introduced into any information storage and retrieval system, in any form or by any means, whether electronic or mechanical, now known or hereinafter invented without the express written permission of copyright owner.

Please Note

The reverse engineering, uploading, and/or distributing of this book via the internet or via any other means without the permission of the copyright owner is illegal and punishable by law. Please purchase only authorized electronic editions, and do not participate in or encourage electronic piracy of copyrighted materials. Your support of the author's rights is appreciated

No part of this book may be reproduced or transmitted in any form or by any electronic or mechanical means, including photocopying, recording or by any information storage and retrieval system, without the written permission of the publisher, except where permitted by law.

Thank you.

Cover Design and Interior format by The Killion Group
http://thekilliongroupinc.com

Meta Data: romantic comedy, humorous women's fiction, cozy mystery, dog lovers, small town romance, series, chick lit, Colorado author, kindle best seller, Kansas, summer, 1950s

DEDICATION

*This book is dedicated to
Todd, Tyler and Nick
My family, my joy, my loves
Thanks for always believing in my dreams!*

JUST ANOTHER MANIAC MONDAY

Edna Allen grumbled as she pushed her ancient bones off the sofa and crossed the living room, her slippered feet slapping the floor with each step. Mondays were her lazy days, and even though it was close to noon, she was still in her pajamas and quite engrossed in her morning shows. Whoever was ringing her doorbell was interrupting the spinning of the prize wheel.

Her mind was busy calculating the difference between the current value of a vacuum cleaner versus a washing machine when she absently opened the front door. The remote control slipped from her hand and hit the floor as she took in the sight on her front stoop. Holding a red rose in one hand and a small dog tucked into the crook of his arm stood a ghost.

He looked like a man, but the man he resembled was dead. He had died a long time ago. Or maybe she was dead. Maybe she had stroked out between the bonus round and the Showcase Showdown and this *was* heaven. Maybe heaven was really just watching game shows in your pajamas all day and having the love of your life appear suddenly on your doorstep.

Except she didn't feel dead. As a matter of fact, she could feel her heart beating strong and quick, threatening to pound free of her sunken chest.

And he sure didn't *look* dead. In fact, he looked pretty good in a gray three-piece suit, his skin tanned and his once blond hair now pure white. Beyond his shoulder, Edna could see old Mr. Ferguson mowing his lawn and she knew there was no way that old coot would ever make it into heaven, so either she was still alive or there was a worse alternative.

If she *was* still alive, then Johnny Collins was really standing on her doorstep.

A hundred memories flooded her mind. She had dreamt of this moment a thousand times. She'd planned a hundred scenarios of what she would do. What she would say. But none of those clever thoughts came to mind as she opened her mouth to speak. "What in the Sam-Hill are you doing here?"

The ghost chuckled softly, the familiar twinkle in his crystal blue eyes. "You haven't changed a bit, Eddy."

Edna's knees threatened to buckle at the familiar nickname that only one man had ever called her. "Of course I've changed. And more than a bit. The last time you saw me, I was a young girl. Now I'm an old woman. It's been almost sixty years since you've seen me."

"It feels like yesterday," he said. "You look as beautiful as the first day I met you."

Heat warmed her cheeks as she took in the sight of the first man she had ever loved. He stood around six feet tall and was well dressed. A satin square of royal-blue handkerchief poked from his breast pocket and the color matched his eyes. The eyes that had looked into hers and pledged to love her until the day he died. And she thought he had.

She blinked, tears filling her eyes. "Johnny? Is it really you?"

He nodded, a slow bob of his head, never taking his eyes off of hers. "Yes, it's me. I'm really here."

Choking back the emotion welling in her throat, she shook her head in wonder. "I thought you were dead."

"I know. That's what I wanted everyone to think." His expression turned deeply sad for just a moment, then the charming smile returned as he tipped his head. "Are you going to invite me in?"

Edna wiped at the stray tear on her face and narrowed her eyes. "I haven't decided yet."

She nodded at the small dog under his arm. He was a cute little guy with big brown eyes and brown and white spotted fur. She recognized the breed as a Jack Russell terrier, but only because the dog looked similar to the one on *Frasier*. "What's with the dog?"

He looked down at the pup and laughed. "I'm not sure. He found me a year or so ago and adopted me. No matter where I go, I can't seem to shake him."

She took a step back and motioned for him to come inside. Reaching out her hand, she brushed his arm as he passed. He felt real. And the moist slobber, where the dog had licked her outstretched hand, was definitely real.

The man walked into the center of the room and set the dog on the hardwood floor. Edna's home was a sprawling ranch style with a full basement. The living room was large, with a hallway leading to three bedrooms. A tall archway led into a generous-sized kitchen with a big center island separating the cooking area from the dining area. An antique china hutch sat against the wall behind a round farmhouse table with chairs for six.

Depending on where you stood, you could see between the living room and kitchen. Edna had her television placed against the wall so if she were standing at the kitchen counter, she'd still see her shows. She had to turn the volume up loud enough for the neighbors to hear it, but she didn't give two hoots what the neighbors thought.

Her decorating style was a cross between country and kitschy, combining antique memorabilia with modern appliances. She loved bright colors and daringly mixed different patterns, crossing polka-dots with plaids. Edna knew what she liked. So what if it was a little outdated and probably too cluttered; it was home.

She watched the little dog run in front of the couch and into the kitchen, where he stopped to sniff at the kitchen table. He finished his sniff then turned, raised his leg, and peed on the table leg. Sitting down, he looked to his master as if expecting a treat for his actions.

Edna also looked at his master. She tilted her head and raised an eyebrow. "Seriously?"

He smiled and shrugged. "Sorry. The silly mutt never listens to me. Hand me a paper towel, and I'll wipe it up." He set the rose gingerly on the table, then leaned down to the dog. "I told you to behave. Remember, this is why I had you go outside before we rang the doorbell."

Edna stepped into the kitchen and pulled several paper towels from the roll under the counter. Handing them to Johnny, she silently watched as he bent to wipe up the mess and deposit the soiled towels in the trash can.

Anyone who knew Edna would never describe her as silent. Ever. She *always* had a comment or a piece of advice to add to any conversation. But for the first time in a long time, she was at a loss for words. It was as if the arrival of this man, this memory from her past, stirred up so many emotions that there was no room for words.

Standing at the counter, her feelings tumbled inside of her like a load of laundry in the dryer. A load with a tennis shoe mixed inside that clunked and thunked against the barrel with every rotation. The soaring joy of seeing him again mixed with a deep sadness of the last six decachaptedes she had missed out on. The shock of his being alive blended with the awe of seeing his face again. Of being able to look in his eyes and hear his low rumble of laughter.

But the shoe still thunked through the exciting tumble of emotions. The heavy shoe filled with the dull thud of anger. Anger at his letting all these years go by without telling her he was alive. And inside the anger, a tiny flutter of fear swirled. Fear that maybe he hadn't really loved her at all.

Her thoughts raged with a million questions she wanted to ask. *How can you still be alive? Where have you been? Why didn't you come back sooner? Why are you back now?*

Multiple questions flooded her mind, but her heart only had one. *Why did you leave me?*

But she didn't ask any of these questions. Instead, she stood silently watching him, feeling surreal as she wondered how the love of her life had just walked through her door and was now cleaning dog pee up off the floor.

He seemed quite at home in her kitchen, crossing to the sink and turning on the water. She watched him squirt liquid soap into his cupped palm and rub his hands together, forming a soapy lather. His hands were good hands, strong hands, the hands of a working man. Edna remembered the feel of those hands sliding across her body as if it were yesterday.

How could he be here? Alive and well, washing his hands in her sink and using her favorite blue-checked towel to dry them. She gestured to the living room and followed him in.

He sat on one end of the sofa and the little dog jumped up and stretched out across his lap, looking at Edna with an adorable expression of "sorry I peed on your floor, but don't you think I'm so darn cute?"

Johnny patted the dog on his head and chuckled. "He does grow on you. His name is Havoc."

"I can see why." Picking up a small pillow, Edna eased herself onto the chair across from him. She held the pillow in her lap, feeling awkward, as if she suddenly forgot how to sit in a chair, as if her arms and legs were separate from her body and she didn't quite know what to do with them.

"Oh, you haven't seen anything yet." He settled back into the sofa and smiled at Edna. "So, how have you been?"

Really? Edna lifted the small pillow and threw it at him. The pillow bounced off the sofa, missing its intended target and fell to the floor. Havoc jumped off the couch, growling, and attacked the pillow, gripping the corner in his teeth and shaking it back and forth.

The man looked shocked and slightly amused. "What was that for?"

Edna shrugged. "It is called a throw pillow."

"But why did you throw it at me?"

"Why wouldn't I throw it at you? Because I'm shocked that you're here. And mad that you let me think you were dead all these years." Her voice faltered and her anger slipped into disbelief. "Or maybe just to prove that you're real. Or that I'm not dreaming." She pinched her arm. "Nope. Not dreaming."

"I can assure you that you are awake, and I am very much alive and real."

Edna sank back into the chair. "How can you be? The Johnny Collins I knew died a long time ago. I went to his funeral." She choked back the emotion welling in her throat. "Is it really you, Johnny?" she whispered.

His blue eyes filled with tears and he nodded. "It's really me, Eddy. I can't tell you how sorry I am to have put you through that." He took a deep breath and cleared his throat. "It's been a long time since anyone's called me Johnny. I just go by John now."

Edna shook her head, the pain of the memories bubbling to the surface in anger and resentment. How much she'd loved him, the plans they'd made, the agony of sitting at his funeral, feeling left behind and knowing she'd never see his face again.

Yet, here he was. He had left her, but it seemed now to have been his choice. "John. Johnny. John Jacob Jingleheimer Schmidt. I don't give two hoots what name you go by. What are you doing here? And how could you have let me believe you were dead?"

Before he could answer, a knock sounded and they heard the back door of the house open. Edna's neighbor Sunny Vale walked in from the kitchen carrying a measuring cup. "I need to borrow an egg, Edna. I was in the mood for chocolate chip cookies but don't have all the ingredients."

Sunny stopped as she spied Edna's unexpected visitor sitting on the sofa. "Oh, sorry. I didn't know you had company."

Edna and Sunny had been neighbors for years and made up two of the five members of the Pleasant Valley Page Turners book club. The women were a close-knit group, though different in age and temperament.

Sunny, Maggie, and Cassie were in their thirties and had been roommates in college. Cassie's seventeen-year-old niece, Piper, had joined the group earlier that summer when her mom deserted her and left her on her aunt's doorstep. Though Edna, in her early eighties, was the oldest member of the group, her spirit was perhaps the youngest, and she liked to keep them all in stitches with her quirky comments and crazy adventures.

The book club had been through a lot that summer, and Sunny, true to her name, kept a cheery disposition and didn't let life get her down. She was an elementary school teacher and had recently found the love of her life. His name was Jake. He loved her dog, had abs to die for, and conveniently lived in the house between hers and Edna's.

Sunny looked from the rose sitting on the table to the man in the three-piece suit and raised her eyebrows at Edna. "Am I interrupting?"

Edna shrugged. "It doesn't matter. Even if I said yes, you wouldn't leave."

Sunny laughed. "No, you're probably right." She approached the man on the couch, stooping to pet Havoc before she held her hand out. "Hi, I'm Sunny."

He took her hand in his. "It's a pleasure to meet you, Sunny. I'm John Collins. I know Edna from a long time ago, when we were practically kids."

Sunny plopped onto the sofa next to John, and Havoc jumped into her lap. "Oh, that's so sweet. How fun for you two to see each other again."

Edna harrumphed. "Yeah, it's been a real barrel of laughs so far."

"Hey, I saw the story about Zoey in the news," Sunny said. "They had a picture of her, and she looked gorgeous."

"Yeah, I saw that too. Her mother called and told me she might show up on the TV." Edna turned to John. "Zoey is my granddaughter. She works as an accountant for some fancy-dancy firm up in Denver and just found some incriminating evidence during a routine audit. She's evidently exposed them for a big money-laundering scheme and ended up in the news."

"How's she doing?" Sunny asked. "It seems like she's getting a lot of press over this thing."

Edna shrugged, the drama of her granddaughter seeming trivial compared to the appearance of John. "I haven't had a chance to talk to her, so I don't really know how big of a deal it is."

"I'm sure you'll hear about it soon enough." Sunny waved a hand in John's direction. "Edna's really close with her granddaughter."

"That's good," John said. "Family can mean everything to some people."

Hmm. What was that supposed to mean? Edna considered asking him but didn't want to get into their history in front of Sunny.

Instead, she nodded to the measuring cup in her neighbor's hands. "Why do you have a measuring cup if you want to borrow an egg? Exactly which ingredients do you *not* have for these chocolate chip cookies?"

"Well, after I mixed in the butter and the sugar, I realized I was out of brown sugar and short an egg. And I'm not sure I have enough vanilla."

Edna laughed. This was not the first time she had played this game. "And...?"

Sunny grinned. "And I may need to borrow a bag of chocolate chips. But I have everything else."

Edna pushed up from the sofa. She crossed to the pantry and pulled the ingredients on Sunny's list from the cupboard as she listened to her neighbor and John talk.

"So, how long are you here for?" Sunny asked.

"That's a good question. My plans are flexible right now."

"Where are you staying?"

"At the Travel Inn out on the highway."

"Well, that's ridiculous. You should stay here. Edna's got plenty of room."

The bottle of vanilla slipped from Edna's fingers and crashed to the floor at the suggestion that he stay here. She stood frozen in place, her heart racing at the idea of Johnny being in the same house, under the same roof.

Sunny jumped from the sofa to help her with the broken bottle, shooing away the dog who was trying to lick up the spilled vanilla. "Are you all right? What happened?"

Edna shook her head. "Of course I'm fine. Just lost my grip." She turned back to the cupboard, hoping Sunny wouldn't notice the tremble in her hand. "I think I've got a new bottle in here somewhere."

John came into the kitchen, grabbing some paper towels and bringing the waste basket to Sunny.

Edna thought he was getting quite adept at cleaning up messes in her house. If only he could have cleaned up the mess he started that summer, so long ago. "I'm sure the Travel Inn is nice."

"Nonsense," Sunny said. "Edna loves having company. She's been complaining all summer that no one has come to visit her."

John looked at Edna. "Is that right, Eddy? Were you hoping for some company?"

Sunny covered her heart with her hands. "Eddy? Oh, my gosh, that is so cute."

"Yeah, it's adorable," Edna said. "And I haven't been complaining about anything. I don't complain."

Sunny arched an eyebrow at her friend, but wisely remained silent.

"I don't want to impose. I think I've already surprised Eddy enough today just by showing up."

Sunny waved her hand. "Nonsense. Edna is the most hospitable person I know. I'm sure she'd love to have you stay with her. Wouldn't you, Edna?"

No way in hell did she want Johnny Collins staying at her house. No. Not a chance. Absolutely not. "Sure, I guess that would be fine. If he wants to."

John smiled at Edna and nodded. "It's settled then. I'll go get my things and be back this evening. Around six, is that all right?"

"Sure, why not?" Edna shrugged. "Six would be great. But sixty years ago would have been better."

Sunny gave her a quizzical look.

Edna sighed. "Six is fine. That'll give Sunny and I enough time to make up the bed in the guest room and clean up around here. Right, Sunny?" *You got me into this mess, you little troublemaker, you're darn sure stickin' it out with me.*

Sunny grinned like the Cheshire Cat. "Oh yeah, of course. I'll bring over some cookies for you all to have later tonight."

John rounded up the little dog and tucked him under his arm. "I appreciate the gesture, but really, don't go to any trouble for me. I've slept just about everywhere. All I really need is a blanket and a patch of floor."

Where? Where had he slept? What floors? The questions whirled in Edna's head. Where had he been all these years? She wanted to bombard him with questions, to make some sense out of what he was doing here. How he was here—and alive? As much as she dreaded the idea of him staying at her house, she hoped that having him under the same roof would at least give her a chance to get some answers to those questions.

She watched Sunny walk John to the door and close it behind him. Her friend whirled on her with a questioning look.

"What the heck is wrong with you?" Sunny asked. "I've never seen you like this. Sure, I've seen you be snarky, but you were practically rude to him. What's going on? I thought you would be excited to have your old friend stay with you."

Excited. Thrilled. Terrified. "Well, I wasn't sure if I *wanted* him to stay here." Edna looked out the window. She watched John walk to his car then turned back to Sunny. "He *was* my first true love, but the last time I saw him, he was being accused of robbery and murder."

John Collins opened the door of his car and set the little dog onto the seat before sliding in next to it. The heat of the summer day had him starting the engine and flicking on the a/c, but he didn't put the car in gear.

Instead, John sat still, lost in the memories of the past and the girl that had been the love of his life.

He hadn't seen Edna in so many years and while his mind knew that she was an old woman, his heart only saw the young girl he had fallen in love with. Her eyes still sparkled when she laughed, and she still had the spunky spirit that had drawn him to her in the first place.

He couldn't believe that he was here. He had done it. He had actually rung the doorbell and seen her face. Spoken with her.

He had considered rushing back to his car before she opened the door, but he was a little old for ding-dong-ditch. He'd probably break a hip if he tried.

It had been a pretty big leap from ringing her doorbell to actually staying at her house, and he wondered if he'd made the best decision there. He scratched the dog behind its brown and white ears. "Too late now. In for a penny, in for a pound. I guess we're in this thing now, so we might as well ride it out and see what happens."

Putting the car into gear, he pulled out into the street. It wasn't like he was getting any younger.

Twenty minutes later, he approached the counter of the County Clerk's office in the Pleasant Valley Court House. An older woman sat at the counter, a pinched expression on her face as if she had just tasted something sour.

"Good morning. I'm Irma Jean. May I help you?" she asked in a clipped tone.

This woman was all business. John studied her for a moment. In his lifetime, he had learned how to size up people. Taking in their expressions, their clothing, and their body language, he could quickly determine if they were someone he could trust or how best to approach them.

Irma Jean wore a light beige cardigan over a pale pink button-up blouse. Her blouse was crisply ironed, and a short string of pearls lay along her neck. Gray hair, pulled tightly into a bun, gave John the impression that Irma Jean was no-nonsense and liked things manageable and in order. The pale colors and simple jewelry told him that she preferred to fade into the crowd rather than stand out.

A tiny set of pink glasses perched on her nose. She looked at him above the rims, obviously waiting for his request.

He lowered his voice, just a little. "Hello, Irma Jean. I'm John Adams, and I'm wondering if you could help me out with something?" He maintained eye contact just a fraction too long then went in for the kill. "I like those pink glasses. They really set off your blue eyes. Has anyone ever told you that you have beautiful eyes?"

Irma Jean's beautiful blue eyes widened and the corner of her mouth turned up just a bit. "Not in a very long time. But the fact that you're telling me leads me to believe that you are about to have an interesting request, Mister..."—she paused for effect, and John's respect for her ratcheted up a notch—"Adams, is it? Like the president? What exactly can I do for you, Mr. Adams?"

John smiled and passed a sheet of paper to her. "I'd like to see these two documents. I don't necessarily need a copy of them. I just want to read what they say. Can you help me out?"

She read the page and peered at John over her glasses. "Marriage licenses are a matter of public record, so that should be easy. But this other one, I'm not sure about it."

"It would really help me, Irma Jean. Is that a family name? It sure has a pretty ring to it."

"All right, Mr. Adams. Here's the deal." She leaned forward, lowering her voice a bit. "You can lose the false compliments. They're not working with me. Complimenting my eyes doesn't pay my mortgage, if you know what I mean."

John's eyebrows rose and he grinned. Evidently the pressed blouse and granny glasses hid a woman with a killer instinct. He'd prepared for several different tactics depending on who was at the counter so he withdrew a twenty from his pocket and slid it discreetly toward her.

Irma Jean looked at it as if the currency were a piece of garbage soiling her counter. "You must think I live in a very small house, Mr. Adams."

A laugh escaped John's lips as he set two more twenties alongside the first.

"That'll do." Irma Jean glanced around the empty hallway, then her hand snaked out and the twenties disappeared below the counter. "But only because I like you, and you tried to charm me first instead of going directly for a bribe."

She pulled her computer keyboard closer and tapped away at the keys. "I can print out that marriage certificate for you. There is a fee for the county, of course."

"Of course."

"But the other one, I'll need to work on that to see what I can find out. It may take me a day or two."

"That's fine. I just got to town and plan on being here a few days."

A few days or a few weeks. Whatever it took to get the answers he was looking for.

Edna stood before the full-length mirror on the back of her bedroom door. Behind her on the bed lay a haphazard pile of clothes. She looked at the dozen outfits strewn about and thought it looked like a tornado had hit her room.

Hmm. That's a pretty fitting thought, all things considered. Thoughts of Johnny and the events of that summer had played in her head all afternoon. The memories felt as strong and sharp as if they had happened yesterday.

Songs playing on the radio, smells of hay and lake water, snippets of conversation, the feeling of freedom riding on the back of Johnny's motorcycle, the anticipation of his lips on hers.

Snap out of it, woman. That was a long time ago.

She looked at the blue dress she'd just put on. Johnny always told her she looked good in blue. She surveyed the clothes on the bed, taking note of the various shades of blue present in each one. Feeling ridiculous for getting so worked up over an outfit, she yanked the dress back over her head and threw it on the growing pile.

She didn't want to look like she'd gone to too much effort, yet she didn't want to look like a frumpy old woman either. He'd already caught her in pajamas that morning. She thanked the Lord she'd been wearing her pink satin shirt and pants set rather than the too-snug purple pair with the hole in the seat and the picture of Garfield stuffing a piece of lasagna in his mouth that she'd had on the night before.

Grabbing a pair of jeans from the mess, she pulled them on, then slipped her feet into her favorite white Keds. She chose the turquoise tunic with the sparkling beaded front she'd pulled out of the closet first. It was one of her favorite 'go-to' shirts, one she always got compliments on, and it lay nicely on her petite frame. She didn't have a lot of cleavage to boast of, but the small amount she did have was encased in a leopard print bra, making her smile at the secret of her wild side. *Oh hell, it isn't really that much of a secret.*

The doorbell rang and she fluffed her hair one last time. She squirted a spritz of perfume into the air and walked through it as she headed for the living room, closing her bedroom door on the mess behind her.

She stopped midway down the hall. What was she doing? She hadn't seen this man in sixty years and she'd invited him to stay at her house. Correction: Sunny had invited him to stay at her house. She knew a boy many years ago, but she had no idea what kind of man he'd become.

She shook her head. Yes, she did. She still knew him. Because he wasn't just some boy to her. She knew his heart and soul. It may have been six decades ago, but he had pledged his love to her and she still saw that boy in the eyes of the man who had stood in her kitchen a few hours before.

The doorbell rang again, and she wondered if John was as anxious as she about seeing each other again. Opening the front door and seeing him standing there took her breath away.

And at her age, she needed all the breath she had. At this rate, she was going to have to find an oxygen tank just to be in the same room with him.

He'd changed from the suit to a pair of jeans and a simple yellow golf shirt. Still so handsome, Edna wondered if he actually played golf. Or tennis. Or badminton. Did he still drink his coffee black? Did he still like his burgers rare? Did he still prefer his ice cream floats with strawberry soda? She realized that although she felt she knew everything about the boy, she really knew nothing about this man.

"Should I come in?" he asked with a smile, still standing on the doorstep.

Edna laughed. "Of course. Sorry, I just got caught up in the past for a moment." She pointed at the little dog. "Has he already done his business or is he waiting to christen another one of my table legs?"

John set Havoc on the floor and motioned for him to sit. "We had a little talk on the way over, and he's promised to be on his best behavior. Can I leave him here a minute while I grab my suitcase?"

Edna eyed the dog with suspicion. He wagged his tail as she questioned him. "Do you really think you can manage? There's not a lot of good behavior that goes on in this house."

John laughed as he headed out the front door. "You're just the same, Ed. You still make me laugh." He gestured at her outfit. "And you always did look beautiful in blue."

Edna's cheeks warmed as she watched him slip out the door. He could still destroy her with one sentence. She wondered again what she was doing. How was she going to spend the whole night with him? She really didn't even know him anymore. Or did she? Would she always know him? When you love someone so deeply, are they always embedded in your heart?

Her heartbeat quickened as he walked back into the house, pulling a wheeled suitcase behind him. The well-worn luggage was black, and the piping was frayed. Edna wished she could ask it where it had been. What kind of things had John packed inside of it, and where had it traveled in his company?

She pointed down the hallway. "First room on your right. The sheets are fresh, and we set out some towels. There's a bottle of water on the nightstand in case you get thirsty later." Geez. She sounded like the bellhop at a hotel. She willed her mouth to stop talking.

"Thank you. That's very thoughtful. I really don't want you to go to any trouble." He dragged the suitcase into the room, and Havoc ran after him, nipping at the wheels of the luggage.

What was wrong with her? She was as nervous as a long-tailed cat in a room full of rocking chairs. She typically prided herself on marching to her own drumbeat. She normally didn't give two hoots about what others thought of her. Suddenly this man from her past shows up, and she's jabbering like a teenage girl, worrying about her outfits and if she used enough fabric softener on the towels.

John closed the guest room door and walked back into the room. She hadn't budged an inch. She still stood in the middle of the floor, halfway between the kitchen and living room. It was as if she were frozen in time and feared that if she moved, he might vanish in a puff of smoke. Disappear before she had a chance to ask him what he was doing here. Why was he back? And where the hell had he been for the past sixty years?

"Have you eaten?" John asked, breaking her free of her musing.

Before she could answer, the doorbell rang. Who in the world was at her door now? The way her day had been going, it could be anyone from the UPS guy to Ed McMahon.

She opened the door. Not a delivery guy and no balloons or a giant check from Publishers Clearing House.

Instead, Sunny and Maggie stood on her stoop, laden with sleeping bags, pillows, and three pizza boxes.

"We brought pizza," Sunny said with a grin.

Not waiting for Edna's response, the two friends pushed through the front door and dropped their sleeping bags onto the sofa.

"Hope he likes pepperoni," Maggie said, dumping the pizza boxes onto the coffee table.

Carrying a plastic container filled with cookies under her arm, Sunny crossed the room to set them on the kitchen counter. She wore loose cotton capris and a pink t-shirt that read "Don't Make Me Use My Teacher Voice." Her shoulder-length blonde hair was pulled up into a curly ponytail.

She pulled open the lid of the cookies and offered one to John. "They're chocolate chip."

John took a cookie, saying nothing, just watching the scene unfold with an amused look on his face.

Maggie did not share Sunny's easy disposition, and she looked skeptically at this new man standing in Edna's living room.

Tall and slender, Maggie cut an imposing figure in her slim cotton t-shirt and figure-hugging yoga pants. She wore her long, dark hair loose and it fell in easy waves down her back.

She had on cute black flip-flops, showing toes that were perfectly manicured and shiny with a cranberry nail polish.

Used to facing powerful men in the courtroom, she held her hand out to John and spoke in her lawyer voice. "I'm Maggie Hayes, a good friend of Edna's and I'm also an attorney."

John took her hand and smiled broadly. "I'm pleased to meet you, and I'm happy to see Edna has such good friends."

Edna was still standing by the open front door, her hands on her hips. "Yes, but what are her *good* friends doing here and why do they have sleeping bags and pizza?"

"Because we're having a slumber party here tonight." Piper Denton, the youngest of the Page Turners book club, walked through the open door. She carried a large blue Rubbermaid tub, the words CAMPING GEAR marked on the side in magic marker.

"Hey everybody." Her aunt, Cassie Bennett, followed close behind, her blonde curly hair bouncing as she walked directly to the kitchen counter and set down a large cake container. A box of microwave popcorn and a small stack of DVDs teetered precariously on top of the cake box.

Always perky and fun, Cassie practically skipped back to the front door, her face full of excitement as she threw her arms around Edna.

At five foot four, Cassie wasn't much taller than Edna and she constantly complained about her plus-size curves. But Cassie had a welcoming personality and was always ready with a shoulder to cry on, a warm hug, and a slice of chocolate cake.

Squeezing Edna to her, Cassie whispered in her ear. "Surely you didn't think we were going to let you spend the night alone with a murderer?"

Edna narrowed her eyes at Sunny, who was the only person she had mentioned John's checkered past to.

Sunny shrugged and smiled, and Edna couldn't help but grin back. There weren't many secrets between the Page Turners, so Edna supposed it hadn't taken long for the news of her house guest to travel among the women.

Edna looked out the front door. "Are we expecting anyone else? Did you perhaps invite any of the neighbors?"

Cassie pushed the door shut. "Nope. Just us." She looked around the room. "Who's hungry?"

Who's hungry? What was going on here? How had her evening gone from a quiet night with John to a slumber party? She knew her friends meant well, but she hadn't had a sleepover since…well, come to think of it, she'd never had a sleepover.

She looked around at her friends, laughing as they passed out paper plates and slices of pizza. They loved her and wanted to protect her. And maybe they were right. Maybe it wouldn't hurt to have them here while she figured out what was going on with John.

She wasn't afraid of him and didn't think he'd hurt her. But in the movies, even the best cops called for backup. And her backup had just arrived bearing food, pillows, and a stack of romantic comedies.

The smell of pepperoni and cheese wafted through the air, and her stomach growled. Maybe she was hungry. She reached for a plate. "Somebody pass me a piece. I hope you brought parmesan."

An hour later, Edna's living room looked like a slumber-party war zone. Pillows and comforters were piled over every surface. In the middle of the coffee table, a half-empty pizza box sat next to a giant bowl of popcorn, errant kernels scattered across the surface. Havoc was running between Piper and Cassie as they each snuck him bites of popcorn and pizza crust.

Cassie held up the stack of DVDs. "Who's up for a movie? I have an action flick, two romantic comedies, a romantic drama, and a romantic suspense."

Sunny laughed. "I vote for a romance."

"I vote to *hear* a romance," Piper said, looking from Edna to John. "I want to hear about how you two met and what your story is." As tough as Piper acted, the girls knew she was a romantic at heart by the choices she recommended for book club reads.

Sitting in the recliner, John watched the women talk and laugh. The dog finally settled down and lay curled against his side, his nose resting precariously close to the empty paper plate sitting on the arm of the chair.

John seemed comfortable and at ease in the company of so much estrogen. Edna wondered if he had a wife. Or maybe daughters. There was so much she didn't know about him.

He cocked an eyebrow at Edna. "I'd like to hear the story as well. Why don't you tell them, Eddy?"

Edna was curled into the corner of the sofa, her legs tucked under Cassie's sleeping bag. She looked questioningly at John, trying to decipher if he really wanted her to tell the tale. He nodded, so she guessed it was okay. She'd been thinking about the past all day, but now she was at a loss for where to start.

She cleared her throat. "I was in my early twenties that summer. I hadn't married yet, and my mother considered me an old maid. It was her idea to send me to spend the summer with my dad's sister, my "spinster" Aunt Janice. My dad had passed away the year before, and I was sad and angry and bored with my life. I thought a change, any change, would be a good idea. But when I agreed to go, I had no idea that summer would change my life forever."

JUST ANOTHER MANIAC MONDAY

It was the summer of 1955 and 102 degrees the day Edna arrived in Coopersville, Kansas.

She'd craned her neck to look out the window of the bus as they drove into town. The sun shone brightly, and the town looked almost idyllic, with bright storefronts and a courthouse in the center of the town square. She saw a hardware store and a movie theater. A grocery sat on one corner, and she spied a red-and-white-striped pole signaling a barbershop.

The sidewalks were alive with people and activity, and Edna secretly thought it looked wonderful.

A tiny stab of guilt hit her for feeling excited, but she was so glad to get out of that house with her mother. Her dad had been gone almost a year, and yet she could still smell the antiseptic the nurses used to sanitize not only her father's wounds but every inch of their home.

His death still settled over the house like a black crow stands over its prey, protecting its meal as it feasts on the carrion. Her mother tried to hide the bottles from which she claimed she only needed an occasional nip. But an occasional nip had turned into an all-day affair.

Her father's illness had postponed her plans for college and instead she'd found a job to help her mother with the monthly bills. She'd spent the last several years working at the drugstore, stocking shelves and serving as cashier.

Since her father's death, her job had been a refuge from the pain surrounding her house. A feeling of dread fell upon her each night as she returned home and tried to anticipate what was in store for her when she opened the front door.

Would her mother be sweet and extra-affectionate, pouring on gratitude for Edna staying home from college to help take care of her ailing father? Or would this be one of the nights her mother had already had one too many sips? When she fell into a mire of depression and despair, crying and railing at the unfairness of the world and her husband's untimely death?

Edna had tried to act affronted at the idea of being shipped off to spend the summer with her aunt, but inwardly she felt a sense of relief mixed with a tiny hint of excitement.

She craved something new and different. Granted, rural Kansas might not be a hot bed of excitement, but anything would be better than staying with her mother. Any place that she could be free to read a book or lie around on the sofa without fear of what her mother was doing. That she could open a window and let in fresh air. That she could breathe.

Breathing was a chore as Edna stepped off the bus into the hot, humid Kansas air. Even though it was almost five, the sun still shone hot in the sky.

It had been several hours since their last rest stop, and the plastic seats of the bus had contributed to her sleeveless button-up shirt now being soaked through with sweat. Adjusting the knot at the center of her shirt, she pulled it down to cover her bare midriff. She was glad she'd chosen pedal pushers and canvas tennies for the trip instead of the skirt and heavy saddle shoes her mother had suggested.

She had run a final load of laundry through the wash last night and had pulled her best white bobbysocks from the dryer that morning. It wasn't until later in the morning that she realized something red must have been in the wash, and one of her socks had a large pink stain covering the better part of the fold. She was sure she would make quite an impression with her damp, wrinkled clothes and one pink-tinged sock.

Her naturally wavy blonde hair was pulled up into a ponytail, and she was sure her bangs had fallen, as she could feel them clinging to her damp forehead. Her cute, perky hairstyle now one more casualty of the hot, humid Kansas summer.

The air itself, so full of moisture, seemed to slam against her as she stepped to the sidewalk and looked around for her aunt.

The bus had pulled up across the street from a drug store that boasted of a malt shop inside. Edna thought she could've given her left foot for a chocolate malted right now. They'd stopped at a diner for lunch, but Edna was careful with her hard-earned wages so had eaten the peanut butter and jelly sandwich she'd packed earlier that morning.

Her stomach growled at the thought of a home-cooked meal, and she hoped her aunt was a good cook. Anything had to be better than the simple meals of soup and sandwiches she frequently put together for her and her mother in the evenings.

The bus driver set her heavy suitcase next to her on the sidewalk and climbed back onto the bus. Only a couple of people got off at that stop with her, and one man was already walking down the street. The other person, a red-haired boy about her age, was met by a small family who immediately surrounded him with hugs and kisses. Edna assumed he was home from college, and tried to quell the tiny prick of jealousy at the loving family waiting to envelope their son.

With a low groan, the bus pulled away from the curb, leaving Edna alone with only her suitcase and cloud of exhaust. She looked around, but saw no one resembling her aunt waiting to pick her up. She supposed she could go across to the drugstore to find a payphone, but she didn't have her aunt's phone number. They had only corresponded through the mail, and it would probably take too long to send a quick letter asking if she forgot to pick her up.

Edna waited another five minutes then pulled her suitcase to the shade of the awning in front of the hardware store. The sidewalk was so hot she could feel the heat through the thin soles of her tennis shoes.

An elderly man came out of the store carrying a bag and a small flat of petunias for a customer. He wore a beige apron tied around his waist, and Edna watched as he settled the plants and the bag on the front seat of the woman's car and gave her a wave as she drove off.

He looked pleasant and had a warm smile as he stepped back onto the sidewalk and turned to Edna. "You look a little lost. I'm Fred; this is my store. Is there something I can help you with?"

"I just arrived in town and my ride seems to be late. At least I hope she's late and hasn't forgotten about me. I'm supposed to be meeting my aunt, Janice Anderson. I don't suppose you might know her?"

Fred laughed. "I know just about everyone in these parts, and if I'm not mistaken, that's your Aunt Janice barreling down Main Street right now." He pointed to an old blue pickup speeding through town, its paint chipped and faded from the sun.

The pickup screeched to a halt in front of the hardware store, and Edna was shocked to see a black-and-white Border collie and a pink pig in the bed of the truck. Neither seemed to be fazed by the erratic driving. The dog panted lightly and the pig stood chewing on a mouthful of the hay that covered the bed of the pickup.

A tall woman climbed from the cab of the truck, her figure hidden by the set of denim overalls she wore over a loose cotton top. Her brown hair was pulled back in a ponytail and tucked under a straw cowboy hat. She smiled warmly at Edna, her face tanned and alive with excitement.

"Hey there, honey. You've got to be Edna. You look a little different from the last time I saw you. Why, you're a grown woman. And gorgeous too." Leaving the pickup door open, she stepped onto the sidewalk and pulled Edna into a huge hug. "Sorry I was late. I got caught up in a few chores at home. But I am so glad you're finally here."

Edna inhaled the scent of her aunt. She smelled like warm sun and hay and a hint of vanilla. Janice talked fast, laughed easily, and always had something positive to say. Edna absorbed her compliment as if it were a ray of sunshine on her skin, and she was reminded of how much she loved her aunt.

She hadn't seen Janice since she was ten years old, when her aunt had come out to Colorado for a rare visit. Edna remembered connecting with Janice, and they had shared a few letters over the years. But still, Edna had been a little worried that she may not be excited about a houseguest for the entire summer.

The giant hug and enthusiastic greeting set Edna's mind at ease. She smiled up at her aunt. At five two, she felt small crushed in the arms of her tall aunt, but it felt so good to be crushed in anyone's arms that Edna relished in this display of affection. "I'm so glad to be here. I didn't think I would ever get off that bus."

Aunt Janice clapped the hardware store owner on the shoulder. "Thanks for looking out for my niece, Fred. This is Edna. She'll be staying with me over the summer. Can you add her name to my account in case I send her into town to get supplies?"

Into town? How far out did Aunt Janice live? Edna looked at the old blue pickup and imagined driving it. Would she have to bring the pig?

"No problem," Fred said. "Do you need help with the suitcase?"

"No thanks, I got it." Janice lifted the suitcase and dumped it in the bed of the truck. The Border collie tentatively sniffed the edges of the bag.

Edna thought of the numerous books she had in that suitcase and was amazed at the ease with which her aunt had tossed it into the truck.

Janice pointed to the animals. "These are my riding buddies. The fat pink one is Mazie and the dog is named Penny." She nuzzled the dog under the chin. "A farmer sold her to me for one cent and it was the best penny I've ever spent."

Edna reached out to stroke the dog's neck and was rewarded with a lick on the hand.

"She likes you already." Her aunt smiled at her.

Edna grinned back. She'd just made her first friend of the summer.

"You ready?" her aunt asked.

Was she ever. She was ready for whatever this summer had in store for her, and she couldn't wait for it to start. Picking up her purse, she headed for the passenger side. The faded blue door had several rows of wire strapping the handle of the door to the cab of the pickup.

Aunt Janice waved her over to the driver's side. "Sorry, that door's wired shut. It had a run-in with an old bull and lost. It's usually just me in the truck so I haven't got around to fixin' it yet. You'll have to climb across."

"That's okay." Edna crossed to her aunt's side and slid across the big bench seat. The truck smelled of hay, engine oil, and a sweet, tangy scent of tobacco. Edna spied a red-and-white pouch of Red Man tobacco and wondered if her aunt actually chewed tobacco or if she occasionally had a gentleman friend riding with her. Either answer seemed kind of neat to Edna.

Her aunt slid in after her, and with a loud grinding of the gears shoved the truck into reverse. She waved to Fred, and they headed back the way she had come, the pickup rumbling over the red-bricked road. "Well, how was your trip? Meet anyone interesting?"

Edna thought of the odd assortment of folks who had surrounded her on the bus. An elderly couple sat across from her and offered her an apple. They said they were headed to see their grandkids in Missouri. She'd also smiled at the red-haired boy who'd got off at her same stop. She had a row of seats to herself and spent most of the trip napping, reading, or looking out the window, daydreaming about the summer ahead. "Not really. I mostly read a book."

"Oh, good. I hope you brought some books with you. I love to read and am always looking for something new."

Edna thought of the stack of romance novels and adventure stories she'd packed and wasn't sure they were exactly her aunt's kind of reading material, but this woman was continually surprising her. "I did bring some along, and I'd be happy to share."

"We'll come into town later this week and get you set up with a library card. Then you can come into town and get both of us new books. I never seem to find the time to get down here during the week." Aunt Janice pulled the truck into Howard's Hamburger Joint, a drive-in carhop restaurant. "You feel like grabbing a hamburger and a soda before we head out of town?"

Edna's stomach rumbled, the apple long ago digested. "I'd love that. I'm starving. And I could sure use the ladies' room."

"You go ahead. I'll get you a burger and fries." Janice stepped from the truck to let Edna slide out. She picked up the little speaker from the display to place their order. "Chocolate soda or strawberry?"

Edna's mouth watered at the thought of the icy soda bubbling over rich vanilla ice cream. "Strawberry, please."

Her aunt pointed to the sign on the outside of the building, and Edna headed for the ladies'. While she was in there, she used a few minutes to wash her face and hands and reset her ponytail. She had tied a big bright blue ribbon around her ponytail, similar to a style she had seen Audrey Hepburn wear in one of the fashion magazines they sold at the drug store.

That morning, the bow had looked starched and neat, but now it hung limp and wrinkled in her hair. It had gone from dreamy to droopy in the heat and humidity of the long bus ride.

Adjusting her purse as she walked back to the truck, she failed to notice the boy leaning against the hood of his car until she almost tripped over the tanned legs stretched out in front of him.

He reached for her, grabbing her around the waist to steady her before she could fall. "Whoa there. You all right?"

Embarrassed at her clumsiness, Edna laughed and tried to play it off. "Oh sure, I'm fine. Just got off the bus and felt like another trip."

The boy laughed good-naturedly. "That's a good one. Are you new in town, then?"

"I'm spending the summer with my Aunt Janice." Edna pointed at the blue truck and her aunt, who appeared to be watching them, and popped up a little wave.

"That's cool. My name's Frank. I'm home for the summer from college." The boy was of average height and build, clean-shaven, and dressed nicely in shorts and a button-up short-sleeve shirt. His black hair was just a little too long and greased back with pomade. He was handsome in a boy-next-door kind of way, and his dark eyes were kind and friendly.

"I'm Edna. Nice to meet you." She gestured to the town. "So, what's fun to do around here?"

Frank laughed. "This is about it. We have the malt shop to hang out in and the movie theater on Friday nights. And the lake, of course."

"The lake?"

"Sure. Watson Pond is right outside of town. It's a giant lake and has a great beach. That's where most of us hang out in the afternoon. You'll have to come out with us sometime."

Edna smiled. She was looking for a fun summer, and within an hour of her arrival, she had met a cute boy and had an offer to go swimming. Not bad. "I'd like that."

"Great. I'll call you out at your aunt's."

"Do you know the number?"

Frank grinned. "It's a really small town. We know everyone's number. Plus, I know your aunt. A couple of my buddies and I help out at her farm when she needs extra work done."

The sound of a motorcycle engine had Edna turning, and her heart caught in her throat. A silver motorcycle pulled into the parking spot next to Frank's car, carrying the cutest boy Edna had ever seen in her life.

He wore faded jeans and thick-soled, black engineer boots. His white t-shirt was tucked into his pants and had a dark smear of grease across its side, as if he had wiped his hand there. He wore dark sunglasses, and his greased-back blond hair made him a dead ringer for James Dean.

He parked the motorcycle and headed toward them. Edna thought her heart would stop, and she willed herself to breathe.

The boy, whom Edna now saw had a thin edge of blond stubble along his chin, ambled up to Frank and threw his arm around his shoulder. "Hey, Franky. What's up?" He nodded at Edna. "Who's your new friend?"

Frank gestured to her. "This is Edna. She's visiting her aunt for the summer. She's staying out at the Anderson farm."

He nodded at Edna. "That's cool. I like your aunt. She's a good lady." He stuck out his hand. "I'm Johnny Collins."

Edna reached out and took his hand, willing herself to appear calm and collected. And not show that she was trembling inside. She had met plenty of cute boys, even gone out on dates with some of them, but no one had ever affected her the way this boy did. Just the touch of his hand sent an electric thrill racing through her body. "Nice to meet you."

Wow. Could she have been any more exciting? Reluctantly, she let go of his hand. She had expected it to be smooth, like

Frank's, but it had the rough callouses of hands that did a hard day's work.

He looked her up and down, his eyes lingering on her mouth then slowly taking in her legs. The corner of his mouth tipped up. "Nice socks."

Stupid washing machine. If only she hadn't been in such a hurry to get to the bus this morning, she might have noticed. Now she just looked like an idiot.

She blinked up at him, trying to think of something clever to say. He was taller than Frank, and she tilted her head to look into his eyes. He had bright blue eyes, a crystal blue cross between the shades of sapphire and ice, and she couldn't seem to tear her gaze from his.

Either the sidewalk was going to need to open up and swallow her whole or she needed to figure out something to say. "Thanks. I did that on purpose. That's the way we wear them where I'm from. It's all the rage in Colorado." She tipped up on her toe, showing off her pink-stained sock as if it were the latest in fashion.

Johnny laughed, his small grin turning into an all-out smile. "I like it. Maybe it will catch on here." He winked at her as if they were in on the joke together.

Edna's mouth went dry. Her previous hunger pains now turned to butterflies, tumbling and turning inside her stomach. Rather than risk another embarrassing word spilling from her mouth, she chose to stay silent.

Johnny leaned against the hood of the car next to Frank, his posture loose and relaxed. "So, did you invite Edna to come out to the lake with us tomorrow?"

"I was getting there," Frank said with a sigh. Later, her aunt, who'd been watching the whole encounter, said she saw Frank deflate in the presence of Johnny, his shoulders sinking in resignation the moment Johnny smiled at Edna and she smiled back.

Johnny looked at Edna, the grin on his face turning her insides to goo. "How about it, Edna? A bunch of us are spending the day at the lake tomorrow. You wanna come with us?"

Edna would go anywhere with him, just to see that grin again. She thought about the two new swimsuits she had purchased last week in anticipation of the summer. She had shown the stylish white one-piece to her mother, but had hidden the pink polka-dotted two-piece in her suitcase. It was her first two-piece and she hoped she had the guts to wear it that summer.

Imagining wearing that swimsuit in front of Johnny Collins had her pulse racing. Knowing her midriff would be bare and his eyes would be on her skin. Her mouth had gone dry again. She swallowed and tried to act nonchalant. "Sure, I guess. I'll have to check with my aunt."

Edna looked toward her Aunt Janice and saw the car hop delivering a tray of burgers and fries. "I better go. We're having strawberry sodas. That's my favorite." Oh gosh. What a stupid thing to say. No one had asked her what she ordered or what kind of pop she liked. She looked at the sidewalk, searching for a crack to disappear into.

"Strawberry's my favorite too," Johnny said.

She looked up, meeting his eyes. Why did everything he say have a sexy tone to it? She couldn't help it; she smiled back, her lips curling in response to his open grin. "I'll remember that."

Her aunt tooted the horn of the old pickup and waggled a French fry in her direction. Edna smiled and waved at the boys. "See you later. It was nice to meet you." In fact, it was the nicest thing that had happened to her in years.

"See you tomorrow," Frank said. "We'll pick you up around eleven. Pack a lunch."

Edna nodded and turned to walk back to the pickup where Aunt Janice was eyeing her with a good-natured look on her face.

She stood back and let Edna slide into the truck. "Looks like you're making friends already." Janice passed her a paper wrapper of warm, greasy French fries.

"Just a couple boys. They said they know you, and they invited me out to the lake with them and a few friends tomorrow. Would that be okay?"

"Of course." Janice patted Edna on the leg. "Edna, I invited you here hoping you might help me out a little around the farm and to feel a connection with my brother. But you're a grown woman; you can do whatever you want. This is your summer."

A weight lifted from Edna's shoulders. She felt the stirrings of hope that this really would be her summer. She popped a fry in her mouth and groaned in pleasure. She accepted the icy glass of soda and took a sip, the frothy strawberry-flavored bubbles sweet on her tongue. "Oh my gosh. This is the best strawberry soda of my life."

Janice laughed. "I'll bet it is."

They finished their meal, Janice tossing her last two bites of burger to the dog and the pig as the car-hop took the tray from the window. Her aunt put the truck in gear and reversed out of the drive-in. Edna stuck her head out the passenger window and waved to Frank and Johnny, who were still standing by Frank's car. "See you tomorrow."

They drove about two miles out of town before Janice turned the truck onto a long dirt driveway, one side lined with cottonwood trees.

Pulling up to a two-story white farmhouse, Edna got her first look at the farm where she would spend her summer.

Except for some peeling paint, the farmhouse was in good condition. A long porch ran the length of the house, a swing on one end and a couple of white rocking chairs on the other. The rockers had colorful quilted cushions and throw pillows on them, as if in invitation to sink in and sit a spell. Pots of multicolored flowers lined the steps leading up to the porch, and everything looked tidy and well kept.

A large barn sat behind the house, its red paint faded from years in the sun. A fenced corral ran around one side of the barn, and Edna could see brown and black cows standing behind the fence. A tall windmill stood to the other side, its giant blades still in the dry early-evening air.

Janice lowered the tailgate of the pickup, and Penny jumped down. Her aunt lifted Edna's suitcase, then the pig, from the back of the truck and set them both on the ground. "I've got some chores to do. Think you can get your stuff inside on your own?"

"Sure."

"Go in the front there and through to the back of the house. I set you up on the sun porch. It's a little warmer during the day, but cooler at night and I thought you might like it back there." Janice headed toward the barn, the dog and the pig following at her heels. "Go ahead and get settled. I'll come inside in a bit."

Edna pulled her suitcase up the stairs and opened the door of the house. The living area was a large room with colorful rugs scattered across the hardwood floors. She could see a big kitchen off to the left, a long wooden table separating the two rooms.

Walking through the living room, she noticed the worn but comfortable-looking sofa and chairs. Stacks of books sat on the floor around a blue easy chair, the seat cushion flattened and sagging from years of wear. A bag of yarn sat in the seat, knitting needles and colorful skeins spilling from its top.

At the back of the house, a staircase led up to the second floor, and a wooden door stood open to the sun porch. Edna stepped into the room where she would spend her summer and immediately fell in love.

The sun porch was a decent-sized room with whitewashed walls and screened-in windows running the length of the wall. A door leading into the backyard was at the center of the outer wall, and Edna could see a vegetable garden and several flower beds overflowing with the bright colors of summer. A wicker rocking chair sat in a corner of the room, and a small dresser lined one wall.

A twin bed with a pink-and-white floral bedspread sat pushed against the corner of the porch. With its white, wrought-iron bed frame and tumble of pink and green pillows, Edna thought it was the most romantic bed she had ever seen.

She dropped her suitcase and flung herself across the bed, anxious to curl into its softness and dream about the summer ahead of her. A summer filled with strawberry sodas and days at the lake and a boy with crystal blue eyes.

The next morning, Edna was up with the sun. She'd slept like a rock, a contented rock, the night before and was excited about what her first day of summer would be like. She'd offered to wash the breakfast dishes and sweep the floors while her aunt tended to the morning chores outside.

Aunt Janice gave her a tour of the farm, and though it seemed small, there was quite a bit of pastured land surrounding it. Between crops of wheat and fields of livestock, her aunt kept plenty busy. Plus, she employed a few hands that came out to help her with the upkeep of the farm. Edna couldn't help but be impressed by the amount of work her aunt did on her own, and wondered if she ever missed having a husband.

Edna was sweeping the front porch when she heard a horn sound and looked up to see Frank's blue-and-white car heading down the long driveway. He had the top down, revealing Frank at the wheel and a young couple in the back seat. Her heartbeat quickened as she recognized Johnny riding in the front with Frank. She waved and tried not to run down the porch steps to greet them.

The car pulled to a stop and Johnny pushed up to sit on the seat back. "Hey, Edna, grab your suit. We're headed to the lake."

Worried about leaving on her first day there, Edna had discussed it with her aunt the night before. They'd sat at the kitchen table, sipping iced tea from the Mason jars Janice used as glasses.

"I do want to go to the lake, but I feel terrible leaving you alone on the first day after I arrived," Edna admitted.

Janice laughed. "You are a sweet girl, but you don't need to worry about me. I was alone yesterday and the day before. I think I'll be all right."

"I'm alone too. That's the only reason my mom wanted me to come. So I could see what my life would be like if I don't find a husband." She winced. "Sorry. No offense."

"None taken. Some women think their only plan in life is to find a man, get married, and have babies. That's never been my goal. I've had plenty of chances to get married, but I'm single by choice. I have a sassy mouth and a free spirit, and I haven't found anyone to keep up with me yet. I don't see myself as a spinster or a failure for not being married. I see myself as a liberated woman, who makes her own decisions and enjoys life."

Her eyes sparkled with mischief as she winked at Edna. "I can still enjoy the company of men when I want to. But I can experience their finer points and don't have to do their laundry or cook for them."

Edna's cheeks warmed at her aunt's implication, and her heart swelled with love for this lady who made her feel less like an outcast and more like an independent woman. "Aunt Janice, I'm so grateful to be spending the summer with you. I love visiting with you and want to do my part to help out. That's why I feel bad going to the lake my first day here. I don't want to hurt your feelings or skip out on any work you need me to do."

"Oh honey, it takes a lot more than that to hurt my feelings. You seem to have the misguided idea that you were sent here to be free labor or that being here is some type of punishment. I *wanted* you to spend the summer with me so I would have some company and so you could experience something new." She narrowed her eyes at her niece. "And I thought it would be good to get you out of that house for a little bit. To give you a little break."

Edna wondered how much Janice knew of her mom's drinking problem. "Thank you. It's been hard since Dad died. My mom can be a little overbearing sometimes."

Janice rolled her eyes. "Okay, we can save the part where we talk about your mom for another night. A night when we have chocolate cake and some strawberry wine."

She leaned forward and took Edna's hand. "But for now, I want you to know that this is *your* summer. It's your time to read, to relax, to find yourself, if that's what you need to do. If you want to pitch in around here, I've always got chores that need to be done. But I asked you here this summer for you. And for me. I miss my brother, and you remind me of the good in him. Plus, I see a little bit of myself in you, and I wish someone would have done this for me. So go to the lake tomorrow. Go every day if you want. Swim and laugh and flirt with that cute Johnny Collins."

Edna looked down at her lap, embarrassed to meet her aunt's eyes. Her voice was soft as she admitted, "I bought a two-piece and am considering wearing it to the lake."

Aunt Janice laughed, a loud and hearty sound. "Good for you. You better wear it." She winked at her niece. "I might consider getting one this summer too."

Edna had lain awake the night before, listening to the sound of the crickets and replaying her aunt's words in her mind. She *could* be anything she wanted. She just needed to figure out what that was. But in the meantime, this was her summer and she planned to make every minute of it count. She would read and swim and help out around the farm. And if she got the chance, she would definitely flirt with Johnny Collins.

Earlier that morning, Edna had put together a simple lunch with a sandwich and a large jar of iced tea. Her aunt had offered to send along a dozen of the chocolate chip cookies she'd made the day before.

She packed everything into a small basket and put on the pink polka-dotted two-piece. She wore white shorts and a blue sleeveless tank top over her suit. Her figure was slim and petite and the white shorts showed off the slight tan that was just starting to color her legs.

Part of her worried that Frank and Johnny weren't going to show up and part of her was terrified they would. She'd swept the porch four times already as she tried to keep busy and act like she wasn't bursting with excitement as she listened for Frank's car.

Grabbing her things, Edna walked to the car as if she didn't have a care in the world. As if she were completely unconcerned about the cute boy in the car wearing a white t-shirt, a faded red swimsuit, and a grin that was setting her insides on fire.

Johnny jumped out of the car and held open the passenger door for her. He pointed at the couple in the back seat, and Edna was surprised to see the red-haired boy who had arrived on the bus with her yesterday. He had his arm around a plain-looking girl in purple shorts, her brown hair pulled into a ponytail. "This is Weasel and his girlfriend, Donna. Guys, this is Edna."

Edna waved and nodded at the boy. "I think we were on the bus together yesterday."

Weasel smiled. He had a light spattering of freckles across his cheeks and hazel eyes. "I didn't think you noticed. You had your head in a book most of the trip."

"Well, it was a long trip and a good book," Edna said, not quite sure how to respond, unsure if he was making a statement or an accusation. "Is Weasel a nickname or was your mom fond of animals?"

The girl sighed. "His real name is Warren. These two lunkheads started calling him Weasel in grade school and now everyone thinks that's his name." Her voice had a slight nasal quality to it, so her statement came out sounding like a whine.

"He was a year younger than us in school, but lived in Frank's neighborhood. He was always coming around, trying to weasel his way into our fun," Johnny explained. "After a while, we just got used to him, and he's been hanging around us ever since."

Weasel kicked at the front seat. "Yeah, and I'm still waiting for them to start having some fun."

Edna smiled. "It's nice to meet both of you." She slid into the seat, holding the lunch basket on her lap, acutely aware of her bare legs touching both Johnny's and Frank's as Johnny slid into the seat next to her.

Frank put his arm around the back of the seat, turning his head to reverse the car and get it turned around. He smiled down at her. "Glad you could make it. It's gonna be cool. You'll see."

The ride to the lake took about fifteen minutes. Between the music blaring from the car radio and the wind whipping their hair, there wasn't a lot of conversation. Edna was happy to look out at the scenery, watching the wheat fields go by. She caught her breath as they passed an entire field of golden sunflowers, their yellow faces reaching to the sun.

The fields gave way to cottonwood trees as they neared the lake. Frank turned down the dirt road leading to the beach. The ride was over too quickly. Edna enjoyed being squished between the two boys, caught between the scents of Frank's aftershave and the clean laundry detergent smell of Johnny's white shirt. They both smelled like soap and pomade, and Edna could have stayed there for hours.

They turned a corner, and Edna gasped as she got her first look at Watson's Pond. It was huge. Blue-green water as far as the eye could see. A few boats were out, and Edna saw a boy skimming across the lake on water skis.

A long, sandy beach ran along one edge of the lake, and a string of red-and-white bobbers cordoned off the swimming area. Umbrellas and bright beach towels lay scattered across the sand as weekenders spread out to spend a day in the sun. A group of teenagers were setting up umbrellas, and two young moms lay sprawled across red towels, chatting away as their toddlers poured sand into buckets a few feet away.

"What d'ya think?" Frank asked, raising an eyebrow at her. "Pretty great, huh?"

Edna nodded, a smile breaking out on her face. "Yes. Really great."

"What are we waiting for?" Johnny pushed open the car door and grabbed a stack of towels from the back seat. "Let's go get wet!"

The group followed Johnny and dropped all of their things in a pile on the beach. The sand was already hot under Edna's feet and she spread out a towel to stand on before pulling off her tank top. She dropped her shirt to the ground and noticed Johnny watching her.

He raised his eyebrows at her, one corner of his mouth lifted in a grin. "Nice polka dots. I like the pink. Somehow I knew you would be a two-piece girl."

A two-piece girl? What in the world did that mean? Edna didn't know, and she didn't care. She loved it. It sounded brave. And a little daring.

Being here gave her a chance to start over, to be someone besides the girl whose dad just died or the girl who still lived at home. Yes, that was a label she could live with. She stepped out of her shorts and threw back her shoulders. Putting a hand on her small waist, she wiggled her hips a tiny bit. "Yeah, I am a two-piece girl. A pink polka-dotted two-piece girl."

Johnny laughed and pulled off his t-shirt. "Let's see if you can swim."

Swim? Edna didn't know if she could even breathe. Looking at Johnny's tanned chest and muscled arms made her throat go dry, and suddenly all the water in the lake didn't seem enough to quench her thirst. His waist was slim, and a fine line of blond hair ran from his navel to the top of his swimming trunks. A long white scar ran down one side of his ribs, and Edna had the insane urge to reach out and run her finger along the smooth scar tissue.

He turned to run down to the water. Edna's hands flew to her mouth as she saw a group of bruises clustered around his lower back.

Before she could say anything, Frank stepped between her and Johnny and gave her a look of discretion. Frank's voice was low as he spoke. "Johnny's a mechanic. He's always getting hit with engine parts."

Oh really? Did engine parts have fists? Edna studied Frank's face, seeing the confirmation of her suspicions in his downcast eyes. She respected his motivation to protect his friend and looked away, unsure how to respond.

"He probably doesn't even know those are there," Frank said.

"Of course. I won't mention it." Edna reached for her towel and saw Donna watching her. The other girl wore a salmon-colored one-piece and by the looks of her pale skin, she hadn't been outside much yet this summer. "I like your swimsuit. That's a pretty color."

"Thanks. It's probably too boring. I guess I'm not much of a two-piece girl." Donna spread out a towel and sat on the sand next to Weasel.

Not sure how to take that, Edna was saved by Frank grabbing her hand and pulling her to the water. She shrieked in joy as they splashed into the lake, the cool water wonderful against her warm skin.

A large raft, made from a layer of bridge planks floating atop fifty-gallon barrels, drifted on the water about thirty to forty yards from the shore. Johnny was already climbing up the ladder affixed to the side of the raft. He waved and called to them.

Edna was used to swimming pools, and cringed at the slimy sludge that oozed up between her toes as she followed Frank into the water. She was a strong swimmer, but that was in a pool where she wasn't worried about a fish touching her leg.

Frank dove into the water and swam toward his friend, his strong arms effortlessly cutting through the water. Edna didn't have a bathing cap and wasn't sure she wanted to get her hair wet or if she wanted to dip her face in the lake water.

She looked toward the raft and saw Johnny standing there, running his hand through his too-long hair, water glistening on his tan chest. She would swim through the Red Sea to get to him. And after all, she was a two-piece girl now.

Edna dove under the surface, marveling at the varying levels of coolness in the murky blue-green water. Her head broke free of the gentle waves, and she shook out her curly hair as she heard Johnny calling to her from the raft. She swam toward him and let the boys haul her up the ladder.

Johnny sprawled out on the warm wooden planks, patting a place beside him. "This is the best way to do it. Lay out flat on your stomach and the sun will warm you right up."

Edna lay down on the raft and Frank plopped down on her other side. The heat from the bridge planks warmed her skin, and the sun on her bare back felt delicious. She grinned at her new pals. "Thank you for bringing me. This is the best day of my summer already."

Johnny winked. "You ain't seen nothing yet. This is Franky's last summer home from college and we're determined to make it the best summer ever. Right, Franky?"

Frank smiled at this friend. "I guess." He nudged Edna. "You ready for the best summer? Ever?"

Edna laughed and pushed up from the wooden raft. "I am more than ready. Count me in," she said, then with a whoop she jumped back into the water.

They spent the day lounging on the raft or playing in the water. Sitting on the beach, they ate their lunch, the ice in Edna's tea long melted and the jelly soaked through the pieces of bread. They all laughed as she listened to the three boys tell tales of their childhood, growing up together in a small town.

Edna tried to engage Donna in the conversation, but the younger woman was quiet and mostly let the boys do the talking. Edna missed having another girl around to talk to. Most of her girlfriends from high school had either left for college or gotten married, and none seemed to have time to chat anymore.

After a few more unsuccessful tries, Edna realized that Donna must see her as an invader on her territory. Obviously Donna was used to having the three males' attention all to herself, and she didn't seem so keen to have this petite blonde from Colorado stealing her show. Donna seemed to always have a hand possessively touching Weasel whenever he told a funny story or made Edna laugh.

Edna sat on a towel between Frank and Johnny. The heat in her cheeks meant she was probably getting sun burned, but she didn't care. Johnny had offered to put suntan lotion on her shoulders after lunch, and she'd almost died at the feel of his hands rubbing the warm lotion into her skin.

His hands were firm and confident as they crossed her back and shoulders. She hoped no one noticed that she caught her breath when he slid his fingers along the band of her bathing-suit top and ran his hand across her skin.

She tried to act like this was no big deal. Like she had shirtless, muscular mechanics rubbing their hands on her back all the time. She'd had men place their hand on her back before, guiding her through a door or holding her while dancing.

This was different. Even though only a few inches of skin showed above the high-waisted bottoms, she felt like she was practically naked and completely exposed in the two-piece bathing suit.

In reality, no man had ever actually touched the skin of her lower back. Especially not the way Johnny had just brushed his knuckles across the bare skin above the waist of her swimsuit bottoms.

A ripple of desire ran down her spine as he gently lifted her hair and pressed his hands along her neck. He leaned forward and spoke next to her ear. "It's getting hot out here. We don't want you to get burned."

He'd passed her the bottle of lotion, and she hoped no one noticed the way her hands trembled as she poured the white suntan cream into her palm. She had never been one to be very nervous around boys, but something about Johnny Collins caused her to come completely undone.

She rubbed the lotion on his upper back, careful to avoid the bruised area, not wanting to draw attention to it if he really was unaware of its presence.

She noticed several scars on his back as she smoothed the lotion into his tan skin. His back was toned and muscular. Edna thought he might have flexed as she ran her lotioned hand down the hard muscles of his arm and smiled at the thought of him trying to impress her.

Frank leaned forward, shrugging his bare shoulders at her. "I think I'm getting a little burned. Would you mind doing my back next, Edna?"

She smoothed suntan lotion onto Frank's shoulders and noted the difference between the two men. Frank was slender and toned but didn't have the rock-solid muscles born of hard labor that Johnny did. Frank's back was smooth and tanned and scar-free.

She rubbed the last of the lotion into her hands and leaned back on her towel. "I think it's neat the way you guys grew up together. I've never had a friend for that long."

"Franky's the closest thing I've got to a brother," Johnny said. "Our dads grew up here too. Went to high school together."

Frank nodded. "We've known each other practically our whole lives. My dad owns the only car dealership in town and Johnny's dad is his best mechanic."

Johnny lay on a striped towel next to Edna's. Dark sunglasses covered his eyes so she couldn't read his expression. "Yeah. The real truth is Franky's dad is the only guy who would hire my drunk of a pops."

Frank sat on a towel on the other side of Edna, his legs stretched out in front of him. He rolled his eyes at Johnny. "That's because he can take an engine apart and put it back together in his sleep—drunk or sober. And he taught his kid everything he knows. Johnny's a first-rate mechanic as well."

"I used to hang out at the shop with my dad, and Frank was always around. We became friends as kids and hung out together all through school."

"Frank and I were on the high school football team together, and Donna was a cheerleader," Weasel said.

Edna nudged Johnny's leg with her toe. "How about you, Johnny? Did you play football and date a cheerleader?"

"Not Johnny," Frank said. "He was always working after school. He couldn't ever make practice."

Weasel laughed. "And Frank's the one who dated all the cheerleaders. Johnny just went out with them."

"What's the difference?" Edna asked.

Johnny raised his dark glasses to look Edna in the eye. "That's means Frank took them on actual dates, and I just went out with them. Went out to the barn, went out to the woods, went under the bleachers." He stared at her, as if daring her to respond.

Edna shrugged noncommittally. "I've been under the bleachers myself a time or two." Okay, it was only once and it was to grab her purse that had fallen between the slats, but she *had* been under the bleachers.

Frank, Johnny, and Edna swam back out to the raft and took a nap in the hot afternoon sun.

Edna's head was turned to Johnny. Her body felt liquid, as if it were actually melting into the warm wooden planks of the raft. Her eyelids flittered open, lazy after her cat-nap, and she was surprised to see Johnny's eyes were open and looking at her.

A slow, easy smile crossed his face and he leaned closer to her. "You look awful pretty when you sleep." He pushed up from the raft, his muscles flexing as he moved.

Edna swallowed as she watched him stretch. The faded swim suit hung low on his slender hips, and the muscles of his abdomen were tight and hard. His skin was bronzed from the sun, and he grinned as he caught her looking at him.

She turned her head and looked back to the beach, anywhere but at Johnny's stomach. "Why don't Donna and Weasel come out here with us? I haven't seen them in the water all day."

"And you probably won't all summer," Johnny said. "Donna's dad is the chief of police, so he's crazy over protective at her doing anything slightly dangerous, which I guess includes swimming. And Weasel won't go near the water. He fell through some ice and almost drowned as a kid, and ever since then, he's been terrified of the water. I don't think he's ever even learned to swim."

Edna shuddered at the thought of a child falling into frozen water and the terror he must have felt. "How awful."

Johnny nodded. "He doesn't ever talk about it. They make a good pair and like to come out here with us. Donna likes to sunbathe, but Weasel never gets in the water. We get it, so we don't ever give him a hard time about it."

"That's about the only thing we don't give him a hard time about," Frank said, his eyes still closed as he lay on his stomach next to Edna. "Everything else is fair game."

Edna laughed and poked Frank in the side. "I thought you were asleep."

He opened his eyes and rolled over. "I was, until you two jabber-mouths started talking." He looked up at the late-afternoon sun. "We should probably head back. We were planning on going to the drive-in movie tonight. You wanna come with us?"

Edna thought about the small nest egg of money she had saved from her job at the drugstore. "How much is it to get in?"

Johnny and Frank exchanged a knowing look, and a grin crossed Johnny's face. "Oh, don't worry about that. It won't cost a thing."

The sound of the car engine coming down the driveway had Edna tossing a lipstick into her purse and racing for the front door. She stopped in the living room, took a deep breath, then calmly opened the front door and stepped onto the porch.

Her heart raced faster than the engine of the car as she saw Frank, Weasel, and Donna in the front seat. Johnny sat in the back alone, an empty seat beside him, waiting for her.

Johnny hopped over the side of the car and opened the door for her to climb into the backseat. "Hi, doll. You ready for some fun?"

"Of course," she answered. He made the word "fun" sound full of opportunities, and she smiled up at him before crawling into the backseat. Thank goodness she had decided to wear shorts instead of a skirt.

Edna leaned forward and greeted the group in the front seat. "Hi, gang."

"Hey, Edna." Frank turned the car around and headed out the driveway. Donna gave her a little wave, and Weasel offered a quick bob of his head in greeting.

Her aunt had told her the drive-in movie theater was just on the other side of town. Considering the size of the town, Edna knew the drive wouldn't take long, so she reveled in the time she had sitting next to Johnny as the wheat fields sped by.

She had taken the time to bathe and wash her hair after they had dropped her off that afternoon. She had pinned some curls and let her hair dry as she ate a light supper of ham sandwiches with her aunt. She found herself spilling all the details of the day to Janice as they ate and laughed over Edna's first adventure at a Kansas lake.

It felt so good to relax and laugh as she enjoyed a simple conversation, without worrying about saying the wrong thing or doing that odd thing that would set off her mother. She missed her mother, but more the mom she used to know. The one who smiled and laughed and sang songs while she cleaned the house. The mother she knew before her dad got sick.

"You look a million miles away," Johnny said, tugging on a lock of her hair. "Are you thinking about all the broken hearts you left back in Colorado?"

Edna laughed. The only broken heart she had was inside of her. And Johnny Collins' grin was working magically to mend it. She shrugged, but before she could come up with a witty reply, Frank pulled the car to the side of the road. "Why are we stopping?"

Frank put the car in park and pulled the lever to release the trunk. He winked at her as he opened the door. "You said you were worried about paying to get into the drive-in. Well, tonight you get in free. You just don't have the most glamorous entry."

Johnny opened the trunk and climbed inside. He patted the empty spot in front of him. "Climb in. Best seat in the house."

When Frank said she didn't have to worry about the price of the ticket, she thought he meant it would be his treat. She hadn't even dreamt they would sneak her in, and especially in the trunk of the car.

What if this was a trick? She didn't really know these kids all that well. What if they were really going to get her in the trunk and kidnap her? Drag her in the woods and leave her stranded or worse.

Get ahold of yourself, girl! She'd read way too many adventure novels. Why would they kidnap her? To rob her? They would be quite disappointed when they found her purse held only two dollars, three lipsticks, and a soiled handkerchief. She had more lip care in her bag than she did money.

Johnny looked up at her, an *I dare you* grin on his face. "Come on. You're not scared, are you?"

Heck yes she was scared. She was terrified. But she wanted an adventure. Climbing into the trunk of a car with a hunky mechanic certainly seemed a good way to start one.

Frank held her hand, and she climbed over the rim of the trunk and lay down, her back nestled against Johnny's chest. She jumped and let out a little shriek as Frank slammed the lid.

Johnny's arm came around her, pulling her tight against him. "Don't worry, I got you. But you better hold on to me, Eddy. We're in for a bit of a bumpy ride."

Eddy? No one had ever given her a nickname, and she secretly loved it. She actually kind of loved being locked in this tight, dark place, nestled against Johnny, his arm wrapped around her. The trunk smelled of exhaust and engine oil, and she felt the scratchy wool blanket they lay on against her bare legs. But she wouldn't have traded this moment for anything.

The car moved forward and she squealed, then giggled as they bumped over the road, tossing the two trunk-mates against each other in the dark.

"Frank's hitting those bumps on purpose." Johnny pulled her tighter to him and laughed out loud. "Don't worry, we'll get him back next week when we make him ride back here."

"Next week?"

Johnny chuckled softly against her ear. "Haven't you realized that I plan to spend the whole summer with my arms around you and my lips against your neck?" His lips brushed the skin under her ear, ever so slightly, sending delicious ripples of sensation down her spine.

Did he just say he planned to spend the whole summer with her? With his arms around her? Had she died and gone to heaven? Could heaven consist of being locked in a hot trunk crushed against an even hotter guy whose hand was holding her waist and whose mouth was temptingly close to hers?

But what if she didn't want to spend her whole summer with him? She had only met him the day before.

Ha! Who was she kidding? Of course she wanted to spend her whole summer with him. She wanted to spend her whole life with him. She would be happy to spend the entire summer locked in this trunk with him.

She had longed for freedom. For something new and different. And in her secret heart of hearts, had hoped to find even an ounce of romance that summer. She wasn't waiting. She wasn't contemplating if this was a good decision or if she would regret this. Regrets were for homebodies, not two-piece girls. She stopped thinking at all and just did what felt right. Absolutely right.

The car slowed and turned a sharp corner before pulling to a stop. Edna realized they must have arrived at the drive-in. She turned her body toward Johnny, not an easy task in the confined space.

She could smell his aftershave and feel the taut muscles of his chest through his t-shirt. She placed a hand against him, resting her fingers above his heart, and tilted her face up to his. "Haven't *you* realized that I plan to spend the whole summer in your arms and kissing you?"

In the dim light of the trunk, she saw his lips curve into a smile and he leaned close to her ear. "You're my girl now, Eddy. I knew the minute I saw you that you were something special. And that I wanted you to be mine."

He leaned down and kissed her, his lips lightly grazing hers. Just enough to tempt her, to send her pulse skyrocketing, to make her ache for more. Her arms wrapped around his neck, and she pulled his face toward hers.

And that was the first time she knew he was a thief. He took her breath away, robbed her of every conscious thought, and stole her heart.

Edna sighed and looked around the room at the Page Turners, who were all glued to her every word.

"And then what happened?" Piper asked, reaching into the bowl of popcorn for the last few kernels.

"Then an old lady got tired and decided she needed to go to bed." Edna stood and stretched. "Turn out the lights before you go to sleep, and no funny slumber-party business. I do not want to find my brassiere in the freezer in the morning."

She glanced over at Johnny. He was smiling at her, and she wondered how he felt about her digging up all their old memories. Did he remember falling in love with her? Did he ever really love her at all?

He stood and held out his arm to walk her down the hall. She took his arm, feeling the warmth of his body through his sleeve. He really was here. Johnny Collins was alive and walking beside her.

"I liked hearing you tell the story of how we met," he said. "I had forgotten about the strawberry sodas, but I remembered everything else. Especially those funny pink socks and that polka-dotted swimsuit. Lord, you were a looker." He looked down at her and squeezed her hand. "I remembered everything else like it was yesterday."

"Well, it wasn't yesterday. It was a long time ago." Edna waved at the guest-room door, trying to tamp down the fresh set of butterflies reeling in her stomach when he complimented her. "You should be all set. But if you need something in the night, go wake up one of those gals in the living room. Don't bother me. I need my beauty rest."

She walked another few steps then turned back and pointed a finger at him. "Dredging up those old memories has me feeling nostalgic, and I'm too tired to think straight right now. But in the morning, I want some answers."

John raised his hand in mock salute. "Aye-aye, captain. We'll talk in the morning."

Edna pounded the dough. She'd had a restless night's sleep, and she looked around the living room at the women who were there to protect her. Sunny was just waking up, but the rest were still sound asleep, curled up on chairs and sofas, and Piper had sprawled out on the floor.

Apparently, none of them had heard her houseguest as he had slipped out that morning before they woke. He'd left a note claiming he had unexpected business to take care of and would be back later that afternoon. He had taken the dog with him.

Now there was a house full of women who all adored her cinnamon rolls and would be ready for breakfast soon. After rolling out a sheet of thick dough, she sprinkled it with cinnamon and sugar. She dropped thin slices of butter across the sheet before rolling it up and cutting it into neat round discs. After placing the rolls in a greased pan, she laid a towel across the top, and set the timer to give them thirty minutes to rise.

She might as well get showered and dressed for the day. It would take another half an hour just to pick out an outfit. She slammed the dishes in the sink. Why did she care what she looked like? A layer of lipstick and a squirt of hairspray wouldn't bring back the years they had lost. Wouldn't tell her where he'd been and why he'd let her think he was dead.

Picking out a shirt in John's favorite shade of blue wouldn't answer the question if he still loved her. Or if he *ever* did.

An hour later, Edna was back in the kitchen, her hair combed and curled, wearing denim capris and a cotton blouse in a gorgeous shade of turquoise. She scooped warm, gooey cinnamon rolls onto plates and passed them out to the Page Turners.

Sunny had run home and showered, then brought Jake back with her. That, or he had been lured over by the seductive scent of cinnamon filling the air. Either way, he was standing in the kitchen, pouring a glass of milk. His presence seemed to fill the kitchen. Between his muscled arms, his incredible-smelling aftershave, and his easy-going charm, he was hard to miss and hard to resist.

Edna passed him a plate, a warm roll sitting in a pool of creamy icing. "So, Mr. Private Eye, how much would you charge me to do a little investigative digging into someone's past?"

Jake took a bite of the roll and closed his eyes in what looked like sensual delight. You could almost hear the gulp of every woman in the room as they watched him take another bite. He opened his eyes and winked at Edna. "I would do just about anything for you if you baked me another pan of these cinnamon rolls."

Edna whacked her palm on the counter. "Done! Now, what do you need from me? I know where he was born and where he grew up. I even know his social security number. But I want to know where he's been all these years that we thought he was dead."

Jake licked some stray icing from his thumb. "I'll start with the information you have and see what I can dig up. There weren't a lot of electronic records in the fifties. But I can go back to old newspaper archives and police records. Would he have a police record?"

Edna nodded. "Oh yes. He was wanted for murder and larceny when he died. Or when we thought he died. But I guess he's just been missing."

"Speaking of something missing," Maggie said as she lifted the sofa cushions and peered underneath, "has anyone seen my silver bracelet? I took it off last night and thought I laid it on the end table next to the lamp."

Sunny popped up from her seat at the kitchen table. "I'll help you look. I'm sure it's around here somewhere."

They searched the living room but found no sign of the bracelet. Edna knew what they were all thinking, but no one spoke the accusation aloud. She had a hard time believing

Johnny would come into her home and steal from her friends. But, she couldn't believe that he had faked his death and robbed a bank either, so maybe she wasn't the greatest judge.

Maggie shrugged. "Maybe I left it at home. I'll check there." She reached for her purse. "I've got to go into the office this afternoon and get caught up on some cases. What time are we meeting back here tonight?" Maggie was a defense attorney but had taken the morning off to participate in the sleep over.

"What do you mean tonight?" Edna asked. "I am perfectly capable of handling myself in my own home. I have Mace, ya know?"

Sunny rested a hand on Edna's arm. "Of course you are. But we want to avoid any instances in which you need to use the Mace."

Edna grunted an acceptance.

"Besides," Sunny said. "I'm making baked ziti, and Cassie said she would bring a pie."

It was hard enough to turn down baked ziti, but when she threw in the pie, that sealed the deal. "Okay. Okay. You can come over again. But someone better be bringing garlic bread."

Cassie raised her hand. "Piper and I will be in charge of garlic bread too. I need to get home and work on the pie so we're taking off." She hoisted a pillow and the empty cake container onto her hip. "We'll see you all back here around six tonight."

Jake swiped one last cinnamon roll before heading for the door. He held it open for Cassie, Piper, and Maggie to walk through. "I'll get to work on seeing what I can dig up on Mr. Collins today. Edna, email me the info you know, and I'll report what I find out at dinner tonight."

"Who invited you?" Sunny asked as she followed Jake out the door.

"You said baked ziti. That's all the invitation that I needed." Jake waved and pulled the front door shut, leaving Edna in the quiet house alone.

She sighed and collected the plates from the kitchen counter.

Not wanting to miss out on Johnny coming back to the house early, she skipped Zumba class for the afternoon and instead putzed around the house, cleaning and straightening up. She figured running the vacuum would count as her exercise for the day, then completed her workout by taking a nap on the sofa.

It took everything she had not to sneak into the bedroom and rifle through his belongings. Twice she caught herself standing in front of the guest room door. Each time, something stopped her from going inside. Maybe she was worried about getting caught if he came back unexpectedly, or maybe she just wanted to hear the truth from his own lips. Either way, she resisted the temptation, and his room remained untouched.

She was freshened up and had the table set by five thirty. Sunny arrived a few minutes before six, a bouquet of fresh-cut flowers from her garden in her hands. On her heels followed a freshly showered Jake carrying a steaming casserole dish in his potholder-covered hands. Edna couldn't decide which smelled better, the ziti or Jake's shower gel.

She directed him where to set the pasta and within fifteen minutes, the rest of the Page Turners had arrived and were seated at the table, ready to dig in.

Edna reached for the basket of fresh bread, the delicious aroma of garlic and butter wafting up as she took a slice. "So Jake, what did you find out today?"

"Not a lot," Jake said. "He's covered his tracks pretty well. I think I got a few hits on him in Europe. I'll keep after it and let you know what I find out."

Piper lifted a forkful of pasta to her mouth, a thin strand of cheese clinging to the tines. "I've been waiting all day to hear more of the story of that summer, Edna. I have a feeling you were just getting to the good part."

If Piper only knew how true that statement was. That whole summer was full of good parts. Edna set down her fork and took a sip of water. "Where was I?"

"You had just gone to the drive-in and told us that Johnny had stolen your heart." Piper spoke around the bite of ziti she had stuffed into her mouth. "You said he was a thief. What else did he steal?"

"Well, my virginity for one thing." Edna laughed and wiggled her eyebrows. "But I'm sure you don't want to hear about that."

"Oh, you know we do," Cassie said. "I love hearing first-time stories. Tell us."

Edna wiped her mouth with her napkin and settled back in her chair. "It was several weeks into the summer and I had been spending a lot of time with Johnny. It was a Sunday afternoon and one of the hottest days of the summer. And I mean that in more ways than one."

Coopersville, Kansas, 1955

Edna reached into the straw and pulled out a warm egg. She'd thrown seed into the pen of the chicken coop like Aunt Janice had taught her, then ducked into the little coop to collect the eggs while the chickens were busy feeding.

She wore a pair of her aunt's rubber boots and had an apron tied around her waist. Her aunt was quite tall compared to Edna's five-foot-two stature, and the boots were several sizes too big. But they beat getting the chicken mess on her only pair of white tennies, and she stood on her tip-toes to reach into the top row of cubby holes.

Trying not to think about the chicken poo in the straw, she quickly reached into each cubby and pulled out the eggs, gently placing them in the basket she held. She had promised Janice that she would collect the eggs and get them washed and to the market by that afternoon.

Janice had errands to run in the city that day, so she had shown Edna how to package the eggs and get them prepared for the grocer the night before.

"I can do all that," Edna had said, "but the only problem is that I don't know how to drive."

"That doesn't seem like too big of a problem," Janice had said. "Get that boy Johnny out here to help you take them into town. Or better yet, get him to teach you how to drive. You can use that old blue truck. There's not much you can hurt in that south field if you want to start out there."

Edna thrilled at the idea of learning to drive and of having Johnny be the one to teach her. "But you're going to be gone for the day. Aren't you worried about Johnny and I being out here alone together?"

Janice had smiled and touched Edna's cheek. "I wish you would see yourself as I see you. You see yourself as a child, still stuck in a house caring for your dying father and your alcoholic mother. And as much as I love that you took care of my brother till his dying breath, you are a grown woman now. One who can make her own decisions and do what she wants."

Edna's eyes filled with tears, and she was too choked with emotion to speak. How much did Aunt Janice really know about her mom? She could only look at her aunt and nod.

Janice grinned. "And if I had a beau like Johnny Collins and could spend an afternoon alone with him, I sure know what I'd want." She laughed heartily and gave Edna an exaggerated wink. "Just make sure you get the eggs to the market."

Edna smiled at the thought of her aunt, with her big laugh and her dirty mind. Talking about sex was taboo, and certainly never discussed by a woman. But nothing seemed off limits with Janice; she would gab about anything.

Edna had never met anyone like her and had never had an adult treat her as an equal before. It was a heady experience, and Edna loved it. She loved everything about her experience on the farm this summer.

Well, maybe not the chicken poop on the side of her hand.

Her heart leapt as she heard the familiar drone of Johnny's motorcycle coming down the driveway. She wiped her hand on the straw and grabbed the last egg, then stepped from the chicken coop, latching the door behind her.

She raised her hand to block the sun as she watched him ride toward her. He wore jeans, a white t-shirt, and a serious expression on his face. His eyes were covered with dark Aviator sunglasses, and Edna's pulse raced as he drew to a stop in front of her and pulled the sunglasses from his face.

She watched as his eyes surveyed her from her loose, curly ponytail to the clunky boots, and his face broke into a grin. "I hope you're wearing a pair of shorts, because from my vantage point, it looks like all you have on is an apron and a pair of rubber boots."

Edna looked down and saw that her aunt's apron completely covered her outfit of shorts and a sleeveless top. She grinned at the thought that Johnny was imagining her in only the apron and wiggled her hips a little. "It's the latest style. All the girls are wearing this."

He laughed and dismounted the motorcycle, kicking the stand into place. He reached for her, pulling her against him in a tight hug. His voice sent delicious waves of pleasure through her as he spoke against her ear. "It's good to see you, doll."

It was still morning, but the sun had been up for hours, and the warm fabric of his t-shirt brushed against Edna's sweat-damped skin. "Sorry, I've been collecting eggs, and I'm all sweaty."

"It's summer in Kansas, we wake up sweaty." Johnny brushed a quick kiss on her lips. His voice softened to a whisper. "I don't mind a little sweat."

Oh goodness. Now she really was sweating. She pushed against him with a nervous laugh. "Be careful that you don't break the eggs. I've got to get them to the market before lunch."

"All right, let's take care of the eggs. I can drive us in to town. Then, this afternoon, I'll teach you how to drive that old pickup." He took the basket from her as they headed up to the house. She had called him the night before, using the need for help with the egg delivery and driving lessons to get him out to the farm.

"You don't mind spending the day with me and teaching me how to drive?" Edna asked.

He stopped and looked down at her. "Mind? Heck no. It's all I've thought about since you called last night and asked me to help you out." He reached an arm around her and leaned down to nuzzle her neck. "*You're* all I've thought about. You keep me up all night just thinking about this spot on your neck right here."

He laid his lips against her skin right under her ear, and Edna let out a breathless sigh. "Yeah, that sure is a good spot."

Johnny laughed. "Let's get these eggs to town so we'll have more time this afternoon for me to spend exploring that spot."

She loved to hear his laugh, full and hearty, and she loved that she was the one who brought him enough joy to invoke that laugh. The thought of him exploring any spot on her body had her pulse racing and her heart thrumming in her chest. *Yes, let's get these eggs to town. Quick.*

They took care of the eggs, dropping them off with the grocer and collecting her aunt's earnings.

Janice had left them the makings for lunch, and Edna and Johnny sat on the porch, eating thick-sliced ham sandwiches and drinking Janice's sweet and tart lemonade. They laughed and talked, Edna telling stories of Colorado and hanging on every word of Johnny's tales of growing up in rural Kansas.

Edna collected their plates and ran a sink of soapy water, dumping their few dishes in to wash. The front screen door slammed and then Johnny was behind her, sliding his arms between hers and dunking his hands into the warm, sudsy water.

His hard, muscled chest was tight against her back. He leaned in, laying his hands on hers and guiding the dishcloth across the plates. His hands gently directed hers in the washing motion, his chin on her shoulder and his breath against her ear. "We'll get done faster if I help."

His voice was like velvet in her ear. She was glad he stood behind her, afraid her knees might buckle from the nearness of him.

She had read historical novels where the damsel was always swooning from the touch of the handsome knight and for the first time in her life, Edna understood the meaning of the word "swoon". His hands on hers, his body touching hers in the most intimate way, the sensuous feel of the warm water—she was afraid she just might swoon into a puddle on the floor right in front of him.

She swallowed, afraid to move, afraid to break the spell of the moment. The wonderful moment of being in his arms. She would never look at washing dishes the same way again.

She wished they had more than six dishes to wash. They could only wash the same plate so many times. She pulled the drain on the soapy water and turned to look up at Johnny. "So, you wanna teach me how to drive?"

He laughed and was still laughing thirty minutes later when she stalled out the pickup for the fifth time.

Edna banged her fists against the steering wheel in frustration. She was too short to reach the pedals *and* see over the dashboard, so Johnny had wired wooden blocks to the pedals and found an old Sears and Roebuck catalogue for her to sit on.

He'd patiently explained the gears and how to start out in the lowest gear called the "grandma gear." He shrugged and sat calmly in the bench seat next to her in the old pickup. "It's no biggie, Eddy. It can take a while to get it, but once you figure it out, it'll be a breeze." He pointed at the gear shift. "Put it back in 'grandma' and try again."

Edna blew her damp bangs off her forehead and set her jaw, determined to get this. "I know why they call it the 'grandma gear,' because I am going to be an old lady before I figure out how to drive this thing."

She started the pickup again, put it in gear, and slowly eased her foot off the clutch as she depressed the gas pedal. The truck pitched and jumped, then the gear caught and they were rolling through the field. Edna whooped in delight. "I did it! I'm driving."

"Now switch to second—pick up your speed, that's it." Johnny called out instructions while Edna increased her speed.

She switched gears and bounced through the field in the old truck, laughing and cheering for herself. "I'm really doing it. I'm shifting. I'm steering. I am driving a truck." She turned the wheel, heading back toward the house, and drove the truck…right into a huge hay bale.

"Well, shit!" She clamped a hand over her mouth, looking wide-eyed at Johnny. The truck stalled and died, wisps of hay floating down onto the windshield.

Johnny looked at her in astonishment, then broke into hearty laughter. "I think that about sums it up." He rubbed his knee where it had hit the dashboard when they pitched into the hay bale. "Are you okay? Did you hurt anything?"

Edna looked down at herself and didn't see any visible scrapes. "Just my pride. And my dignity." She peered up at him. "Sorry for swearing. That was a little unladylike."

He scooted closer to her, putting his arm around her shoulders, and drawing her close to him. "I am the last person you need to be lady-like in front of. In fact, there are a few things I would like from you that are decidedly *un*-ladylike."

The afternoon clouds had rolled in, and a slight breeze blew through the open windows of the pickup. She could feel his heart beat under her hand as she rested it on his chest and looked up into his eyes.

She had wanted daring. She had yearned for adventure. She was tired of her life being in the grandma gear. She wanted speed and excitement, and this looked like her chance to grab it.

She took a breath, her voice low, barely above a whisper. "Like what kind of things?" She was answered with a loud crack of lightning and a flash of thunder. She shrieked as another crack lit the sky and fat raindrops hit the windshield.

"Looks like somebody wants me to take a *rain check*," Johnny said, and lifted Edna's petite frame over his body and dumped her on the other side of the seat. He gave her a quick kiss and slid into the driver's seat. "Hold that thought while I get us back to the house."

By the time Johnny had started the truck and reversed it out of the hay bale, the rain was coming down in sheets. The sky had darkened and was lit with intermittent flashes of lightning as he drove out of the pasture. The field quickly turned to mud and the tires spun a few times as he expertly maneuvered the truck back to the house.

He pulled as close to the back of the house as he could then took Edna's hand. "We're gonna have to make a run for it," he shouted over the clattering rain on the tin roof of the truck's cab.

Edna grinned. This felt like an adventure to her. "That's okay. I won't melt."

"You are one crazy chick," he said with a chuckle, then released the door handle and grabbed Edna's hand.

Their clothes were soaked clear through by the time they ran across the yard and onto the sun porch. The screen door slammed behind them and they stood, catching their breath, as the rain pounded on the roof of the porch.

Johnny looked around. "Is this your room?"

"I guess. It's where I've been staying. It's cooler out here at n-n-night." Her teeth chattered, and she rubbed her wet arms.

He took a step closer and wrapped his arms around her, surrounding her wet body with the warm heat of his. He wiped her dripping bangs from her forehead and laid a kiss against her skin. Holding perfectly still, he kissed her again, gently, next to her eyebrow. Once more, on her cheekbone. Another. The edge of his lip just glancing against hers.

Her breath came ragged and her chest heaved against him. She arched into him, aching for his next kiss.

His mouth closed on hers, then he was pulling her tight against him, his arms locked around her, lifting her to him. He feasted on her mouth, her neck, her chest. She clutched at his back with one hand and drove the other through his wet hair, gripping his head.

This was full speed, and she was no longer in an old pickup, but a sleek race-car rocketing down the highway. Heat pulsed through her body, coiling in her stomach and causing an ache, a need that only Johnny's touch could fill.

No longer shivering, her body warmed from desire. She wouldn't have been surprised to see steam rise from their clothes. Johnny reached for the buttons of her blouse, glancing first at her for permission.

She nodded. He undid each button, achingly slow. His skilled mechanic's hands easily working each button loose. He pushed the wet fabric from her shoulders, and she dropped her arms, letting the sodden shirt fall to the ground behind her.

She stood before him, trying to act bolder than she felt, knowing the dark outline of her breast was visible through the soaked white fabric of her bra.

This was the new Edna. The one who wore two-piece swimsuits and polka dots, who drove a truck and had a boyfriend with a motorcycle. She took a deep breath and reached for his t-shirt, pulling the drenched fabric over his head.

He shook his head, sending droplets of rain from his soaked hair flying into the room. He looked down at her, desire in his eyes but also a look of concern. "Are you sure about this, Eddy? I want you like I've never wanted another woman in my life. But I don't want to pressure you. I am in this thing with you for always. We have plenty of time."

She had spent the last several years of her life wasting time. Spending her days trapped in her home with her parents. She wouldn't have traded those last years of time spent with her dad, but he was gone now and she was ready to live. To experience life and beauty and joy.

They had only known each other a few weeks, but she knew, as certain as she was that the sky was blue, that she was in love with this man. He awoke a desire in her that she never even knew was possible. She loved the way he patiently taught her things, whether it was driving a truck or explaining how to catch a firefly in a jar.

He laughed with her, and when they were alone, he talked to her. Really talked to her about his dreams, his hopes to someday have a garage of his own. To get out of Coopersville, out of Kansas. To have a family and be the kind of father that his old man never was.

She wanted him like nothing she had ever wanted before in her life. He made her feel special. Feel alive.

She wrapped her arms around his neck, laying her lips along his skin, the rain dripping down his neck from his hair. "You are *not* pressuring me. I want this. I want this more than anything." She pulled back, looked into his crystal blue eyes. "I want *you* more than anything."

He trembled in her arms and leaned his head against hers. Drawing a breath, he closed his eyes. "I know it seems sudden, but I have never felt like this with anyone but you. I swear my heart fell out of my chest the first moment I saw you at the drive-in. With that lopsided bow in your hair and those funny pink-splotched socks that you acted like you did on purpose. I've never met anyone like you. Never given my heart to anyone before. This scares the daylights out of me."

Edna touched his cheek. "Open your eyes. Look at me." She peered up at him, trying to convey the depths of her feelings into words. "Johnny, I'm scared too. But you can trust me with your heart. I promise you I won't break it. And I will give you mine in return."

He looked deep into her eyes, into her very soul. Without speaking another word, he moved back, toed his boots off, and unzipped his jeans. He pushed both the jeans and his briefs to the floor, then stepped free of them.

All she could do was stare at the beauty of his naked body. He was tan and toned everywhere. The thought of his muscled body against hers took her breath away.

Reaching for her, he wrapped his arms around her and flicked the clasp of her wet bra. He peeled it from her body, leaving her exposed skin damp and sensitive to the cool breeze coming through the screened-in windows.

She pushed back her shoulders, determined to feel brazen and reflect bravery, even as she trembled under his touch. Running his hands lightly down her back, he kissed her neck, her shoulders. He skimmed his hands under the elastic waistband of her shorts and her cotton underwear and across her bare bottom. He slid them down her legs, bending and laying a soft kiss against her exposed belly.

She shivered, only partly from the cool room. Resting his hands on her hips, he looked up at her, his thick blond hair falling onto his forehead, and whispered sweet words: "You are so beautiful."

He stood, scooped her into his arms, and carried her to the twin bed. He laid her across the thick quilt that she had thought so romantic on her first day here. She couldn't have guessed that pink quilt would be wrapped around her naked body when she experienced a man for the first time.

The bed squeaked and creaked as Johnny climbed onto it and lay next to her. He laughed. "Not a real smooth entrance."

Edna lay next to him, unsure what to do with her hands. She wanted to touch every part of him, but didn't want to do the wrong thing. "I'm scared," she whispered against his chest. "I don't want to mess this up."

He tipped her chin so she was looking at him. "Hey, don't be scared." A light went on behind his eyes, as if he'd just realized the reality of the situation. "Is this—? Am I—your first?"

She nodded. Two quick bobs of her head.

Johnny dipped down and laid a gentle kiss on her lips. "Are you sure you want to do this? With me?"

The corners of Edna's mouth tipped up. "I am sure you are the *only* one I want to do this with."

He grinned. "Then don't worry. There's no way to mess it up. Sex is messy and noisy and scary and a lot of fun. But it's also kind of beautiful. Like you. And I will try to make your first time beautiful."

Edna's heart swelled with love for this man who gently took her in his arms and laid a trail of light kisses down her throat. His hands moved lightly across her skin and a delicious quiver ran the length of her body. She wanted him to touch her. To touch every part of her.

Johnny shifted and rose above her, lowering his body onto hers. She wrapped her arms around his back and pulled him to her. He leaned in to kiss her, and a fire ignited inside of her. She kissed him back with everything she had, feeling him, touching him, trying to convey through her actions the depth of her feelings.

He feasted on her mouth and groaned in pleasure as she arched up underneath him. He leaned his forehead against hers, his breath ragged, his eyes open and staring into hers. "I want to tell you something. Before anything happens, I just want you to know that I'm crazy in love with you. I have been since just about the first moment we met. I never really believed in all that love- at-first-sight baloney, but that was before I saw you."

Edna ran her hands lightly across his back. Everything about this moment was terrifying and exciting. She felt like she couldn't breathe. He had just told her that he was *crazy* in love with her. How could that possibly be?

Actually, she didn't care. She didn't care if he only loved her for tonight or for the rest of her life. She was seizing this moment, this one piece of time, and she was holding on with everything she had. "I am crazy in love with you too."

He laughed out loud and kissed her again. Lowering his body onto hers, his arms wrapped snugly around her, he moved against her. Then with her.

The only music in the dim sun porch was the rhythm of the rain on the rooftop. Johnny and Edna found their own music, their own measure of time. The scent of fresh rain and honeysuckle filled the room, and they were lost, in the moment, in each other.

7

"I can picture that day in my mind as if it happened only yesterday," Edna said, a tear rolling down the wrinkled skin of her cheek.

"So can I," John said. He stood in the doorway of the living room, the little terrier resting in the crook of his arm. The book club had been so engrossed in Edna's story that no one had heard him come in.

Edna brushed the tear from her cheek. "Oh, for goodness' sake. When did you get here?"

"I've been standing here for a while. The screen was open. Don't you ever lock your doors?"

Edna shrugged. "No, it's a small town, and what if someone needs something? I don't even know if I could find a key if I wanted one."

John shook his head. "Yeah, I get it. I'm from a small town too. I just worry about you being here alone."

Edna raised an eyebrow. "Now you're worried about me?"

Wisely ignoring her comment, John easily changed the subject. "I like hearing you tell the story of that summer." He smiled at the book club members. "Although she may have exaggerated my patience and her skill at driving that old truck. She was a terrible driver."

"She hasn't improved with age. She's still a terrible driver," Piper said, earning a swat with Edna's napkin.

"I'll have you know that I am an excellent driver," Edna said. "Other people just don't always watch where they're going. None of those accidents were my fault."

Sunny laughed and gestured at the empty seat at the table. "Have you eaten, John? Can I heat up a plate of baked ziti for you?"

John slumped into the chair and set Havoc on the floor. "That would be great. I've been running all day and haven't had a chance to eat. It smells wonderful."

Sunny dished cheesy pasta onto a plate, and Cassie got up to serve the pie.

Edna watched Johnny take the plate and fork from Sunny, her eagle eye scanning for clues. As if the way he took a bite of pasta or how much salt he sprinkled on his food might tell her his whereabouts over the last sixty years.

John took a bite of ziti and closed his eyes in contentment as he chewed. "Delicious. Just as good as the traditional pasta of Italy."

Oh really? Edna thought. Now we were getting somewhere. "Have you spent a lot of time in Italy? 'Cause that's not where I thought you'd been the last sixty years."

John looked at her, amusement evident in his eyes. "I have spent some time in Italy. I went overseas for a bit when I was younger, and I must say floating down the canals of Venice is pretty close to being in heaven." He gave her a sideways glance. "Unless you meant you thought I had been in the other place."

Edna's eyes narrowed. "I haven't decided."

His face took on a serious look. "Well, I was there after the war so I spent a fair amount of time in that other place as well."

"What parts of Europe have you lived in?" Sunny asked, scratching the ears of Havoc, who had jumped into her lap and was trying to lick her plate.

"You can shoo him away if he's bothering you," John told her, neatly avoiding the question before taking another bite of pasta.

Sunny nuzzled the little dog. "He's cute. I like him." She gestured to Jake, who was quietly observing the newcomer. "John, this is my boyfriend, Jake Landon. He lives next door in the house between Edna's and mine."

Jake reached a hand across the table to shake John's. "Did you spend a lot of time in Europe? I don't detect much of an accent."

"No, you wouldn't. I was there a long time ago, when I was a young man and hiding from the world. I've spent most of my life back in the states."

"Which states exactly?" Edna asked, not even trying to be sly about her curiosity.

John studied Edna, and his blue eyes filled with sorrow. "I'm sorry, Eddy. I know I've hurt you, and I know you have a lot of questions. I was tempted to stay away and let you believe that I really had died all those years ago. But I'm an old man now, and I have questions of my own. You talk about how that summer changed you. Well, it changed me too."

Edna listened, and for once, stayed quiet and let John talk.

"So many things happened that summer. Some that I could influence and some that were completely out of my control. I thought I was a man by then, but I was just a kid. A boy who had no idea about the real world outside of Coopersville, Kansas. I look back and know that was the best and the worst summer of my life. I met you. I fell in love for the first time. I learned about responsibility and what being a man and making hard choices was all about."

John never took his eyes from Edna's. "I was never good in school, but I was good with my hands and I picked up things quickly. My dad wasn't good for much, but he was a great mechanic, and the things I learned from him and from your Aunt Janice were enough to help me survive all these years and build a life for myself. I know you believe that I saved your aunt's life that summer, but really, she helped to save mine."

He looked around the table. "Has she told you about the storm yet?"

Coopersville, Kansas, 1955

The day started innocently enough, the sun waking Edna as it shone warmly through the screen porch windows. She'd spent her morning helping her aunt around the farm, collecting eggs, sweeping out the muck in the stall of Janice's favorite mare, and laying fresh hay in its place.

The heat seemed oppressive that morning, and Edna's shirt and hair had quickly dampened with perspiration.

She knew she would be meeting the gang at the lake for the afternoon, so she ignored the heat and worked quickly to complete her chores. The low hum of the engine of Johnny's motorcycle was a welcome sound, and she called out to Janice that she would be home later that night and not to wait for her for supper.

Wearing her pink two-piece under her clothes, she grabbed a couple of the oatmeal cookies cooling on the counter, and hurried to where Johnny sat in the driveway. She leaned in, gave him a quick kiss, stuck a warm cookie in his mouth and flung her leg over the back of the motorcycle.

The vinyl was hot against her shorts-clad legs, but she scooted up against Johnny and wrapped her arms tightly around his waist. She loved to ride on the back of his bike. The feel of the engine rumbling underneath her and being so close to Johnny was a thrill like no other.

Johnny shifted into gear, and they flew down the road, the wind quickly drying her sweat-dampened hair. Edna laughed into the wind, thinking she had never had a summer as great as this one.

"Are you okay if we swing by my place?" Johnny yelled the question into the air behind him. "I just got off work and need to grab my swim trunks."

"Sure," she yelled back, secretly thrilled that she would finally get to see where he lived.

She knew the area of town, but in the weeks they had been dating, he had never offered to have her over. He had always come out to the farm or met her in town. It felt like a milestone that he was letting her into this part of his life and allowing her to see the home he shared with his father.

They pulled up in front of a small, nondescript house. The faded paint, which looked as if it used to be yellow, was now as beige as the dead grass in the small patch of lawn in front of the house. The only green visible in the yard was on the leaves of a few scattered dandelions.

Johnny held her hand as he helped her off the back of the bike. "My dad's at work," he said, indicating the empty driveway leading up to the house.

He led her inside and waved a hand around the small living area. The kitchen was visible through a wide doorway, the sink full of dirty dishes. "Home sweet home."

She glanced around, noting the sagging brown sofa and the faded blue recliner. A small television sat on a cinder-block shelf, tin foil wrapped tightly around its rabbit-ear antennae. The house smelled vaguely of bacon grease and motor oil. A small grease-covered engine surrounded by loose parts covered the Formica-topped kitchen table. "It's nice."

Johnny laughed, a dry huff of breath. "No, it's not. But *you're* nice for saying so."

A short hallway held three sets of doors, and Johnny led her to the farthest one. They passed a tiny bathroom, and Edna assumed the other closed door belonged to Johnny's father.

Johnny opened the door and ushered her into his bedroom. It was sparsely decorated, with only a bed, a dresser, and a small nightstand. But the room was tidy, and the bed was neatly made. The floor seemed to have been recently vacuumed, with the room smelling of laundry detergent and Johnny's cologne.

The one window in the room stood wide open, and Johnny turned on the small fan resting in its sill. "Sorry, it's so hot in here. I wasn't exactly expecting company."

Edna raised an eyebrow. "Oh? You always keep your room this neat?"

Johnny looked around the room as if assessing it from her eyes. "I guess. It's the only part of the house that's completely mine. Nobody else really comes in here, except the guys every once in a while. It's the one place in my life that I can keep in order."

He plopped down on the bed while she wandered around his room, touching his things, soaking up this new side of him. She ran her hands along the few shirts hanging in his closet, fingering the fabric of a red plaid button-up. "I like this one."

"Thanks. It's a hand-me-down from Frank." He gestured to his closet. "Most of my clothes are. He started doing it when we were little kids and has never stopped. We'd be at his house, and he'd hand me a shirt that was practically new and say it didn't fit him anymore and that I could have it. He was so easy going about it that I never realized it was charity. It just seemed like a guy giving me a shirt he didn't wear anymore."

Edna smiled. "Aren't you both about the same size?"

"Yeah. So I eventually figured it out. And by then, I realized it was mostly Frank's mom. She knew my size, and when she bought jeans or shirts for Frank, she would always grab an extra set for me. He would rip off the tags and pass them off like they weren't his style or that his mom was annoying for buying so many clothes that he didn't need. I would wear a shirt around his mom, and she would look pleased and tell me it looked nice. It made her so happy, and it was just easier to take the clothes than to hurt her feelings."

"She seems like a really nice lady."

"She's the best, actually. She's always treated me like one of her own kids. I can't tell you how many meals she fed me then sent the leftovers home to feed my dad. She's the closest thing I've had to a mom since my own mother took off."

Edna could sense the bitterness in his voice when he spoke of his mother's desertion. "How old were you when she left?"

"I don't know. Eight or nine."

The tone of his voice told her he knew exactly how old he had been when his mother left. "Were you close? I mean before she left?"

"I guess not close enough." He gave a bitter laugh followed by a sigh. "I thought so. She used to read to me every night. And she used to sing. All the time. She loved to sing anything, songs from the radio or church hymns. It didn't matter. Sometimes, in my mind, I can't exactly picture her face, but I can remember the way she sounded when she was singing."

He smiled. A sad smile. "I can also remember her crying. She cried a lot. She didn't sing as much when she was having one of her sad spells. Then right before she left, she seemed to get real happy again. Cleaning house and dancing to the radio. She must have been planning to leave and that made her happy again."

"Do you have a picture of her?"

He nodded.

"Would you be okay showing it to me?"

"Geez, Eddy. I've been basically pouring my heart out to you for the last half-hour. I think I've told you every sad-sack detail of my life. It's not gonna embarrass me now to show you her picture."

She shrugged. "I was just trying to be polite."

"Polite is the last thing you need to be with me." He narrowed his eyes at her. "I mean it. I love you just for you, and I always want you to be yourself with me. And I'll try to do the same with you. My dad said he never knew what my mom was thinking. I don't want that. I want something real where you can just be yourself around me. No fakey niceness. If you feel nice, just be nice. If I make you angry, tell me you're mad and we'll figure it out." He winked at her. "Then I'll kiss you and make you forget why you were ever angry."

Wow. Did she ever love this man. Never in her life had anyone told her to just be *her*. She always felt like she was expected to act a certain way. Be obedient. Be a good daughter. Listen to your elders. Do as you're told. Johnny had just given her permission to completely be herself and her heart soared with love for him. "Got it. But I can't imagine ever being mad at you."

"Oh, you will be. I plan to spend my whole life with you and sometimes I can be a total bonehead."

He just said he planned to spend his whole life with her. Happy butterflies soared and dipped inside her stomach. She grinned. "Maybe I'll just act mad so I can get you to do some of that anger-erasing kissing you were talking about."

He popped up from the bed and grabbed her around the waist, hugging her to him and planting a noisy kiss on her neck.

She giggled and feigned weakness. "Why Johnny, I can't even remember why I was mad at you."

"I told you." He laughed then opened the top drawer of the dresser. He pulled out a small picture frame and a gold brooch in the shape of a peacock, its feathers studded with colorful glass jewels.

His mood shifted from fun to sadness as he handed Edna the frame. "This is pretty much all I have left of my mom. She used to wear this pin all the time, and I loved to play with it. I liked the way the jewels caught the light and made rainbows on the wall. She left this pin and a note on my dresser the day she left. The note said she would always love me." His bitter tone was back. "Just not enough to stay."

Edna looked at the picture in her hand. It was of a pretty blonde woman holding the hand of a little boy, his light blond hair a match to hers. She was looking down at him, and they were laughing. "She's beautiful."

"Yeah. She was." He took the picture from her and put it and the peacock pin back into the dresser and shut the drawer. He turned to her, taking her into his arms. "I think you're beautiful."

"You make me feel beautiful." She rested her hand on his chest, feeling the outline of his muscle through his white shirt. "And I'm not going anywhere. I will stay with you as long as you will have me."

"How about your whole life?" He leaned down and nuzzled her ear. "I mean it, Eddy. I've never felt like this with anyone. I never talk about my mom or the way that Franky's family helped me. But with you, my mouth just opens, and my entire soul pours out."

"I like that you talk to me. It makes this more real."

"This is real. And this is my real life. I want you to know what you're getting yourself into. I want you to see all of me, all of my scars. No surprises. I want you to make the decision to be with me with your eyes open."

Edna took his face in her hands, looking deeply in his eyes. "My eyes *are* open. Wide open. And all I see is the man I love. And I do love you, Johnny Collins. Just for you. Nothing you can tell me or show me is going to change that."

His face seemed to hold a mixture of hope and fear. "Are you sure? You understand that I want a life with you? Like I want to get married to you and grow old with you."

She smiled. "Yes, I understand. And if that was a proposal, my answer is yes. I am not ever letting you go, Johnny. I want to fall asleep every night in your arms and wake up to your smile every morning. I want to make babies with you that have your blonde hair and your beautiful blue eyes."

He leaned down and kissed her, his lips soft against hers, but his arms wrapped tightly around her. He drew back and rested his forehead against hers. "That *was* a proposal. An awkward one, but still a proposal. I'll do it again, and better, when I actually have a ring."

"It was perfect." She brushed the hair from his forehead. "You think you're scarred. But what about me? Are you sure you want me? I'm practically a spinster, I'm not going to get any taller, and I have tiny breasts. I'm just discovering myself and figuring out that I don't think like other girls. I don't want the same things that they do. Staying home and cooking meals and having babies isn't enough for me. I want to go to college. To learn and absorb knowledge. To experience life."

"Do it. Go to college. We can live anywhere you want. I'm a mechanic. I can always find work. You can go to school during the day while I work and then you can come home and tell me everything that you learned. I want you to be whatever you want to be. I want you to have those experiences. I just want to go along for the ride. To experience life with you."

She touched his cheek. "It wouldn't be a life without you in it."

"Then let's do it. Apply for some colleges in the fall. It will take me about ten minutes to pack, and we can go anywhere you want."

Anywhere she wanted. A few weeks ago, she couldn't imagine leaving Colorado, and now every dream she imagined was coming true. She was in love. With not just any boy, but a crazy-handsome boy who loved her back and wanted a life with her. A life where she could go to school and be accepted for who she wanted to be. She was over the moon with happiness. "Yes."

"Yes, you will marry me or yes, you want to apply for some colleges in the fall?"

"Yes to everything!" She threw her arms around him and kissed him with abandon. Conveying every feeling in her heart through her lips. She loved him, and she desired him. Oh, how she desired him.

He pulled back, his breathing ragged. "Do you think we should head out to the lake? Those guys will probably be waiting."

"Let them wait." She grinned up at him, feeling alive and complete in his arms. He wanted to know the real her? To know what she was really thinking? Well, here goes. "I'd rather stay here and get naked with you."

His eyes widened in surprise, then he let out a loud laugh. "I think that's a great idea." He grabbed the hem of her shirt and pulled it over her head, leaving her standing in only a pair of shorts and her pink swimsuit top.

She wiggled her eyebrows and reached for his t-shirt. He leaned down and let her tug it over his head. She gasped as she saw the fresh purple bruise across his shoulder. Her feelings of desire changed to a fierce protectiveness, the emotion evident in her voice. "Johnny. Oh my gosh."

He brushed her hands away. "It's okay. It's no big deal."

"It *is* a big deal. He's hurting you. Why do you let him do this? You're strong. I know you could stop him. You're a man. You don't have to take this anymore." Her voice choked with tears.

Johnny smiled down at her, tears welling in his own eyes. "Don't you see, Eddy? I *am* a man, and that's *why* I take it. I love my dad and somehow this is what makes *him* feel like a man. Even for a little bit. I can take a punch. It's no big deal. He's usually sorry afterwards, and then he gives me a hug and offers me a beer." He looked down at his chest, wiping at the bruise as if he could brush it away. "This is nothing if it gets me time spent with my dad and he seems okay for a while."

Edna's heart swelled with love for the poor, broken little boy inside of the man who stood before her. She wanted to take him in her arms. Take him away from this life where he suffered pain to receive love. Where he sacrificed his pride to build up another's. "I'm sorry."

"Don't be sorry. It's not your fault. It is what it is." He took her chin in his hand and tilted her face up to his. "I want you to know these things about me. I want you to know me. To know what you're getting yourself into. But I also want you to know that I would never lay a hand on you. Just because it happens to me doesn't mean I will do it to you, or anyone else. I hate violence."

"Really? But you seem so—" She shrugged, looking for the right word. "So dangerous, I guess."

He smirked. "It's all an act. People expect me to be like that, and if I act really tough, no one messes with me. Or with Frank, or Weasel. I can fight, if I have to. But usually I just give them the look and they back off." He narrowed his eyes and sneered at her. "That's my mean look."

"Yes, I see what you mean." She giggled. What was it about this boy that had her constantly giggling? She felt like she hadn't had anything to even mildly laugh at in the past few years, then she got around Johnny and seemed to always be giggling like a schoolgirl. Must be love.

His eyes went from the mean look to an amused one. "Are you telling me my mean look has no power over you? You Colorado girls are tough." He reached down, swept his arm under her knees and lifted her, cradling her against him.

Carrying her to the small twin bed in the corner of the room, he set her on the mattress and climbed onto the bed, leaning over her. He dropped his head to her neck and laid a trail of small kisses up to her ear. His voice was low in her ear, sexy and teasing. "I guess I'll have to find a different way to show you how dangerous I am."

She pushed back and looked up at him, a feeling of fear quickening her pulse. "You *are* dangerous, Johnny. I believe that you would never physically harm me, but you do have the power to hurt me. You're holding my heart in your hands and Johnny, it's so fragile. You could break it so easily." She gripped his arms, pleading to him with her eyes. "Please don't hurt me. Don't break my heart, Johnny."

"Your heart is safe with me, Eddy." He lay down next to her, pulling her body in close to his. Holding her chin in his hand, he gazed at her, and she could feel the love in his eyes. "I love you. With everything in me. I won't hurt you. I would die for you."

She gasped. "Oh, Johnny. I don't want you to die. For me or for anyone. I want you to live, with me, forever."

"I know. I'm not saying I'm *going* to die. I just don't know how else to explain how *much* I love you. I've never felt something so huge in all of my life. I don't know any other way to say it. You are mine now, and I take care of what's mine. I would do anything to protect you. To keep you from harm. Even if it hurt me. Anything."

She was overcome with the emotion in his voice, and her heart ached with love as she watched a lone tear roll down the side of his cheek. She rolled over on top of him, her arms on either side of his head. Bending forward, she kissed away the tear. "I am yours. Everything in me and all of who I am belongs to you. Forever. I promise I will never love another man as much or as deeply as I love you."

She sat up, never taking her eyes from his. Reaching behind her neck, she pulled the halter straps of her two-piece and let the top of her swimsuit fall. Her shoulders hunched forward: she felt suddenly modest at her small chest.

"Don't," he said. "You don't have to be shy with me. I love you, and I love that you say what you think. I want you to be proud of yourself. Always."

She pushed her shoulders back, his words giving her the power to be bold. She took a shuddering breath as he reached behind her and slowly unclasped the lower straps, allowing the swimsuit top to drop to the floor.

He looked up at her, straddling him and hunger displayed in his eyes. "And just so you know, I think your breasts are perfect."

She grinned, feeling the truth of his words rising underneath her. She moved against him. Slowly rocking her hips forward and back, the denim of his jeans rough against her bare legs, her shorts the only thing she still wore. She felt him at the core of her body, the center of her womanhood, as she continued to move against him.

His eyes closed, and a groan escaped his lips. Her confidence soared and she leaned forward, sliding her body against his naked chest. His hands moved up, grasping her waist and holding her hips firmly against his.

She kissed him then, no holds barred. Kissed him with a ferocity she didn't know was inside of her. The touch of his bare chest against hers was like fire igniting between them. Her hips moved against his, inciting a hunger in Johnny, evident by the way his hands gripped her back and the crush of his lips on hers.

She pushed back, still straddling him, and watched his face as she rode him, slowly moving back and forth as waves crash on the shore of the ocean. Knowing her hair was wild around her shoulders, she reveled in the look of desire and need on his face. Passion flared in his eyes, and he groaned with want as she slid across his manhood.

Feeling bold, gaining courage from his obvious pleasure, she picked up his hands and guided them to her breasts. Gasping at his touch, she leaned her head back, arching her back against his firm grip. Her hips moved again, in rhythm with the way his hands kneaded her breasts, breathless as his fingertips brushed against her erect nipples.

As if unable to take another moment of the sweet torture, Johnny raised up and, with strong arms, flipped her over and underneath him. His lips crushed hers, and she felt his fingers fumbling with the clasp of her shorts. He shed his jeans and rose above her, finally freeing the zipper and tugging her shorts and swimsuit bottoms down her legs.

Then he was against her, his bare skin touching every part of her naked body. She couldn't get enough of him. Her arms wrapped around him, and she pulled him tightly to her, gripping his shoulders, scratching at his back.

Rejoicing in his moans of want, she shifted under him, enticing him with her movements and tempting him with the glory of her body.

His lips were everywhere. Moving from her throat to her breast. Nibbling and sucking. His mouth taking as his hands touched and squeezed. Fondled and caressed. His teeth brushed her neck, his breath ragged in her earlobe. "I want you, Eddy. I want you so much. I can't get enough of you. Of your skin. Of the way you taste. The way you smell. God, you smell amazing."

His words sparked a passion inside of her. She wanted this man. Wanted every part of him. Needed to be one with him. To share her body, her soul, her very being. "I want you too, Johnny. I need you. I need you inside of me."

And then he was. And she almost wept with relief. And joy. And a love she thought would tear her body apart with the enormity of it.

He felt so good. Around her. Inside of her. She moved against him, their bodies in perfect rhythm with the beat of their hearts.

Everything else fell away. The scars of their parents, the weed-choked front yard of the tiny house, the past and the future. Nothing mattered except this moment. This boy and this girl, their bodies wrapped together in a tiny bed with threadbare sheets and a sagging mattress.

They were oblivious to everything around them. The world melted away, leaving only fragments of time, of motion. Of the sweet, desperate yearning for that moment of connection. Of oneness.

The unbearable pleasure shattered, leaving them weak and breathless, the sheets tangled around their legs and Johnny's body collapsed onto hers.

His voice against her ear, raspy and rough. His words raw with emotion. "You are mine. Now and always. No one will ever love you the way I do. I will love you till the day I die."

An hour later, finally making it to the lake, they lay on the beach, sprawled across the towels that Frank seemed to always have in the back seat of his car. Spent and energized at the same time, Johnny lay on his stomach beside Edna, his eyes closed and one hand resting across her bare stomach. His fingers absently traced circles around her navel, sending delicious shivers arcing through her spine.

Frank and Weasel had been there for an hour, and Weasel's cheeks were already tinged with the pink of too much sun.

"Where's Donna?" Edna asked Weasel, turning on her side to look at the boy as she passed him a tube of sunscreen.

"Had to work at the bank today. She's gonna meet us at the drive-in later, though." He squirted some sunscreen in his hands and rubbed it into his cheeks.

Donna worked at the First State Bank of Coopersville as a teller and had been putting in more hours lately to fill in for another employee who was out on vacation. She and Edna had formed a cordial and, at times, even pleasant friendship. Edna had continually worked to win the other girl over, anxious to have a girlfriend to share stories with, and she thought Donna might be softening to her a little.

The four friends languished on the beach. Johnny, Edna, and Frank played in the water, soaking up the summer sunshine.

By mid-afternoon, the feel of the air changed as heavy thunderclouds rolled in and darkened the sky. A flash of lightning lit the sky, followed by a crack of thunder a minute later.

"We'd better pick up our stuff and get out of here," Johnny said. "Looks like a storm is moving in."

Frank was already gathering their towels and empty pop bottles. Edna could feel the urgency in their movements. She pulled on her shorts and reached for her top. "What's the big deal, guys? So what if it rains? We're already at the beach; it's not gonna hurt us if we get a little wet."

Johnny tossed her the towels and stuffed his feet into his engineer boots. Edna would have laughed at the sight of him in his swim trunks and boots if he didn't have such a serious look on his face.

He reached for her hand. "This isn't that kind of storm, Edna. If you were from Kansas, you would know. You can feel it in the air. We need to get back to your aunt's farm. Right now."

Another flash of lightning. This one closer, the crack of the thunder following within seconds.

Frank and Weasel ran up the beach and threw their things in the car. Johnny and Edna followed on their heels. Frank grabbed for the convertible top, pulling it up and over the seats. A loud siren filled the air. Johnny and Frank exchanged grim looks.

"What's going on?" Edna cried, the intensity of the boys and the shrill sound of the siren creating a bad feeling in the pit of her stomach. "You're scaring me."

Johnny's normal good-natured tone was gone, replaced by a commanding one as he shouted out orders. "Weasel, you go with Frank. You guys head to town. We'll take the bike and try to get to Miss Janice. We need to warn her if she hasn't heard the siren."

"I need to get to the bank and check on Donna. She freaks out in storms like this," Weasel said, securing his side of the convertible top and climbing into the front seat.

"I'll drop you by the bank. I need to find my mom and make sure she gets to the basement." Frank looked at Johnny. "You sure you wanna take the bike? You can come with us, and I'll bring you back out later."

"I'm sure. I can cut through a couple of fields, and we can get to the farm quicker. I want to be able to help Janice if she needs it." Johnny waved Frank away and grabbed Edna's hand, pulling her to the bike. "We gotta go. That siren means there's a tornado coming."

A tornado? But how? They'd just been swimming and lying in the sun less than half an hour ago. How could the weather change so quickly? And that drastically? Edna's heart raced as she climbed onto the back of the bike and secured her arms around Johnny's waist.

He gunned the engine of the bike, gravel spitting as they peeled out of the lake's parking area and sped down the dirt road toward Janice's farm.

Fat droplets of rain began to fall.

"Hold on," Johnny yelled above the sound of the wind. He turned off the road into a field, and the bike bounced through the ruts of a tractor-made path.

Edna tightened her arms around his waist, her teeth clacking together as they hit a bump in the field. They flew through the pasture and came out the other side, the bike losing momentum as it climbed the slope of the ditch lining the road.

They were on the highway now, and the leaves from the cottonwood trees lining the road flew in their faces. The big trees swayed as the wind kicked up another notch. A branch broke off a tree and fell to the road in front of them.

Johnny swerved to avoid the fallen limb, leaning his body to counterbalance the tilt of the bike. Edna screamed as an oncoming truck honked and veered off the side of the road, narrowly missing the motorcycle.

The rain was falling harder now and whipped into their cheeks as they sped down the road. Edna was soaked to the skin, shivering against Johnny's back. Her hands shook as she held on to Johnny's waist, trying to mimic his movements as he leaned with the motion of the bike.

Her aunt's farm was in sight. Johnny took his hand from the handlebars for just a moment and pointed at the sky behind the farmhouse. He gunned the engine. The bike burst forward with a jolt of speed that rivaled the beating of Edna's heart as she saw the monstrous black funnel cloud filling the sky and bearing down on the farm.

Leaning against the turn, mud flying against their bare legs, the motorcycle banked the corner into the driveway as Johnny tore down the dirt drive. He braked in front of the house, the wheels spinning, and for half a second, Edna was afraid that he had lost control and they were going to crash. He leaned back and drew the bike to a shuddering stop.

He and Edna jumped off, and he dropped the bike to the ground. Running toward the barn, Edna searched frantically for her aunt as she screamed her name. The gusting wind and rain soaked up her cries and the panic inside of her built with the force of the storm.

The windmill above her head shrieked. The sound of tearing metal was deafening as the blades tore loose and the head of the windmill flew through the air. It crashed into the side of the barn, wood splintering, pieces of metal and wood flying through the air, picked up by the intense wind.

Relief flooded Edna as she saw her aunt run from around the side of the barn, a pink pig cradled in her arms. Penny ran beside her, barking at the storm. Edna ran to her aunt. She threw her arms around her, not daring to imagine the possibility of something happening to Janice.

"We need to get to the storm cellar," Janice yelled above the din. She pointed toward the side of the house, where Johnny was already wrestling to lift the door set into the ground. The fierce wind and rain worked against him as he pulled on the door, slamming it down each time he lifted it a few inches.

The women ran to the shelter. Edna stepped in beside Johnny and grabbed the handle of the door. Her hands were below his and her muscles strained as she lifted with all of her might.

Between the two of them, they raised the door just enough for the wind to get under it. Johnny knocked her hands free and pushed her back as the door flew open, slamming into the ground, the wooden frame cracking with the impact.

Janice ran down the cellar stairs, the dog on her heels. Johnny grabbed Edna's hand and thrust her ahead of him into the dark pit of the storm cellar.

The storm raged and howled above them as Johnny fought to pull the cellar door closed. The sky was black and thick with clouds, tumbling and twisting against each other. Edna screamed as a flash of lightning lit the sky above Johnny's head, and thunder followed immediately in its wake.

Johnny managed to gain purchase on the door, and it slammed closed, knocking him down the few steps into the cellar. Edna heard him clamber up the steps to bolt the latch, securing the door.

The storm cellar was pitch black and shut out some of the noise of the raging storm. Edna heard crying and realized the sound was coming from her as her chest heaved and pitched, trying to suck in air as she cried from a terror she had never before felt in her life. She felt Johnny's arms around her, and she clung to him with one hand and reached for her aunt with the other.

"It's all right, Edna." Aunt Janice spoke in the dark. "We're going to be okay. This is the safest place for us to be."

A shudder passed through Edna as she tried to calm her breathing. The wind and storm seethed above them, shaking the door of the cellar as if trying to get in and snatch one of them out. A moment later, a plank from the wooden door was ripped free, letting in a shaft of dim light as it was sucked into the air above them.

Through the hole in the door, they could see the wind swirling and knew the tornado was right on top of them. Debris spun through the black funnel. Edna recognized one of the white rockers from her aunt's porch as it flew by.

The noise was like nothing Edna could have ever imagined or described. The fury of the storm's wrath was unbiased in its destruction, obliterating everything in its path. Screaming and howling in a rage as it tore through the landscape of the farm.

Nothing was safe. Edna saw a flash of green paint as a tractor swirled by in the funnel above their heads. The ferocity of the actual tornado lasted for only minutes as it passed through Aunt Janice's farm, but it felt like hours as they waited, huddled together in the dark, the smell of rain and the dirt of the cellar walls mingling in the air.

The wind and rain stopped as if suddenly turned off by a switch. It was eerily quiet as Johnny climbed the cellar steps and threw back the latch of the door.

"Wait! Don't go out there!" Edna screamed.

Her aunt's arm came around her shoulders in reassurance. "It's okay, Edna. It's over now."

"How do you know?"

"Because I've lived in Kansas my whole life. This isn't the first tornado I've seen, and since God let me live through this one, it probably won't be the last." She still held the pig in her arms, and it snuffled against her shoulder. She put her foot on the cellar steps and accepted Johnny's hand as he reached down to help her. The Collie ran up the stairs and out into the yard. "Come on. Let's go assess the damage."

Edna blinked as she followed her aunt up the steps and out into the daylight. Speech escaped her as she took in the destruction around her. The house stood intact and untouched in front of her, but the barn was just simply gone. As if the huge red building had never been there in the first place.

Debris and fallen branches littered the driveway. The green tractor Edna thought she saw in the funnel cloud now hung from the boughs of a tall cottonwood tree next to the headless windmill.

Lady, Aunt Janice's favorite mare, came galloping around the edge of the house, scared but otherwise unharmed. Had it only been a few hours ago that Edna had cleaned out her stall and laid fresh hay on the barn floor that no longer existed?

A large swath of field lay flattened behind the barn, evidence of the path of the tornado. Looking across the pasture, they could see that the neighboring farm stood intact.

Stunned, the three stood speechless, taking in the scene around them. They had come so close to being casualties of the destruction. If Johnny hadn't have cut through that field, if that fallen branch had delayed them, if they had been only three minutes later, they might have been too late. The implications of those thoughts overwhelmed her, and Edna's knees threatened to buckle.

She shook her head, unable to grasp the enormity of what had just happened. She reached out to her aunt. "I'm so sorry, Aunt Janice. What will we do?"

Janice set the pig down and pulled Edna into her embrace. "It's all right, honey. We'll do what we always do. First, we thank the good Lord that we're all alive and nobody got hurt, then we pick up the mess and go on. A barn is wood and nails. It can be rebuilt. Nothing can replace you." She reached for Johnny and drew him into the hug. "Or this one either. I am so glad that you're both okay."

Edna's eyes filled with tears at the tremor of emotion she heard in her aunt's voice, and she snuggled against her. "I'm glad you're okay. I was so scared that you would be out in a field or something and we wouldn't be able to find you."

"I was," Janice said. "I'd been down in the southwest pasture repairing a fence line, and I ran out of wire. I'd just started back to the house when I heard the tornado siren go off. By the time I got to the barn and grabbed Mazie, I could see the funnel cloud coming across the field."

"It looks like the tornado headed for town," Johnny said. "I need to go check on my dad."

"I'm worried about the town, as well," Janice said, heading for the truck. "We'll all go in and see if there's anything we can do to help."

Johnny looked around. "I need to find my motorcycle. It doesn't seem to be where I left it."

Edna spotted the motorcycle against the house, resting between the porch and a pink peony bush. "There it is. Thank goodness the tornado didn't take it."

Johnny found a loose plank from the barn and used it as a ramp to wheel his bike into the bed of Janice's blue pickup. Penny jumped in and settled against the cab.

Janice shrugged and reached for the pig, who seemed to follow her everywhere. "Well, there's no barn to leave her in, so I guess the pig's coming with us too."

They drove slowly into town, assessing the damage to neighboring farms as they went. Edna gasped as she saw the extent of the destruction.

The tornado had gone through the edge of the town, touching down in random spots, destroying one building and leaving the one next to it undamaged. Dozens of townspeople wandered the streets, either pitching in to help or walking aimlessly in shock, glazed expressions on their faces.

Frank's family's car dealership had been left untouched, but the insurance agency next to it was destroyed. One of the cars from the lot had been lifted in the tornado and lay upside down in the middle of the insurance office destruction, its shiny red paint now covered in dust and mud.

Multiple cars lay on their sides, and fires burned sporadically up and down the street. An upside-down modular home lay diagonally over the top of the demolished hair salon, a blue sofa sticking up out of a crack in the home's walls.

The windows were down, and the sound of multiple sirens filled the cab of the truck. Edna stared at the debris. The fallen homes and businesses. How could the ambulance or fire engines know where to respond to first? How could they judge the need of one family's despair over another?

The bank was on this side of town and now stood in a pile of rubble, the steel vault the only thing standing amidst the broken planks of what had been the bank's lobby. Edna said a silent prayer that Donna had not been in the building during the tornado.

"I had never witnessed anything so terrible in all of my life," Edna said. She looked around the table at the Page Turners and wasn't surprised to see Cassie wiping a tear from her face.

"So," Piper said, "was she all right? Was Donna in the bank when the tornado hit?"

"Yes, she was. It was a Saturday so they had a small staff working. It was only Donna and one of the bank officers," Johnny explained. "When the siren went off, they tried to run to the vault to lock themselves inside. But the tornado hit so fast that only Donna made it to the vault. The bank officer was killed when the funnel suddenly hit the building."

"Oh no. Poor girl," Sunny said. "Was she okay?"

"She was totally in shock." Edna looked down, a little in shock herself to see that John's hand was covering hers. "She escaped the vault, climbing over the rubble to get out. Evidently, she was in such a fog that she left the door open, and in the chaos of the storm and the aftermath, someone got in there and robbed the vault of all the cash. Got away with over fifty-thousand dollars. Which was a lot in the fifties."

"It's a lot now," Sunny said. "Did they ever catch the guy?"

"Not as far as I know." Edna looked up at John and pulled her hand free. "Some said he must have disappeared after the storm and others say that he died."

"There's usually more to a story than people realize at the time." John peered at Edna.

"Seems to me there's been plenty of time between now and then to tell that story," she said.

An awkward silence settled around the table.

The silence was broken by a loud crash as a rock the size of a toaster came smashing through Edna's front bay window. The window shattered and broken glass flew into the room followed by the large rock. It landed with a thud on the carpet, rolling to a stop against the coffee table.

Sunny screamed, and Jake went into federal agent mode, on his feet and throwing his arms out to protect the women. Within seconds, he had the kitchen table tipped on its side and the members of the book club herded behind it. He instructed John to stay with the women.

Edna was surprised to see him pull a handgun from the back waistband of his jeans as he moved to check things out. He threw the front door open and slipped outside.

Within a few minutes, he was back, reaching for Sunny and drawing her into his arms. "It's all clear. Is everybody okay in here?"

"We're okay," Cassie said, one arm wrapped around Piper's shoulder.

Edna nodded at the gun in Jake's hand. "Do you always bring a gun to dinner? Or just when we're having ziti?"

Jake's gaze leveled at John. "I bring a gun when I think I might need one."

"What the hell was that?" Maggie asked. She turned to Edna. "Who did you piss off now?"

Edna shrugged. "It could be anybody."

Jake slowly approached the rock. "I don't think it was meant for you, Edna. It's got a piece of paper stuck to it with a message on it, written in red marker. It says, 'I know you're alive.'" He raised an eyebrow at John.

Edna took in the worried look on John's face. "Hell, that could mean anything. Maybe they're talking about Jesus. Those religious groups might have grown tired of handing out pamphlets, and they're trying a new approach."

As usual, Maggie ignored Edna's sarcasm. "We need to call the police."

"We can't," Edna said.

"Why not?"

Edna looked at John. "Because someone out there might know that John's alive, but it isn't the police. If the police knew, they'd arrest him."

John took Edna's hand. "It's okay. I knew once I came back, that everything would come out. I wasn't expecting this, though." He gestured at the broken glass. "I don't want to put you in danger. I think you should call the police."

"No. You're here. After sixty years of believing you were dead, you are standing in my living room. I'm not ready to let you go." She squeezed his hand.

"We could call Mac," Cassie suggested.

Officer McCarthy was a local policeman who had helped the Page Turners book club earlier this summer. He'd been the one on call and shown up to help Sunny when she'd been assaulted. And he was also the officer assigned to the murder case that Maggie's boyfriend had been the prime suspect in. He was a good man and had a soft spot for the Page Turners. Especially Maggie.

"We don't need to bother Mac," Maggie said.

"Well, we need to call somebody," Jake said. "This is a serious rock. If Edna had been sitting in this chair, it could have killed her." He narrowed his eyes at John. "I'm not sure what kind of trouble you're in, John. I'm a pretty good judge of character, and I don't think you're a bad guy, but my first priority is these women. I can't have them put in danger."

"I agree." John looked down at Edna. "You need to file a police report. Plus, you'll need it to file an insurance claim."

"Listen to you, all Mr. Responsible, worrying about insurance claims."

John smiled. "I have grown up a little, Eddy. And I agree with Jake. This is obviously a threat aimed at me and I don't want to put you or your friends in harm's way."

Edna sighed. "All right, let's call Mac. I think we can trust him." She nodded at Maggie.

"Don't look at me. I'm not calling him." Maggie pointed at her friend. "It was Cassie's idea. Let her call him."

"Oh for heaven's sake, I'll call him." Sunny dug her phone from her front pocket and found his number.

Fifteen minutes later, Jake greeted the handsome police officer and ushered him into the room. Well over six feet tall, with his serious eyes and clean-shaven head, Officer McCarthy commanded the attention of the room. His eyes cut first to Maggie, taking in that she was all right, then he swept the room with his gaze.

The living room remained untouched; the rock still lay amidst the broken glass scattered across the floor. They had righted the kitchen table, and the Page Turners and John sat around it.

Mac walked directly to Edna. His eyes were soft as he looked down at the tiny elderly woman. "Are you all right, Ms. Allen?"

Edna winked at the police officer and shook his hand. "Of course I am." She hoped her offhand comment would disguise the trembling in her hand.

But Mac was smart. He folded his other hand on top of her smaller one, and gave her a reassuring nod. "If there's trouble to be had, you always seem to find it."

Edna smiled. "I always say a little trouble keeps you young."

"Well, I assume you're knee deep in this, otherwise your cohorts wouldn't have asked me to come alone." He nodded at the Page Turners before turning back to Edna. "You want to tell me what's going on?"

Edna gave Mac an abbreviated version of the story, leaving John out of it as much as she could. She told him they had been sweethearts, but hadn't seen each other in years. "Listen, Mac, I still trust this man with my life, and I will do whatever I can to protect him."

Mac pulled on a pair of rubber gloves and removed the paper from the rock. He held it by the corner and placed it into a Ziploc bag, then nodded at John. "Do you have any idea who sent you this message?"

John shook his head. "No, sir. I have literally been off the grid for the past sixty years. I arrived in town a few days ago and only the people in this room even know that I'm here. I don't use a computer and have a prepaid cell phone. I haven't told anyone my real name in years."

"This might be my fault, then," Jake said.

"Your fault?" Sunny said. She had grabbed a broom from the closet and was sweeping up the broken glass. "How could any of this be your fault?"

"I do know your real name, and I've used it on the computer. If you were into some kind of trouble or really dangerous, I couldn't have you around these women," Jake said to John. "I've been digging into your past to see what I could find and I've entered your name and social security number into several databases. If someone was monitoring your social, it may have come up as a hit and led them here."

"What kind of trouble were you in that's taken you off the grid for sixty years and has someone monitoring internet activity for your whereabouts?" Mac asked.

Edna sighed. "Why don't you all sit down? It seems like we need to tell you the rest of the story."

Cassie headed for the kitchen and grabbed some dessert plates. "Oh good. I'll serve the pie."

Coopersville, Kansas, 1955

It had been two weeks since the storm. The town pulled together and had been working to repair and restore. Those that weren't hit offered shelter and aid to those who had been.

Johnny, Frank, and Weasel spent their evenings out at the farm, helping Janice to rebuild. It seemed that folks from the town showed up every day, helping to clean up debris and erect a new barn. New fence line had to be run, and the windmill needed to be repaired. Different townspeople arrived as different skills were needed. Edna was amazed at the feeling of community and the way they all pitched in to help each other.

She kept busy making food and doing an assortment of tasks. She would have done anything to help her aunt, and eagerly accepted any job, from putting together sandwiches to filling the truck with downed branches and broken lumber.

The guys came out to help, which made the chores easier. Frank's relaxed manner and Johnny's sense of play made most jobs seem more fun. Weasel was on the quiet side, but he worked hard and could always be counted on to pitch in.

"You guys have made such a difference out here," Edna told Johnny one evening as they loaded debris into the back of the pickup.

"We want to help," Johnny said. "Your aunt is a good lady, and she doesn't deserve this. Not everybody would take a chance on the poor kid of the town drunk, but your aunt's offered me odd jobs out here every summer since I was fourteen. Frank and I have come out and helped with harvest and calf branding, whatever she needed. Even Weasel has done some jobs for her."

"Still, you've been out here every night. And we're not paying you anything."

"I wouldn't take a dime. Even if she offered." Johnny threw a broken tree limb into the bed of the truck. "Janice has always been there for me, helping me when I needed it. I'm glad to be able to repay some of her kindness by helping her get the farm back in order."

Edna warmed at the sincerity of his words. He looked so tough, with his greased hair and muscled arms. It often took her by surprise when he made heartfelt comments, expressing his thoughts and feelings. She smiled up at him. "I know she really appreciates it. We both do. And if you won't let her pay you anything, maybe you'll let me think of a way to repay you."

Johnny's eyes widened at her bold comment. He laughed and wrapped an arm around her waist, drawing her close and placing a quick kiss on her lips. "How about you pay me by agreeing to go to the Harvest Dance with me Friday night?"

A thrill raced up her spine as his lips touched hers. She couldn't get enough of the feel of him. Being in his arms. Having him so close to her. Being able to touch him and kiss him whenever she wanted. She couldn't believe this man was hers. Having him sweep her around a dance floor sounded like heaven. "Of course I will. Are you sure they're still having it?"

"Yeah, I heard them talking about it in the drugstore. They have it every summer, and they think it'll be good for the town to get together and have something fun to look forward to. I guess they talked about canceling it but decided it might help the morale of the town."

"Count me in. I'm all for helping out morale," Edna said, already planning which dress she would wear.

Of the two she brought, she chose the pale yellow one. It had a full skirt and a snug bodice with a row of embroidered daisies lining the thin spaghetti straps. She wore a string of white beads to offset the color of the petals, and yellow pumps completed the outfit. Johnny whistled in appreciation when he and Frank picked her up that Friday night.

The dance floor was hopping by the time they walked into the Elks Lodge. It seemed the whole town had shown up for the event. Punch was flowing, both spiked and unspiked, and the sound of laughter filled the room.

Edna spied Donna and Weasel at a table in the corner of the room and they made their way through the crowd to join them. Donna's hair was curled and set, and she wore a green taffeta dress.

"You look lovely, Donna," Edna said, sinking into the chair next to her friend. "Your dress is beautiful. It looks great with your skin."

Her compliment earned a rare smile from Donna. "Thanks. Yours is nice too."

"I missed you on the ride over. I thought we would have picked you up."

"You don't have to pick us up anymore." Donna gave Weasel an adoring glance. "Warren has his own car now. He just got it. It's a Buick."

"Yeah, got my own wheels finally." Weasel grinned and gestured at Frank. "No more bumming rides off this clown."

"I saw it out front," Frank said. "It's nice. You must have been saving like crazy to afford that beauty. But I wish you would've checked with me or my dad. We could've got you a bargain."

"Ahh, Donna knew a guy who was selling it. He gave me a good deal." Warren reached into the side pocket of his blazer and pulled out a silver flask. He tipped back a swig then offered it around the table.

Frank shook his head. "Nah, I'm driving tonight."

"I'm not." Johnny grabbed the flask, took a quick pull, and passed it to Edna. "It's some of his dad's scotch. Want a swig?"

Edna took the flask. She'd watched her mother fight the debilitating effects of alcohol for years, and she'd always abstained. She recognized the slack jaw and glassy eyes on Weasel and knew he was already drunk. Not wanting to make a big deal, she took a small sip. The liquid burned and left a warm trail down her throat. She passed it to Donna, who waved it away.

Weasel grabbed for it and took another swallow before tucking it back into his pocket. He grabbed Donna by the arm. "Let's dance."

Johnny held out his hand to Edna. "May I have this dance?"

What a gentleman. She took his hand and let him lead her out onto the dance floor. He pulled her into his arms and swayed to the music. His breath was warm against her ear, and she could smell the faint scent of Weasel's dad's scotch. Tucked into his arms, moving with the rhythm of the band, Edna felt the magic of the evening. The magic of the summer.

Too bad there was no such thing as magic.

The group of friends danced and laughed. Keenly aware of the effects of alcohol, Edna noticed that both Johnny and Weasel passed the silver flask between them several more times as the night wore on.

Being such a cute catch, Frank had no shortage of dance partners. He took turns dancing with Donna and Edna when the other guys snuck out back for a cigarette or to refill the flask.

Frank was not as tall as Johnny, but Edna felt comfortable slow dancing in his arms. "It seems like you're having fun tonight. I think you could have your pick of any woman in this room."

Frank ducked his head in modesty. "Nah. They're only interested in me because my family has money. It doesn't have anything to do with me."

"That's not true at all. Your family might have wealth, but you're very handsome, Frank. You must know that."

"Yeah, right. Handsome as my wallet and the nice car I drive."

"Oh, stop it. You would make a great catch, and I think every single girl in the room has flirted with you tonight. Except maybe Ms. May, the librarian, and that's only because she's eighty."

"Oh no, I danced with Ms. May a little bit ago."

Edna laughed. "You didn't."

Frank grinned. "Yes, I did. But I think she just wanted to remind me that I still had library fines due from back in high school."

Edna swatted him on the arm. "Seriously, Frank. You're a great guy and super cute. Why don't you have a girlfriend? Have you just not met the right girl yet?"

Frank looked down into Edna's eyes. "Maybe I did meet her, and she fell for someone else?"

Oh.

Before Edna could respond, she was jostled into Frank as Donna ran by her and into the ladies' room. Edna took a step back from Frank. "She didn't look so good. Maybe I'd better go check on her. See if she's okay."

Frank smiled, but a hint of sadness crossed his face for just a moment. Then he waved her on. "Yeah, sure. I'll catch up with you in a bit."

The sound of retching could be heard as she entered the ladies' room. Edna wet a paper towel as she waited for Donna to exit the stall. The girl emerged, her face pale and her hair damp with sweat.

Edna held out the moist towel. "Are you okay?"

"What do you care?" Donna asked, ignoring the paper towel and rinsing her mouth with water.

"Of course I care. You're the only girlfriend I have in Coopersville." She reached a tentative hand out to touch Donna's shoulder. "I'd like to help if I can."

Edna was surprised to see the girl's face crumple and big tears fill her eyes. "You can't help me. Nobody can."

"Oh goodness," Edna said, unused to any kind of emotion from the other girl. "What's happened? Did you have too much to drink? Are you worried your dad will get upset?"

Donna laughed. A slight, wry sigh. "Yes, I am worried my dad will be upset. I'm worried that *everyone* will be upset. I'm not sick because I'm drunk. I haven't had anything to drink tonight. I've been puking all month."

"All month? But you haven't seemed sick."

Donna waited, as if watching Edna's face for a reaction.

"Oh-h-h." The realization slowly dawned on Edna. "Oh no. You're pregnant?"

"Bingo. Give that girl a prize."

"What are you going to do? Does Weasel know?"

"His name is Warren. And of course he knows. Why do you think he's getting pissed drunk tonight? We're going to the courthouse next week to get married."

"Can I do anything to help?"

"Like what? Make me un-pregnant? Explain to my parents that their pride and joy is not married and having a baby? Explain to my dad, the chief of police, how I snuck out and got drunk and let a boy touch me?"

Her tone changed to one of snide condescension. "What could you possibly do to help me? You show up for two months in the summer and sashay around like you're all Miss Downtown with your fancy polka-dotted two-piece swimsuit and blonde curls. You don't know what it's like to grow up here—to feel trapped by your own circumstances."

Edna knew all too well what that felt like. "I do understand. Donna, I want to be your friend."

"Why? You don't even know me." Donna brushed at the tears flowing freely down her face. "You're leaving at the end of the summer and probably won't ever look back. Just leave me alone." She wrapped her arms around herself, a picture of despair as she sank into the corner of the restroom.

Edna tried once more, reaching out, but the other girl batted her arm away. "I mean it. Just leave me alone."

"I'll go get Weasel—I mean, Warren. I'll be right back." Edna backed out of the ladies' room. She turned and scanned the crowd for the boy. Figuring he must still be outside, Edna ducked out the back door.

She found herself in a dark alley between the buildings. Stepping over trash and cigarette butts, she called into the dark. "Weasel? Johnny?"

The alley was quiet, and Edna took a tentative step forward. The silence was broken by the sharp crack of a wooden matchstick, and a round flame of light lit Weasel's face as he held the match to a cigarette. "What are you doing back here? Come to see how the simple folk live?"

Geez. Why did everyone seem to think she was better off than they were? If they only knew how many nights she had searched the kitchen for something to eat and found nothing but a half-empty jar of peanut butter and a stale loaf of bread.

"I was looking for you. Donna's not feeling well. I thought you might want to take her home."

"I'll bet she's not feeling well." He took a step toward Edna and stumbled forward, reaching for her to steady himself. He looked down at Edna, and she could smell the liquor on his breath. "Did she tell you the happy news?"

"Yes. Although you don't seem particularly happy about it."

"What do I have to be happy about? I worked so hard to get into college. To have a chance to get out of this town. For what? To get my girl knocked up and move back here anyway."

"Maybe she could go with you, back to school. You can get your degree and move anywhere you like."

Weasel laughed, a hard, brittle sound. "The days of doing anything I like are over. You haven't met Donna's dad. I will be under his thumb for the rest of my life. I'm such an idiot." His voice cracked, and he leaned into Edna, dropping his head to her shoulder.

She folded him into her arms, half afraid he might start to cry. She could hear the desperation in his voice, and she rubbed a comforting hand over his back. "It's gonna be okay."

Weasel's hands encircled her back, drawing her close to him. Instead of breaking down, he nuzzled against her neck. "You smell so good. You always smell so good. Different from the girls around here. Why do you smell so nice, Edna?"

"Must be my shampoo." A tiny flicker of panic set off low in her gut, so she stepped back, trying to disentangle herself from his arms.

He pulled her tighter, his words slurred from the alcohol. "You know, I saw you first. I rode here with you on the bus. You even smiled at me. Why couldn't you have been my girl, Edna? Just for the summer." He reached up and slid his hand across her bare shoulder and under the strap of her dress. "How 'bout you be my girl just for tonight?"

A shiver ran through Edna as she tried to push him away. This wasn't like him. It must be the stress of the baby combined with the alcohol. "Weasel, come on, stop it. You're drunk. Let's go back inside."

"I don't want to go back inside." His tone turned belligerent and whiny. He gripped her shoulder tighter, breaking the strap of her dress. "I wanna stay out here. With you. Stay with me for just a little bit. Come on, Edna."

He broke her dress. The stupid oaf! It didn't matter how much he had to drink, she wasn't putting up with this. She pushed hard against him, trying to break free of his grasp.

"Don't be like that, Edna. No one will know. It's just us out here." He turned her around, trapping her between his body and the brick wall of the building. Pressing against her, he leaned down to kiss her, his hands already pulling at her dress, lifting her skirt.

"Weasel, don't." She twisted her face away from his, scraping her cheek against the rough brick wall. That small flicker of panic was turning into a full-blown flame as she realized how helpless she was against the much taller man. She pushed at his hands, fighting him, terror creeping into her. "Warren, stop it!"

His one hand was on her leg and the other pressed against her breast, grasping and groping as he pushed her against the wall. He tried again to kiss her, his scotch-scented breath hot against her cheek as she turned her head.

"Get off me!" she cried. Tears coursed down her cheeks, and she bucked against him, scratching at his face with her nails. "Please, don't do this."

"Get the hell away from her."

A wave of relief hit her as she heard Johnny's voice, and Weasel's weight was lifted from her. Through her tears, she saw a flash of color as Johnny threw Weasel to the ground. In a rage, Johnny fell on him, swearing and throwing punches at his face.

Edna cried out at the crack of Weasel's nose breaking while a spray of blood landed across the rumpled skirt of her dress. "Johnny, stop."

The next few minutes happened in a blur of sound and colors. A rush of voices as men poured into the alley, shouting at Johnny and reaching to pull him off of Weasel. A burst of bright red blood on Johnny's knuckles. A scream from Donna as she raced to Weasel's side, falling on the ground and cradling his bleeding face against her green dress. The flicker of blue of Frank's jacket as he was there, pulling Johnny away from Weasel and down the alley. Away from the dance and the eyes of the town.

He yelled at Edna to follow them, his muscles bulging as he tried to restrain Johnny.

"Don't you ever touch her again!" Johnny yelled, his face flushed with rage. "If you so much as look at her again, I will kill you. You hear me, you little Weasel? I will kill you."

Frank wrestled Johnny to his car. He and Edna got him inside.

Johnny shoved against Frank. "I'm fine. Leave me alone." His words were slurred, and Edna could smell the alcohol on him as he reached for her. "Are you okay? Look what he did to you."

Edna could feel the tremble in his hands as he picked up the broken strap of her dress and touched her scraped cheek. She saw the anger fade from his face, replaced with a terrible sadness and a look of defeat. "I'm okay," she assured him. "You got there just in time."

"What the hell happened? Why would he do this to you?"

Her teeth chattered, a sign the shock of the situation was setting in. The realization of how close she had come to being seriously hurt. "I don't know. I went out there to find him for Donna. I thought you were all out back. Donna told me she's pregnant, that they're getting married next week. Weasel's really drunk. He started talking nonsense about seeing me first and then he was trying to kiss me. I don't know what happened. He ripped my dress and got me against the wall. I tried to fight him." She broke down, crying, and Johnny pulled her against his shoulder.

"I'm so sorry. I'm sorry I didn't protect you. No one gets to hurt you. Ever." He took off his sports coat, a borrowed white jacket of Frank's. Drops of blood and dirt smudges now covering the front lapel as he pulled it around Edna's shoulders.

"It's not your job to protect me," she said.

"Yes, it is." He tipped her face up to his, running his thumb across her trembling lip. "I love you, Eddy. I have never loved anyone or anything the way I love you. As long as I have breath in my body, I will do whatever it takes to protect you. To keep you from harm or any sort of pain."

She took his hand, conscious of his swollen knuckles and held it to her cheek. "I know. I love you too, Johnny. Thanks for getting him off of me."

Johnny shook his head, releasing a heavy sigh. "You know I hate violence. That I've been the punching bag for my dad as long as I can remember. But, when I came out and saw you pinned against the wall and crying, a rage overtook me like nothing I've ever felt before. I seriously think I could have killed that kid."

He turned to Frank. "Thanks for getting me out of there. I know I shouldn't drink like that. It makes me do stupid things. Thanks for pulling me off of him, brother."

Frank nodded. "I think you and Weasel both had too much to drink tonight. But he pulled an idiot move and I don't blame for you taking a swing at him. Why don't I take you guys home? I'm ready to call it a night."

"Nah, I think I'm gonna walk over to Weasel's place and check on the guy. I think I might have broken his nose." Johnny reached for the door handle of the car. "Why don't you take Edna home so she can get cleaned up? The fresh air will help sober me up. I'll come out to Janice's later on the bike to check on you."

"Are you sure?" Edna asked. "Why don't you wait? You can check in on him tomorrow. I'll come with you."

Johnny wrapped his arm around her shoulder and pulled her to him. He laid a gentle kiss on her lips. "I love you for worrying about me. But, I'm okay now. It'll be good for me to walk this off."

He was right. The fresh air might be good for him. Edna pulled the sports coat from her shoulders and pressed it into Johnny's hand. "At least take your jacket."

He smiled down at her then opened the car door and got out. He leaned in, directing his words to his friend. "Thanks again, man. Take good care of my girl, Franky."

And then he was gone. Swallowed up by the darkness of the night. It was the last time Edna would see him.

Frank drove her home, and in the morning, Weasel was dead and Johnny had disappeared.

Within twenty-four hours, Weasel's new car would be dragged out of the lake. Witnesses would claim they saw Johnny driving it as he sped out of town, and one old-timer would declare that he saw Johnny at the wheel minutes before he saw the car go over the bridge and plunge into the water.

The afternoon of Johnny's funeral, a package arrived at the farm for Edna. Inside, she would find a simple jewelry box. Lined with blue felt, the box contained the peacock brooch that belonged to Johnny's mother and a short note.

Her tears fell on the white page as she read his last words to her. *Eddy, I will do whatever it takes to protect you. I will always love you. Yours forever, Johnny.*

"I wish I would have listened to you that night," John said. "If I only would have let Frank drive me home, everything would have been different."

Edna looked at the old man sitting across from her at the table. His hair was white, but his blue eyes remained the same. She could see his pain, and her heart filled with a tenderness for him. But she was also hopping mad. How could he have left her without even saying goodbye?

Just thinking about that night dredged up so many memories. So much pain at the loss of her first love and so many questions about what really happened that night.

"So, I guess you didn't actually drown in the lake," Edna said.

"No. I did not." John looked down at his hands, folded on the table in front of them. "At the time, I felt I had no other choice but to disappear. By the time I came back, it was too late."

"You came back? Where the hell was I? I would have remembered you ringing my doorbell."

"Like I said, it was too late. By the time I made it back, it was years later. You were married. To Frank. You had a family. You seemed happy. You and Frank were the two people that I loved most in the world. I wasn't going to ruin your happiness for my own selfish gain."

"We both loved you. We would rather have known you were alive."

John spoke to Edna as if they were the only two people in the room. "The last thing I asked of Frank was for him to take care of you. And it seems like he did. It just seemed easier for everyone if I stayed dead."

"Your death was not *easier* on anyone." Edna's voice rose to a shrill pitch, and Havoc raced to John's side, as if to protect him.

"It's not your death that concerns me now, it's your life," Mac said, breaking the tenseness of the moment. "There's no statute of limitations on murder. Even if it was sixty years ago, if you killed this guy, I've got to take you in."

Edna waved a hand at Mac. "Of course he didn't kill anyone. Don't be ridiculous." She looked to John for confirmation. "You didn't really kill Weasel, did you?"

"No. Absolutely not."

"Do you know who did?" Mac asked.

"Sure. I was there."

Mac held his empty cup out to Edna. "You got any more coffee?"

"Darn tootin' I do." She grabbed the mug and filled it from the carafe on the table. "You can have all the coffee you want, just let the man talk. I've been waiting sixty years to hear what happened that night."

"I've only been waiting, like, sixty minutes, and I'm dying to know what happened," Piper said.

"Well, then," Johnny said. "You better pour me another cup too. It's not a very pretty tale."

"You want something a little stronger in your coffee?" Edna asked. "Maybe an ounce of liquid courage?"

John shook his head. "I gave up drinking that night and I haven't touched a drop since."

"Well," Edna said as she got up to retrieve a bottle of Bailey's Irish Cream from the refrigerator. "I'll tell you, I do love Jesus, but on occasion, I still drink a little. And I think tonight is one of those occasions."

She poured a dab of Irish Cream into her coffee, looked up at John, then poured in another little dab. She swirled it twice, the clinking of the spoon on the edge of the mug the only sound in the otherwise silent room.

She set the spoon on the table and gingerly took a sip. "Okay, go ahead. I'm ready."

Edna held up her hand. "Wait." She narrowed her eyes at John. "Just remember, Johnny, that I am a very old woman, and I have a weak heart. You broke that heart once already. Try not to do it again."

Johnny nodded. "I never want to hurt you again, Eddy."

"That woman does *not* have a weak heart," Maggie whispered to Cassie. "She'll probably outlive us all."

John took a sip of coffee and cleared his throat. "I felt pretty bad as I walked away from Frank's car that night. I was still a little drunk and pretty ashamed of myself. Ashamed that I'd let something happen to my girl and hadn't protected her. Ashamed that I'd let the rage inside of me slip out and that she'd seen it. I hated violence of any kind, yet I had just beaten a kid to within an inch of his life. A kid I'd known my whole life."

"Don't be so hard on yourself. You were just a kid too," Sunny said. She always had a soft spot for children from broken homes, which is what helped to make her such a great teacher. "And you got to Edna just in time, so you did protect her. Sounds to me like he deserved it."

John shook his head. "He might have deserved a punch in the nose, but he didn't deserve to die. I may have been a kid as I walked away from the car, but by the end of that night, I'd become a man."

Coopersville, Kansas, 1955

As Johnny walked up to the door, he felt a queasiness in his belly. The effects of the alcohol were wearing off and he was left with a swirling pit of nausea in his gut and a pounding headache.

Weasel's parents had remodeled the space above their garage into an apartment for their son. They were spending the month visiting his grandparents and had been out of town when the tornado hit. They were due back sometime next week.

The new car sat in the driveway, and the apartment lights were on. Like he had done a hundred times before, Johnny knocked then pushed the door open.

But the scene that met him inside the apartment was definitely *not* like anything he'd seen the hundred other times. Shopping bags and boxes of every color filled the sofa and floor. An expensive new television sat against the wall, the wooden console gleaming. New clothes lay across the end of the sofa, the price tags still attached and hanging from the sleeves.

The apartment had an open layout with a sofa, bed, and small kitchenette. Weasel sat at the table and Donna stood above him, a wet cloth in her hand as she dabbed at his bloody face. She looked at Johnny with scorn and disdain. "What are you doing here? Come to get in another punch?"

Weasel's face was swollen, with a purple bruise blossoming under his left eye. He waved Donna's hand away. "Hey, I'm sorry. I deserved this. I was drunk and don't know what I was thinking."

On the table lay a canvas bag, a stack of hundred-dollar bills spilling from its mouth. The butt of a pistol stuck out the edge of the bag, like a very dangerous paperweight holding down the money.

"What's going on? Where'd all this stuff come from?" Johnny asked. "Why do you have all that money?"

"Look, we can explain," Weasel said. "It's the money from the bank robbery. Remember the money that was taken from the bank during the tornado?"

John nodded slowly, trying to process his friend's words. His head was a little muddled still from the alcohol, but he couldn't believe what he was hearing.

"Well, Donna's the one who took it."

What? Donna robbed the bank? How could this be happening? Johnny shook his head. "Listen buddy, you have to give that money back. Maybe you can say you found it or something, but you can't keep it. You'll go to jail."

"We were gonna give it back. But then we decided to spend just a little. And then we got kind of carried away."

"Carried away is an understatement. You have hundreds of dollars' worth of stuff here." Johnny's eyes widened. "Is this how you got the car?"

Weasel nodded. "Listen, the bank is totally insured. We're not hurting anybody."

"Then why do you have a gun?"

"The gun is one of Donna's dads. We only have it as protection."

"Protection from what? The shopping police?"

"Shut up, Warren," Donna snapped. "You don't have to tell him anything. We don't need to explain ourselves to you."

"Donna, come on. Johnny's one of my oldest friends. We can trust him."

"Oh, really? Well, your *oldest friend* just broke your nose," she said.

Johnny shrugged. "Yeah, sorry about that. I just saw red."

"It's okay. I was out of line," Weasel said. "I got way too drunk tonight. Tell Edna I'm sorry."

"Why are you apologizing to him? You're the one sitting here bleeding," Donna cried. "And don't you dare tell that girlfriend of yours Warren's sorry. What was she doing in that dark alley alone with him anyway? *She* probably came on to *him*."

Donna's eyes were darting everywhere in the room. She had the look of a caged animal. Johnny knew that look. He recognized desperation. "Look, it's all over now. We can all get a good night's sleep and everything will look better in the morning."

"Oh, will it?" Donna asked, her tone heavy with sarcasm. "Will things really look better tomorrow, Johnny? Will I not be unmarried and pregnant tomorrow? Will Warren and I suddenly *not* have committed a felony?"

"Why don't you turn the money back in? Just leave it anonymously on the bank president's doorstep. Then no one will know it was you."

"We can't turn the money in. We need this money!" Donna's voice turned shrill. "We're having a baby, and we need it to survive. My parents are going to disown me once they find out, and Warren and I will be on our own. If we turn in the money, we'll have nothing."

"Okay, calm down."

"Don't you dare tell me to calm down. I had everything under control until your slutty girlfriend started this mess with Warren tonight. We were leaving in a few days. Taking this money and the new car and finding a place to start over."

"Maybe that's a good idea." Johnny continued to use a calm, easy tone with her. She seemed like a ticking time bomb and the last thing he wanted was to set her off.

"Now you're just patronizing me." Donna looked down at Warren, still seated at the table. "What are you going to do about this? He knows we have the money."

Warren looked confused. "What am I supposed to do about it? It's Johnny. He's not gonna tell anyone."

Donna's disdain turned on Warren. "You are such a fool! Of course he'll tell Edna and then she'll go to the police. She's probably already filed a report for tonight." Donna looked at

Johnny, her eyes wide and panicked. "Did she already go to the police? Did she tell my dad? Is he on his way over here now?"

She dropped the wet rag and scooped the money toward the bag. "Warren, the police are probably on their way. We've got to get out of here. Get our stuff. We'll leave tonight."

Johnny took a tentative step toward her. "Donna, it's all right. Edna didn't go to the police. But maybe we should call your dad. He could come over and help get all this straightened out. I'll stay and help you guys."

"No! We're not calling my dad." Donna was in full-on panic mode. She grabbed the gun and pointed it at Johnny's chest. "We're not telling anyone. *You're* not telling anyone."

"Whoa." Johnny raised his hands. "Okay, I won't tell anyone."

"Donna, put the gun down," Weasel ordered. "Don't be stupid."

Her eyes were wide, and her voice rose to a fevered pitch. "Don't call me stupid! You're the one who got me pregnant because you couldn't figure out how to use a rubber. You're the one who went out and bought a new car. I told you we should lay low, not draw attention to ourselves. If you'd just listened to me, everything would have been fine. Now Johnny knows, and my dad is gonna find out. I can't let my dad find out that I'm pregnant and stole money from the bank. I just can't!"

"Donna, honey. Everything's gonna be okay." Weasel held out his hand. "Just pass me the gun. Nobody needs to get hurt."

Her eyes darted between Weasel and Johnny. "I don't want to hurt anybody. But we can't let him go to the police. Don't you see? We can't let him tell my dad. He'll kill me. Or he'll arrest me. He'll arrest both of us."

Her hand shook as she raised the gun to Johnny's chest. Tears filled her eyes. "I don't want to hurt you, Johnny. But this baby is my main priority now, and I don't want to have it while I'm in jail. I won't." She pulled back the hammer of the pistol, the click of the mechanism deafening in the quiet room.

Weasel took a small step toward her, his hand still outstretched. "Donna, you don't want to do this. Now give me the gun."

He was within a foot of her now, and Johnny saw what he was trying to do. He looked wildly around the room for a way to distract Donna so Weasel could take the gun. He reached out, knocking a hatbox off the coffee table.

The sound of the hatbox falling was followed by the sound of a shot as Weasel leapt forward, reaching for the gun. Instead of the gun, he reached for his chest, a bright red stain blossoming under his hands.

Weasel pitched forward, and Donna dropped the gun and fell to her knees. She rolled Weasel over, cradling his head in her arms as she broke down sobbing. "Oh, no. Oh, baby. I'm so sorry. I'm so sorry."

Johnny knelt at her side. He pulled off his jacket and pressed it to the wound, trying to stop the bleeding.

Donna looked at him in desperation. "Help him!"

"I'm trying." Johnny's hands were covered in blood as he held the jacket to his friend's chest, trying to stanch the flow. "Hang on, buddy." His vision blurred with tears as he looked into his friend's eyes and realized they were glassy and lifeless.

"Oh, no. No. Buddy, please don't die on me." He reached up, feeling for a pulse, leaving a red smudge of blood against Weasel's throat. No pulse. No beat of his friend's heart. Only his blood, draining from his lifeless body.

Terrified, he looked up at Donna, and his terror increased ten-fold.

She was staring at him with hatred, tears running down her face, her eyes steely and focused. "Look what you did, Johnny."

"Me? I didn't do this. You shot him."

She shook her head. "No, I didn't. You did. You came here, in a rage. You came to finish what you started. Half the town heard you tell Warren that you were going to kill him." She reached up and tore her dress, exposing the top of her plain white bra. "You shot Warren and tried to rape me. As payback for Warren attacking Edna."

Johnny stared at her, hearing the words coming out of her mouth, but unable to believe what she was saying. "No. I didn't touch you. I didn't shoot Weasel. He was my friend."

Donna laughed, a hard, cold laugh. "Who do you think they're going to believe, Johnny? You? The son of the town drunk? The troublemaker? Or me? The daughter of the police chief." She stared at Johnny, her face contorted with rage. "You did this, Johnny. This is your fault. It's your fault that my baby's father is dead."

"No."

A light went on in her eyes, and Johnny trembled at what fresh hell she had just dreamt up. "But now my baby will have a new daddy. You. Johnny, listen, we still have all the money. We could make a life together. We could pack up the car and leave town right now. We could dump Warren's body in the lake, and no one will ever know. We could get married. Raise this baby as our own, and I won't ever tell anyone that you killed Warren."

"I didn't kill Warren. You did." Johnny scooted backwards. "I'm not going anywhere with you. I don't want to be married to you or be your baby's father. I'm in love with Edna."

"Edna? That stupid bitch. She came here this summer and ruined everything! I saw how Warren looked at her. How you all look at her. She's here for a few months and you all think she's some newly discovered mystery. She's going back to Colorado when the summer's over and leaving you behind. But I'll still be here. I was always here."

"She's not leaving without me, Donna. I already asked Edna to marry me. I'm sorry. She's the one I want to be with. Not you."

Donna's eyes narrowed. "Well, she's not gonna want to be with you. Not when you're in jail for murdering Warren. And not when she thinks that you raped me and that's why I'm pregnant. My dad won't be mad at me if I'm pregnant because I was raped."

She looked down at Weasel, his head still cradled in her lap. Then she lifted her head, a wicked smile on her tear-stained face. "I've got you, Johnny Collins. You left a bloody handprint on Warren's neck. Your fingerprints are in blood right on his body. No one will ever believe you over me. Not now."

Johnny sat still, stunned at her words. Everything she said sounded plausible, and he knew that everyone would believe her story over his. What was he going to do? His mind scrambled, trying to think reasonably. "I wouldn't hurt Weasel. And I would never rape you, Donna."

"Why not?" Her face twisted into a mask of pain and anger. "What's wrong with me? Am I not good enough for you, Johnny?" She pushed Weasel's head from her lap, and it hit the floor with a dull thud. Her eyes flashed to the pistol where it lay on the floor.

She looked at Johnny then back to the pistol. He could practically see the wheels turning in her head, and he knew this night was not going to end in his favor. He had one chance. He had to grab that gun before she did.

They moved at the same time. She pushed off from the floor, arms outstretched, reaching for the gun. But Weasel's head and shoulders had landed on her dress and her body was whipped back, knocking her off balance. She fell, her head hitting the corner of the kitchen table with a hard smack.

Oh no.

Donna slumped forward, her body landing atop Weasel's, her head twisting sideways and blood already dripping from a gash over her eyebrow.

Please don't let her be dead. Shock took over his body, and Johnny fumbled for his jacket, pulling it loose from under Donna's motionless body. He used the jacket to pick up the gun, careful not to touch it. Wrapping the pistol into the coat, the jacket that he had borrowed from Frank, now stained and hardening with the blood of their childhood friend.

He looked frantically around the room, thinking back to if he had touched anything. It was a pointless task. He'd been here many times over the summer; his fingerprints could be anywhere in this room.

Trying to avoid leaving a bloody handprint, he used the corner of the jacket to open the door of the apartment. He pulled the door shut and looked around the house, anxious about a nosy neighbor or late-night dog walker seeing him.

What the hell was he going to do? Where was he going to go? He was on foot. If anyone had heard the shot, the police could already be on their way. He ran for Weasel's new car, sending up a silent prayer of thanks that the keys were in the ignition.

Setting the jacket on the seat beside him, he started the car and backed it out of the driveway. He hit the gas, putting as much distance between him and his murdered friends as he could.

As if on autopilot, he drove toward the lake. It was well past midnight and the beach was deserted when he pulled Weasel's car into the lot. Opening the door, he stumbled from the car and fell to his knees, heaving and retching into the sand. The bile burned his throat as he threw up again, his body trying to dispel the poison that he'd just witnessed. The poison and the remains of Weasel's dad's scotch.

Johnny lay back on the sand, his body spent and sweating. His hands were sticky, and even in the light of the moon, he could see the dark smudges of crusted blood.

Weasel's blood. Visions of his friend popped into his mind. Playing kick-the-can on warm summer nights. Building a snow fort that one winter when it snowed for a week and they had three days off school in a row. Sitting in detention together after school. Eating peanut butter and jelly sandwiches his mom had made.

Johnny rubbed at the blood, a sob escaping his throat. He lurched forward, staggering to the water and falling in. He splashed the lake water onto his hands, his arms, rubbing at the blood. Trying to wash away the last few hours. If he could just get rid of this blood, he could make it all go away. Weasel would be alive and this would all be a nightmare.

He stumbled from the water, his clothes soaked, and fell onto the beach. The coarse granules bit into his cheek as he lay in the sand. What the hell was he going to do? He'd never felt so alone in his life.

He couldn't go to his dad. He had enough trouble just making it to work sober. He refused to involve Frank in this. He was going back to college in a few weeks. He had a future. He was getting out of this town. No way was he going to be the reason Frank got dragged into staying.

He longed to see Edna. To rest his head in her lap and have her tell him everything would be all right. To hear her say that she loved him, no matter what.

Another sob tore through his body. She did love him. She would stick by him no matter what. That was why he couldn't go to her. He couldn't involve her in this mess. She deserved better. Better than some two-bit mechanic. He knew she would stay with him. Watch him go through a trial and visit him in jail.

And he knew that was where he was headed. All of Donna's accusations spun in his head. If she were alive, she would tell everyone those lies. And if she were dead, he was still the most likely suspect. Everyone had heard him threaten to kill Weasel. He would be the first person they would come after.

He had to get out of here. He ran up the beach, stumbling and falling as he crossed the sand to where he'd left Weasel's car. He unbuttoned and peeled his sodden shirt from his body. He searched the car for something to use to dry off.

Popping the trunk, he hoped to find a blanket or some beach towels. Instead, he found a faded brown suitcase and a cardboard box. Lifting the folds of the box, he peered inside, tipping the box toward the light of the trunk. Stacks of money slid forward, each banded with colorful straps bearing the stamp of the First State Bank of Coopersville.

Piper gasped. "Oh my gosh. What did you do?"

Always the mother hen, Cassie put her hand gently on top of John's. "You must have been so scared."

John turned sad eyes to Cassie. "I have never been so frightened in all of my life. Not before and not ever after. As I sat in my dead friend's car that night, I'd thought nothing in life had prepared me for the choices I had to make."

He looked up at Edna, his wrinkled face now filled with love and tenderness. "And then I realized that *everything* in my life had been preparing me for that very moment. My mother had left when I was young, so I was familiar with the sadness and loneliness of letting people go. My dad had used me as a punching bag, so that served to make me stronger. Gave me a harder will to survive. I knew cars and was a good mechanic. Janice had taught me to work on a farm. I had the skills to earn a living wherever I went. I grew up with Frank, a best friend whose family taught me generosity and grace. More than that, he helped me get through school. Frank's mom was the one who taught me how to read."

His voice caught with emotion as he pulled his hand from Cassie and reached for Edna's. "And you, Eddy, you gave me the greatest gift of all. You taught me how to love. To love someone without expecting anything in return. To unselfishly care about someone else's happiness more than your own. Your love is what gave me the strength to do what I had to do."

"What did you do?" Sunny asked.

"I hid out the next day, trying to come up with a plan. The suitcase was full of Weasel's clothes. He must have had it packed in preparation to leave with Donna. I took the money and the suitcase with Weasel's things. I rigged Weasel's car with gasoline-filled Mason jars then raced through town so at least a few people would see me in the car. I set it on fire right before I pushed it off the bridge and prayed that people would believe that I was inside."

A tear rolled down Edna's cheek. "Your prayers were answered. We all believed you died in that car."

"I know, darling. And I'm sorry." Johnny looked around the table. "But tell them what happened the next day. Tell them what happened with Donna."

Edna looked away, into the living room, as if she couldn't face the memory overtaking her. "Donna had only been knocked unconscious. She came to lying across Weasel's dead body, and pretty much lost her mind for a while. She did exactly what she told Johnny she was going to do. She told the police that Johnny had shown up that night, drunk and in a rage. He had a gun with him and shot Weasel. She told her father that she and Weasel had secretly gotten married and were expecting a baby and Johnny had killed the father of her child. I guess playing the role of the grieving widow with a new baby overshadowed the unwed mother one."

"I couldn't come back, even if I wanted to," Johnny said. "I was sure there was warrant out for my arrest, so I couldn't take a bus or get a car. I snuck into my dad's place and grabbed a few things, the pin from my mom, and some stuff my dad had given me. Then I hitchhiked to Colorado thinking I would wait for Edna to come home and make sure she was okay. I was scared to death every time I got into someone's car that they would either turn me in or kill me for the close to fifty grand that was stashed in my suitcase. I made it to Pleasant Valley and got a cheap hotel. I kept only enough cash to live on and hid the gun and the rest of the money."

He held Edna's gaze just a beat too long, as if conveying a silent message. "You talked about that jewelry box you got in the mail after I died, the one with the note and my mother's pin? I bought that in the drugstore where you'd worked. I wrote that note and wrapped it up, then addressed it to your Aunt Janice's farm and bribed a postal clerk to postmark it for the day I supposedly died. I thought it would give you all the answers you would need. I still do."

"I walked by your house every day, waiting for you to show up or to see if I could learn anything about what was going on. You didn't come back, so the next week, I knocked on your mom's door and told her I was looking to do some yard work to pick up extra money for college. She hired me, and I spent the next few days working in your yard. She would offer me iced tea and I would sit on the porch with her and talk. I'm pretty sure that her tea had a little extra juice in it. I used to sit and talk like that with my dad and knew how to steer the conversation the way I wanted, which was toward you. She told me everything that was happening in Coopersville, and I knew they were still looking for me. Once I realized you were okay and that you'd moved on, I took off."

"Wait," Piper said. Even though it seemed Johnny was speaking only to Edna, the rest of the book club was listening intently. "What do you mean by 'moved on'?"

Johnny looked sadly at Edna. "She knows what I mean."

Edna took a sip of her coffee, which was cold by now. "He means that I 'moved on' because, three weeks after his so-called death, I married Frank."

Sunny gasped. "You did?"

"Oh for goodness' sakes, Sunny. You knew I married Frank. He only died five years ago. We've been your neighbors for as long as you've lived in your house."

"I already saw that coming," Maggie said. She was always the one who leaned over in the movies and whispered too loudly that she'd already figured out the plot.

"Well, yes," Sunny said. "I knew you were married to a guy named Frank, but I guess I wasn't connecting all the dots that it was *this* Frank."

Edna huffed. "And you're responsible for teaching the future leaders of our country."

"All right now, Edna. Don't be mean," Cassie admonished. "I'd figured out that you eventually married Frank but didn't realize it was that same summer."

Edna shrugged. "We both missed Johnny so much. We spent the next few weeks together, grieving our mutual loss. It was just the next logical step."

John raised an eyebrow. "Oh, was it?"

"Hold on," Maggie said. "I've never known Edna Allen to do anything 'logical' in her life. There's got to be more to the story. Did you really believe that Johnny had shot Weasel/Warren/whatever-his-name-was?"

"No, of course not." Edna toyed with the handle of her coffee mug. "Donna was in the hospital and her family wouldn't let us talk to her. Frank and I threw around every possible scenario we could think of, but we both knew in our hearts that Johnny couldn't have shot Weasel, at least not on purpose. It has taken sixty years, but now I finally know the truth about what happened that night." She looked at John. "Thank you for that."

Officer McCarthy cleared his throat. He had quietly listened to the whole tale, refilling his coffee cup and eating the piece of pie that Cassie had placed in front of him. "Regardless of what your story is about how things went down that night, the fact remains that there is an outstanding warrant for your arrest. There's no statute of limitations for murder. I'm going to have to take you in."

"What? You can't," Sunny said. "You just heard what happened. John's innocent."

"That's not for me to decide," Mac said. "I'm an officer of the law, and I'm duty-bound to arrest him."

Maggie turned toward John. "Unfortunately, he's right. But I'll be happy to represent you. I'll try to get you out on bond as soon as possible."

John nodded. "I understand. I knew that if I came back, I was taking a chance on getting myself arrested."

"Then why did you come back, you old fool? You could've just sent me an email from a coffee shop, called me from a burner phone, found a way to contact me that would have kept you hidden." Havoc sat in Edna's lap, and she absently stroked his fur as she admonished John.

He eyed her thoughtfully. "You know why I had to come back, Eddy. I needed to see you. To see your face. To ask you what happened after I left. Apparently, I wasn't the *only* one who's kept things hidden all these years."

Edna looked from Mac to John. Anyone that knew her well could see the wheels turning in her head. She stroked the little dog's fur and looked intently at John. "Just so you know, if you ever have to go away again, even just for a little while, Havoc could stay here. He would be well taken care of."

John nodded. "Thanks, I appreciate that."

"Well, you better just get it over with it," Edna said to Mac. She pushed her chair back and set Havoc on the floor. Picking up the coffee cups, she headed for the sink. "It is your civil duty and all that."

John stood up and held out his hands.

Mac reached for the handcuffs attached to his belt.

Crash!

The group turned as one as the cups Edna had been holding hit the floor and shattered. Edna grabbed for the counter as she crumpled to the floor.

Mac was the first to move, his quick reflexes grabbing her before her head hit the floor. Jake was moments behind him, and the Page Turners rushed to her side, all carefully stepping over the broken glass on the floor.

Edna's head lay cradled in Officer McCarthy's lap.

Jake reached for her wrist to gauge her pulse. "Her heartbeat is steady," he reported.

Slowly Edna's eyes fluttered open. "Where am I? Am I dead? Is this heaven?"

"No," Cassie assured her. "You're not dead. You just fainted."

"Oh good, I'd hate to think I'd have to spend all of eternity in this kitchen. I should have changed that wallpaper years ago."

"Take it easy, Miss Allen." Mac's voice held the authoritative tone of someone used to being in charge. "I think we should call an ambulance. You may have suffered a stroke or broken something in your fall."

"Oh, I don't think we need to go to all that fuss. Just let me lie here a minute." Edna looked around at the broken glass that

Sunny was already sweeping up from the floor. "Who broke something?"

"You did," Maggie answered. "You dropped the cups before you collapsed. We're hoping that's all you broke. Can you move your legs? Your arms? We know you can move your mouth."

Edna stuck her tongue out at Maggie. "I hated those old cups anyway. And I think I can move everything." She waved her arms and legs, making an imaginary snow angel in the dust bunnies on her kitchen floor. "Yep, everything's fine. Why doesn't somebody help me up?"

Mac gingerly helped her to her feet, a concerned look on his face. "Are you sure we shouldn't call you an ambulance? You may have had a heart attack."

"I doubt it. I just went to the doctor and my heart is as healthy as a horse," she told him. "It's all that Zumba and salsa dancing I do. Good cardio, you know." She turned her back to the policeman and gave the Page Turners an exaggerated wink. "It must have just been all the excitement. Or maybe low blood sugar. I'll just eat another piece of pie, and I'm sure I'll be fine."

A low whine arose from the living room, and they all turned to see Havoc sitting by the front door. A quick glance around the room revealed that the little dog's fugitive owner was nowhere in sight.

14

The next evening was the routine night of the Page Turners book club meeting, and you could guarantee not one of the members was going to miss it.

They gathered around the table in Sunny's kitchen. Cassie and Piper wore their yoga gear, having just come from a class they were taking together at the Y.

Maggie looked fashionably sharp, still in the charcoal-gray power suit she wore to court that day. The coral blouse accented her tanned skin and her dark hair fell in shiny waves down her back. She might look like an ad for *Lawyer's Weekly*, but her sharp intelligence made her a formidable foe in the courtroom.

Her sleek leather briefcase sat at her feet, and Havoc sniffed at the front pocket. As if remembering the little dog's reputation, Maggie lifted the briefcase and set it on the counter.

Edna had brought the dog over, and it spent the last fifteen minutes chasing Sunny's golden retriever, Beau, around the back yard. Beau now lay on the floor, his energy spent while Havoc raced around the kitchen in a frenzied attempt to sniff everything in sight.

The scent of cinnamon and vanilla filled the air as Sunny pulled a fresh batch of snickerdoodles from the oven. Using a spatula, she moved the soft, warm cookies to a cooling rack. As fast as the gals were grabbing them, she could have saved herself the step and dumped them right into the mouths of each book club member.

"So did you hear from John today?" Cassie asked Edna as she reached for a cookie.

"No, not yet. But I spent the afternoon in the attic digging through boxes and found the jewelry box that he sent me all those years ago. I never threw it away, I found it packed into a trunk of old mementos."

Edna pulled a jewelry box from her bag and set it on the table. It was ordinary to look at it, a small wooden box that could be found at any drugstore.

Piper reached out and ran a finger down the side of the box. "What's so special about this box?"

"I'm not sure," Edna said. She lifted the lid to reveal a blue velvet lining. Otherwise the box was empty. "But I felt like John was trying to give me a clue last night. He said this box would give me all the answers I would need."

"The answers to what?" Maggie asked. "How to buy a cheap jewelry box?"

"There was a note from Johnny inside of it, and all I ever cared about was reading his words. I never really gave much thought to the box itself. Maybe the answer is somehow in the box." Edna pulled at the lining and the ancient adhesive easily gave way. She peeled it all the way back and gasped at what was underneath.

Under the lining, taped to the bottom of the box, was a flat gold key. Edna tugged at the corner of the tape, releasing the key. She held it up for the others to see.

"A key," Piper said. "What the heck is it to? A secret apartment where he's been living? A locker at an airport? How does this answer anything? It just brings up more questions."

Edna narrowed her eyes as she studied the key. "Remember, he sent me this key back in 1955, so I doubt it would be anything like a locker at an airport. It has to be to something that would be around and stay the same for a long time. It looks like a safe deposit box key. That would be a great place to hide something."

"The only bank in town that's been around long enough would be the Pleasant Valley Bank and Trust," Maggie said.

"Ohhh, wait." Cassie pointed at her bag hanging off the back of Piper's chair. "Hand me my purse."

Piper handed her the bag, and she dug out a large set of keys with a jeweled handbag charm hanging from the ring. She rifled through them, then held up a flat gold key. "I have a safe deposit box at that branch. Here's my key. It looks just the same."

"Johnny said he hid the gun and the rest of the money. He was in Pleasant Valley for several weeks but the murder happened in a different state." Sunny nibbled on a cookie as she talked out her mental reasoning. "Maybe he hoped a bank teller wouldn't recognize his name, or he wore a disguise or something. It was sixty years ago. You probably didn't need all the crazy five forms of ID like you do now. People were more trusting. Plus he was cute and charming. He could have gone into the bank and sweet talked a teller into setting up a box for him using a fake name or even in Edna's name. If he was sending you this clue, maybe he put your name on the box rental agreement."

Edna turned the key over in her hand. "What if the gun and the money is in this safe deposit box? He said he never touched the gun, so it could still have Donna's fingerprints on it. Or her DNA. What if the gun is the key to proving his innocence, and it's just been sitting in a bank for the last sixty years?"

"If ballistics could match the bullet that killed Weasel to the gun that John had, that would be admissible in court," Maggie explained. "We need to see what's in that box."

Edna looked at her watch. "It's five thirty. How late do you think they stay open? We should call them."

"No need," Piper said, holding up her phone. "I just googled them, and they stay open until six."

"It's just off Fourth and Main. If we leave now, we can be there in five minutes." Cassie grabbed for her purse and shoved another snickerdoodle into her mouth. "Let's go," she said around a mouthful of cookie.

Five minutes later, the Page Turners walked into the Pleasant Valley Bank and Trust. The lobby smelled like old paper and canned air freshener. A Neil Diamond song piped through the sound system and with the original gleaming gold teller stations, it felt like stepping back in time.

Sunny approached the closest bank teller. She looked about twelve and was chewing gum hard enough to throw her jaw out. Her cell phone was in her hand, and it appeared the text that she was sending was more important than any customer. "Excuse me, can you help us with a safe deposit box?"

The teller looked up, and her smile of recognition was filled with a shiny set of braces. "Oh, hi, Miss Vale. Remember me, I'm Veronica Howbert. I was in your second grade class." Now that her head was up, she looked around at the rest of the group.

"Oh my goodness. Why yes, of course I remember you, Veronica. And now I feel about as old as this bank. We were wondering if you could help us with getting into a safe deposit box."

Veronica looked at the big clock above the door and frowned. "We close in about fifteen minutes. You might want to come back tomorrow."

Edna bustled forward. "Listen, missy, we drove like a bat out of hell to get here. Your bank is open for another fifteen minutes, so if you can spare time away from texting about what you had for lunch today, I'd like to see my safe deposit box. Now."

The teller slid off her stool, opened a drawer, and pulled out a set of keys. "Okay. Geez, it was just a suggestion. Do you know your box number?"

"I forgot it. And like you said, it's getting late and I'm not getting any younger. Can you look it up for us, Veronica? It's under..." Edna looked at Sunny.

"Edna Allen," Sunny said. "Check for a box under the name Edna Allen." Sunny leaned toward her and whispered, "If John gave you a key, I'm sure he would have put it in your name."

"But my name wasn't Edna Allen then. It was still Anderson," Edna whispered back.

Sunny shrugged. "If it works, it's one more mystery to ask John about."

"Shh." Maggie gave them a glare and a quick shush.

The teller punched a few keys on her computer and came up with a number. "It's box 67, and it's registered to you and a John Adams. Is that the one?"

"That's it," Edna said, and smiled sweetly at the girl. "Can you possibly push a couple more buttons and tell us the last time someone was in this box?"

The girl glanced at the clock and let out a sigh. "I guess. They updated our computers about ten years ago and manually added all the safe box activity from when each box was purchased. I can usually print out all the activity." She clicked a few more keys. "Actually, it's only been accessed twice, ever. Both times in the summer of 1966. Do you want me to print off the statement?" She asked the question as if Edna were requesting she move the pyramids, one stone at a time.

"Sure, if it's not too much trouble for you." Edna waited while the girl hit print and handed her a single sheet of paper. She folded it and stuffed it in her purse. "Thanks so much for going to all that work. Now can we see the box?"

Veronica unlocked a steel door and led them into a large vault room. "I can only take one of you in to get the box, but we have a viewing room and the rest of you can wait in there." She pointed to a door on their left just outside the vault.

A viewing room? That made it sound like a funeral. Was that a premonition? Would the contents of this box give her a heart attack, and she was about to die?

Edna handed the girl the key that she had taken from the jewelry box and watched as she inserted both keys into the box and turned the lock. Edna held her breath, hoping the key would work. She had waited sixty years to hear the truth about what happened the night that Johnny disappeared. And this box could hold the proof to back up his words.

Johnny's story made perfect sense to her. In her head, she could clearly hear the snide tone of Donna's annoying voice, threatening Johnny and making him feel worthless. It had been so long ago, but she could feel the fear that he had felt as he fled the only town he'd ever lived in, leaving behind his girl, his friends, and the only family he had.

With a click, the lock turned, and Veronica opened the rectangle door and pulled a long box from the slot. She carried it back to where the Page Turners stood, and Cassie opened the door to the viewing room. It was a small room with a table and two chairs and a framed print of George Washington on the wall.

Veronica set the box on the table and backed out of the room as the others crowded in. "You have about ten minutes. I don't mean to rush you or anything, but the bank closes at six, and I have a date tonight."

The door closed behind the bank teller. Edna looked at the picture of George Washington, as if gathering strength from the founding father. She took a deep breath and lifted the lid.

The box contained two items. A yellowed newspaper article from the *Coopersville Gazette* dated July 12, 1966 and a clear plastic dry-cleaning bag. Edna gingerly lifted the bag from the safe deposit box. It held a white sport jacket, now faded to a dull beige and stiff with dark brown stains.

"Is that blood? Weasel's blood?" Piper asked, covering her mouth with her hand. "I think I'm going to throw up."

Edna set the bag down, and it made a dull thud as it hit the table. "It's too heavy. There's something inside the jacket. It's got to be the gun."

Sunny reached for the top of the bag, but Maggie slapped her hands away. "Don't touch it. It's evidence. I think we should call Mac now."

"We need to know if it really is a gun inside of the coat." Edna set her handbag on the table with a clunk and started digging through its contents. She held up a small plastic packet with a flourish. "Ta da! I always carry an extra rain bonnet in my purse."

"A rain bonnet?" Piper asked. "What are you? Eighty?"

Edna ignored the sarcasm and fluffed at her silver curls. "Don't want to mess up my perm if it rains. Make fun if you want, but I pay a lot for this style." She unfolded the little packet and shook out the rain bonnet.

"What about your other hand?" Maggie asked. "You don't want your fingerprints on any of this."

Rummaging through her handbag once again, Edna came up with a plastic sandwich bag full of M&M's. She dumped the chocolates on the table and stuck her hand inside, forming a second makeshift glove.

Piper reached out, grabbed a few of the candies, and popped them in her mouth. "What? Five-second rule," she said to her aunt, who was giving her a disgusted look.

Edna opened the top of the bag. A faint metallic smell wafted up, and she wasn't sure if it was from the dried blood on the jacket or the gun she was hoping it hid. With both of her hands now encased in plastic, she reached into the bag and gently peeled back the white sports coat. The fabric was stiff and unwieldy, so she gave it a quick tug.

"Geez, be careful," Maggie cautioned. "If it is a gun, it could still be loaded."

"Good thinking." Edna grabbed a different part of the jacket and pulled it back. It moved easier and revealed the dull gray metal of a pistol. "There it is. Just like Johnny said."

Cassie reached for her phone. "Okay, now we're calling Mac."

Sunny dug in her purse. "And Jake."

Edna looked down at Piper. "You're always on that silly phone of yours. Don't you have someone you want to call?"

"Heck no. I don't want to be on the phone and miss any of the action." Piper scooped up a few more chocolates and shoveled them into her mouth.

Maggie grinned mischievously. "Who wants to inform Ms. Customer Service-Veronica that she's going to be late for her date?"

Twenty minutes later, Officer McCarthy walked into the Pleasant Valley Bank and Trust, accompanied by a young, dark-haired officer.

Tall and clean-shaven, Mac wore his uniform well. His muscular arms filled out his uniform shirt, and his dark Aviator glasses gave him an air of authority with a dash of bad-ass. The younger officer was shorter but stocky and good looking. They could have posed for a Boys In Blue calendar.

The sulky bank teller perked up a little after having spent the last fifteen minutes intermittently glancing at the clock and sighing.

Mac pulled off his sunglasses as he approached the book club members. "All right, what's going on now? What's this important *evidence* you need to show me?"

The Page Turners stepped aside and revealed the table holding the bag with the bloody jacket and the gun.

Mac looked down at the bag. "I have a feeling this is the gun involved in the murder. How did you just happen on this critical piece of evidence?"

"We didn't *happen* on anything," Edna said. "We used our brains and deduced information. You remember John told us last night that the jewelry box he sent me would have all the answers I was looking for? Well, I dug out that box this morning and found a safe deposit box key taped under the lining. The key was to this box and here's what we found."

"And what's all this?" Mac pointed at the baggie, rain bonnet, and the remaining chocolates. "Did you decide to have a snack while you were busy *deducing?*"

"Edna used those so she didn't touch the evidence," Piper explained. "You can have some of the M&M's, though."

"I'll pass."

Edna nodded at the table. "You should really wear gloves if you're going to touch it, so you don't contaminate the crime scene."

Mac rolled his eyes. "Thanks. Have you ever thought about joining the police academy? We could use a few more senior citizens with your sharp eye on the force." He pulled a set of plastic gloves from his pocket and pulled them on.

He picked up the weathered newspaper article. "What's this?"

The women had read the article while they waited for the policeman to arrive.

Edna pointed at the title. "It's a newspaper clipping from the *Coopersville Gazette* dated back in 1966. It's a nice little story about how an anonymous person dropped an envelope with over fifty-thousand dollars into the night depository of the First State Bank of Coopersville. The envelope also had a note explaining the money was being returned from the robbery during the tornado of 1955. They claimed to have returned all the money plus interest for the ten years that it had been missing."

Mac raised an eyebrow. "Sounds like quite an upstanding citizen." He opened the bag and examined the coat and the gun.

"Careful, it might still be loaded." Edna shrank back at the look Mac gave her. "Okay, sorry. You probably know what you're doing."

"This gun is definitely old, and it looks a little rusty. That's amazing to think it's been wrapped in a blood-soaked jacket and hidden in this box for sixty years." Mac flipped open the chamber, revealing one missing round and five remaining bullets. "This thing *is* still loaded."

"I told you so." Edna gave him a smug smile.

Mac tilted the gun and dumped the bullets into his hand. He pointed to the younger officer. "Go out to the car and grab a couple of the larger evidence bags. Let's get this stuff down to the lab and let them run some tests on it."

He turned to Edna. "Now we just need to find your boyfriend. Any idea where he might be?"

Edna shrugged and did her best to look innocent. "He hasn't been my boyfriend in sixty years. How should I know?"

15

An elderly man shuffled up the steps of the courthouse. He wore a faded brown fedora, a baggy gray suit, and bedroom slippers. His cane hit each step with a sound thud. Bent and stooped, he made his way down the hall to the County Clerk's desk minutes before closing time.

The older woman at the counter wore a pair of thin reading glasses attached to a pearled chain around her neck. She looked up from her computer and peered at the man over the top of her glasses. Her expression was unamused. "Hello, Mr. Adams. I was wondering when I was going to see you again."

John's shoulders slumped. "I worked really hard on this disguise, Irma Jean. How'd you know it was me?"

"I may be old, but I'm not stupid," she said in a clipped tone. "How's Edna?"

"She's fine. Wait, I mean, Edna who?"

"Mr. Adams, it's a small town. I've heard an elderly man has been staying at Edna Allen's house, and her name is on both of the forms you wanted to see. It's not rocket science."

John grumbled. "I hate small towns."

"It's also rumored that she may be harboring a dangerous fugitive." Irma Jean looked him up and down. "You wouldn't know anything about any fugitive, would you, Mr. Adams? Dangerous or otherwise?"

"Hmm. I haven't heard anything about that. But just in case there's any truth to it, I better take a look at those documents and get on home."

Irma Jean took a folder from her drawer and slid it across the desk. She held it down with one pink-painted fingernail. "About these documents. With all the danger going around, they seemed to have accrued an extra filing fee. Due upon receipt. As in now."

John shook his head. He leaned his cane against the counter and reached for his wallet. "You may look sweet as apple pie, Miss Irma Jean, but underneath all those pearls and cardigans, you are a feisty little minx."

She took the two twenties John set on the counter and released the folder. "Why thank you, John. It's nice that you noticed."

John opened the folder, his eyes quickly scanning the information. He tipped his fedora at Irma Jean in thanks, grabbed his cane, and shuffled back down the hallway.

An hour later he was tapping on Edna's back kitchen window. Night had fallen, and he could see clearly into the lit house. He watched Edna enter the kitchen, his little dog running along at her feet. She opened the back door and he quickly stepped inside.

She looked out the door, then pushed it shut behind him. "Did anyone see you?"

"I don't think so." He reached down to greet Havoc, rubbing the dog's ears and sending him into a frenzied spin. "Are you here alone?"

"Practically," Sunny said, as she and the other Page Turners stepped into the kitchen. "Where have you been all day?"

"We've been worried sick about you," Cassie said.

"Nice disguise," Maggie said. "Really changed up your look. I never would have recognized you dressed as an old man."

John took off the fedora and set it on the table. "I didn't have a lot to work with."

"How about some coffee? You still take it black?" Edna asked.

He nodded. "Yeah, but it's after supper, so you better make it decaf."

"That goes without saying." She poured him a cup and set it on the table in front of him. Looking up at him, she grinned.

"I'm old too. Decaf and only one cup after six o'clock. Otherwise, I'm up half the night, either wide awake or making extra trips to the potty. And I don't need any more trips to the potty. At my age, nature calls more often than telemarketers."

John chuckled. She still made him laugh.

Even though it had only been a day since he had last seen her, he was taken aback by how lovely she still was to him. His mind looked past the gray hair and wrinkled skin, and his heart saw only the beautiful young girl filled with spunk whose blue eyes sparkled with a mixture of joy and mischief. His heart might be old, but it picked up its beat when he looked at her.

He pulled out a chair and sat down. Lifting the cup to his lips, he took a sip of the coffee. "So, what did you ladies get up to today?"

In a rush of motion, amidst the sound of coffee cups and pulled-out chairs, the book club members were seated within moments and a container of cookies had appeared on the table.

"Edna dug out the old jewelry box that you gave her, and we found the key to the safe deposit box," Sunny said.

John turned to Edna. "Is that right? You still had it after all these years?"

"Of course," she said. "Except for my memories, that box and the peacock pin were all I had of you."

Piper reached for a cookie. "We figured out the bank and found the gun and the bloody jacket. Which, by the way, was disgusting and almost made me barf."

"I understand," John said. "It actually *did* make me barf."

Havoc jumped into Maggie's lap, and she fed him a corner of her cookie. "We gave the evidence to the police. We called in Mac, the guy who was here the other night, and they're running tests on it now. If Donna's fingerprints are the only ones on the gun, especially on the trigger, that will go a long way toward proving you're innocent."

"What I don't understand," Sunny said, "is if you had the evidence to prove your innocence this whole time, why didn't you ever turn it into the police?"

"I was going to," John said. "Once. I felt bad that I used the robbery money, so I saved everything I could to make up what I'd used and what Donna and Weasel had spent. I figured paying back their portion was the least I could do. It always felt wrong to me to use that money, but I was desperate."

Edna put her hand on top of John's. "No one's blaming you. You did what you had to do in order to survive."

John turned his hand over and entwined his fingers with hers. The slightest touch from her still sent butterflies racing through his stomach. "I knew that to disappear, I needed a new identity. Needed to appear common and forgettable. John is one of the most common names there is, so I kept that and changed my last name to Adams."

"John Adams? Like the president?" Edna asked.

He shrugged. "I never said I was creative. Anyway, after I left Colorado, I hitchhiked around the country for several months. I got to know some people, some good, some not so good. The kind of people who would let me do some work and never ask for a social security card or driver's license. The kind who could get me a fake birth certificate, ID, passport, that sort of thing. As soon as I had legitimate papers, I took off for Europe and spent several years backpacking across the continent."

He squeezed Edna's hand. "You have to understand. I had nothing. No home, no family. I had a canvas backpack, a few sets of clothes and a broken heart. I was alone and defeated. I spent a lot of years feeling sorry for myself and searching for the soul I thought I had lost."

"You were so young," Maggie said. "Not much older than my son. You must have been scared."

"After all I'd been through, there wasn't much left to scare me. I tried to keep my nose clean and steer clear of trouble. I fell in with a group of American college students studying abroad. Drank a lot of wine, talked a lot of philosophy, and when they came back to the United States, I came back with them. Traveling was different then. Customs was easier. One of the guys I met was going up to Montana to work on a dude ranch, and I tagged along. Seemed like a good idea at the time, and it was work that I really took to. The ranch was run by a widow named Annie, and she didn't care about IDs and filing for taxes—she cared about the land and getting the horses taken care of. She paid cash, and when the summer was over, my buddy went back to school and I stayed on. I saved my money, and when I had enough to pay the bank back, I came back to Colorado."

Edna pulled her hand free. "If you came back, why didn't you contact us? Let us know you were alive?"

John shook his head, the memory of that trip back to Colorado still fresh in his mind. The excitement of seeing Edna. The anticipation of welcome hugs and smiles. "I tried. That was my plan. It had been ten years since I'd disappeared. I thought enough time had gone by that the investigation would have died down, and no one would be looking for me. I researched where you lived and knew that you had moved to Colorado after Frank graduated and bought a house. You and Frank were the closest thing to family that I had ever had, and I'd missed you both so much. But I couldn't do it."

"Why not? We missed you too. We loved you."

"I know. And I loved you. Both of you." John's voice choked with emotion. "That's why I couldn't do it. I came to your house. This house. It was summer, and you and Frank were outside. I could see you in the backyard, playing with a little girl. You looked so beautiful, Eddy. So happy. You and Franky had built a life together. A family. How could I waltz in, ten years later, and tear that apart? I couldn't. I wouldn't. I loved you both too much. I took the rest of the money from the safe box, drove to Kansas, and dropped it in the bank's night depository with a note. They'd rebuilt the bank after the tornado, but it was still in the same spot."

"How come no one recognized you?" Piper asked.

"By that time, I was a man. I'd grown a beard, filled out. I wore western clothes and looked like a different person than the bad boy kid that had ran out of town a decade before. No one in Coopersville recognized me. I checked in on my dad and Aunt Janice. I spent a couple of days in town, saw the article in the paper and knew the money was back. I felt lighter. That money had been like a weight around my neck for years. I felt absolved of the guilt of at least one part of that night. I clipped the article and decided to head back to Montana."

"Did you see Donna? What happened to her?" Sunny asked as she reached for another cookie.

He shrugged. "I don't know. I didn't want to know. She was the reason I was in this mess. I really didn't care what happened to her. Besides, I was keeping a low profile and didn't want to talk to a lot of people or ask too many questions. I heard that her dad was still the chief of police, so I guess she was doing okay."

He stopped and looked at Edna. "I wanted to see you again, so I drove back through Colorado and stopped in Pleasant Valley one last time. I watched you take your daughter to the park. You had a picnic that day and lay on a blanket side by side and read books together. You were so beautiful."

Edna looked away, her eyes tearing with emotion.

"That must have been the second time you signed in to the safe deposit box at the bank," Piper said. "We saw the record."

John nodded. "I wanted to keep the article about the money being returned to the bank, but I didn't want to ever be found with it and have it connect me back to Kansas or the robbery. I stopped at the bank to put the newspaper clipping in the safe box, and I never went back to it again." He turned to Edna. "I also changed your name on the box from Anderson to Allen, just in case you ever figured it out."

"But if you returned the money, then why didn't you turn in the gun and prove you were innocent?" Piper asked. "Then you wouldn't have to run anymore."

"Because if he turned in the gun, everyone would know that he was alive," Maggie answered.

John nodded. "It was easier to let sleeping dogs lie than to open up all those old wounds. Everybody else had moved on. Who was I to ruin everyone's lives with my own selfish needs? Eddy, you had a family, a little girl. I couldn't destroy your happiness."

Edna got up from the table and carried her coffee cup to the sink. The Page Turners silently watched her. The only sound in the room was the faint tinkle of the cup against the saucer as Edna's hand trembled.

She set her cup in the sink and turned back to John, anger flashing in her eyes. "My happiness was destroyed the night I thought you drove off a bridge and drowned in the lake. Why did you get to decide if we could handle knowing you were alive? What gave you that right?"

"I did what I thought was right at the time," John said, his voice rising in pitch. He looked directly into Edna's eyes. "And before you get yourself too worked up, think about the fact that you made a few important decisions on your own too. I'm not the only one that's been keeping a secret all these years."

Edna's face drained of color. She reached for the counter to steady herself.

His gaze was steady, and he didn't move to help her.

This was it. His stomach churned, and his hands trembled. He knew he was close to finding out the answers that he had risked everything and come back to town for.

He took a deep breath and tried to keep his voice from wavering. "You have yet to ask the most important question, Eddy. Why did I come back to town now? What could be so important that I would risk my freedom and reveal that I was alive after all these years? Can you think of anything that could be so valuable that I would risk everything for? Or *anyone*?"

Edna's eyes filled with tears, and Sunny moved to her side. The rest of the Page Turners sat spellbound at the table, as if the tension in the room held them securely in their chairs. Sunny eased Edna into her chair and poured her a glass of water.

Edna never took her eyes off John. She searched his face, as if gauging how much he really knew. Her voice was barely above a whisper. "You came here for her? For them?"

John nodded, a slight shake of his head.

"But how did you know? How could you?"

He shrugged. "I didn't for sure. Not until today when I got my hands on her birth certificate. I really only guessed about a week ago. I try to keep up on the Colorado news and a story came across the internet the other day. A story about an accountant who had stumbled upon a money-laundering scheme during a routine audit. Her picture came up on my computer, and I thought my heart would stop. She looked so familiar. The blonde hair, the same crystal blue eyes I see every day when I look in the mirror. She looked exactly as my mother did about the time she left my dad and me. But the thing that clenched it was the scarf around her neck. It was blue and held together with a jeweled peacock pin."

16

Coopersville, Kansas, 1955

Edna sat on the little twin bed on Janice's sun porch. The remains of a tissue lay shredded in her lap. Her head ached, and her eyes burned from crying. She had cried so much in the last few weeks she couldn't imagine that she had any tears left.

The back screen door opened, and Frank stepped in. He looked almost as miserable as she did as he crossed the room and sank onto the bed next to her. She leaned her head on his shoulder. What would she have done without Frank these last two weeks?

He had been by her side through everything. The news from the sheriff's department about the shooting, the terrible rumor that Weasel's car had crashed into the lake, the confirmation that witnesses had seen Johnny driving the car right before it crashed, the funeral. The worst day of her life, rivaled only by the day her father had died.

But her dad had been sick. They had watched him wither away for months. When he finally died it was with an ache of relief that his suffering was over.

Johnny wasn't sick. He was in the prime of his life. Healthy as a horse.

Nothing in her could accept the reality that the only two men she had ever loved were both gone. Was her heart cursed? Was she doomed to live a life of solitude, never daring to give her heart away again, for fear that the recipient would end up in the ground?

She didn't have to worry. On either account.

She wouldn't give her heart away again. She couldn't. Because it had been shattered into a million tiny pieces and the fragments had been lost with Johnny. The last remnants of her devastation falling to the ground in the tears that she wept.

But she would not suffer in solitude. In fact, she would never be alone again. Her heart may have been lost, but a tiny piece of Johnny's now fluttered inside of her.

That piece was all she had left. A few mementos. A faded wildflower. She had nothing to hold onto that signified he was ever even here.

They had no body to bury. There was no casket, no gravesite to visit.

After the crash, the police pulled the car from the lake, and divers searched for him for three days. They found his shirt and one of his engineer boots floating in the water.

The reservoir had originally been built by filling in a deep valley. Rather than clear all the trees and debris, they filled it in with water. One area had been cleared to use for the beach, but the rest was cordoned off and swimming was prohibited. Beneath the lake, trees still stood, and searching amongst them proved difficult and dangerous.

Because they couldn't find his body, they held a simple memorial service. Attendance was low for the service of an accused murderer. Edna shared a pew with her Aunt Janice, and Frank and his family sat in the row behind them. Johnny's father sat in the first row, alone, his body reeking of alcohol, his shoulders slumped and shaking with tears as he silently wept through the brief service.

Edna had walked aimlessly through the days since. Eating only if Janice made her and sleeping as often as she could. She would have stayed in bed every day if it weren't for Frank.

He showed up each day. To sit with her. To hold her while she cried. To walk with her in the evenings. To hold her hand. To silently share in the combined grief that Johnny's loss left behind.

They didn't have to speak. Sometimes they would just sit together and stare into space. Sometimes they would talk.

Frank would share stories of growing up with Johnny and the trouble they would get into.

Sometimes they talked about that night. Edna had analyzed every detail of that last night, replayed each scenario, each *what if*. What if they had made him get back in the car? What if she had gone with him to confront Weasel? What if Donna was lying? What if she was telling the truth?

Frank squeezed her hand. "How are you holding up today?"

Edna shrugged. "Same as yesterday. I'm still here, and Johnny still isn't."

"Me too." He gave her a weak smile. "I was thinking maybe we could go in to Howard's. Get a cheeseburger. If you feel up to it."

Edna hadn't eaten since early that morning when Aunt Janice had handed her a piece of toast and she'd absently stuck it in her mouth. She thought about a cheeseburger. The melted cheese, the aroma of the grilled meat, the grease dripping from the ground beef.

The toast from that morning came hurtling back at her, and she grabbed the tin waste basket next to her bed just in time. Afterward, she pushed the trashcan away and reached for a tissue to dab at her mouth.

"Okay, I guess a cheeseburger is out," Frank said, a worried look on his face. "Are you all right?"

She nodded. "Yes, just quit saying *cheeseburger*." She took a drink from the glass of water on the table beside her bed. "Sorry. That wasn't very pleasant."

Frank shrugged. "It's no big deal. I'm in college. I see guys throwing up every weekend. But you look really pale. Maybe you're coming down with something. Is this the first time you've been sick?"

She had to tell him at some point. He was bound to find out anyway. This child was all she had left of Johnny and there was no question if she was keeping it or not. Soon everyone would know.

She offered him a shaky smile. "No, it's not the first time. I get sick every morning."

"Every morning? Have you seen a doctor?"

She waited, watching his face for her words to sink in. "I guess Donna's not the only one who wasn't careful enough this summer."

"Oh no. You're pregnant?"

She nodded.

"What are you going to do?"

"What do you think I'm going to do? I'm going to have the baby. It's all I have left of Johnny. For me, there's no other option."

"But where will you live? Will you go back to Colorado? How will you support yourself?" His questions came fast, and they were all concerning things Edna had already been thinking about.

"I don't know. I could go back to Colorado. Have my mom help me raise the baby. Or I was thinking about asking Aunt Janice if I could stay here with her. She's the strongest woman I know and doesn't care what anybody thinks. I love this farm. I think I could make a life here."

Frank leaned back against the wall and sighed. They sat quietly for a long time, both lost in their own thoughts. A warm breeze blew through the screened-in windows, and Edna caught the scent of honeysuckle in the air.

Taking a deep breath, Frank slid off the bed and bent on one knee in front of Edna.

"What are you doing?"

He picked up her hand and held it in his. "Edna, will you marry me?"

"Of course not."

"Well, those aren't exactly the words that a guy dreams of hearing when he proposes to a girl."

"Proposing? Why are you proposing to me? Because you feel sorry for me? I can take care of myself, Frank Allen."

He chuckled. "I have no doubt about that, Edna. I don't feel sorry for you. I care about you. I want to *take* care of you." He looked at her stomach then back into her eyes. "Both of you."

"Why? You have your whole life ahead of you. You need to go out and find a nice girl to fall in love with. One that will make you happy. That you can be proud of."

"Edna, I *would* be proud to have you as my wife. And you *do* make me happy. I've been giving this some serious thought, and I think we could be happy together." He lifted his hand and gently caressed her cheek. "I don't need to go out and find another girl to fall in love with. I already did. I fell for you the first day I met you. But I knew once you met Johnny that I didn't stand a chance."

Her brain was spinning. He was in love with her? She knew he cared about her, but not that much. He was such a good guy. Stable and kind. He would be a good husband and father. Could she consider his offer? Would it be fair to him?

She shook her head. "It's not fair to you. I would make a terrible wife. You know I'm not like normal girls."

Frank laughed. "Who asked you to be? And maybe I'm tired of normal. Maybe that's the thing I like about you."

"My aunt has taught me this summer the importance of being myself. That I'm okay just like I am. Johnny let me find myself, let me figure out who I was, and I realized that I am *not* a doormat. I don't want to spend my life cast in the shadow of my husband. I don't want to be a flower that fades into the wallpaper. I want to embrace life. To live it to its fullest. I want to be able to speak my mind and say what I feel."

"I want that too. Edna, that's what makes me want to marry you. I love all those things about you. I love being around you. You're fun, and you see life differently. You make every day seem like a new adventure."

Edna's eyes filled with tears. She cared about Frank. He was offering her everything he had. But how could she marry him? She didn't love him. She knew she could never love another man the way she loved Johnny. She never wanted to. Her voice choked with emotion. "I still love Johnny. I will always love Johnny."

"I know. That's okay. I love him too."

She reached out, touched his face. His cheek was smooth, so unlike the rough stubble of Johnny's face. "You're my best friend. You're the best friend I've ever had. I can't ask you to give up everything for me."

"You're not asking. I'm offering. Edna, I am in love with you. That's enough for me. I know I'm not Johnny, and I know you'll never love me like you loved him. But I know you care about me. You consider me your best friend, and we always get along. That's more than some marriages I know."

What he was saying was making sense to her. She didn't think her mother ever considered her father as a friend. And she and Frank never argued. They genuinely enjoyed each other's company.

Maybe.

"I can give you a good life, Ed. We can make a fine life together. I can be a stable provider. I know I can be a good husband and a great father to the baby."

His words were touching her. Wearing through her hard wall of defense and weaving their way into her heart. Frank would be a good dad, and she knew that he would take care of her and the baby. "Where would we live?"

"We can live anywhere you want. I have one year of school left, then we can go anywhere. We can stay here or move back to Colorado. Hell, we can move to Alaska if you want." He set his hand on her stomach, still flat and slender. "Edna, you make me happy. I promise I will cherish you and do my best to make you happy too. I love you. I loved Johnny, and I will love his child as if it were my own. Please let me take care of you both."

A tear rolled down Edna's cheek. "He did what he said. He gave us a good life, and I loved him for it."

"I loved Frank too," Sunny said. She had stepped into the kitchen for a Kleenex and was blowing her nose. "You guys have been great neighbors. Frank always took care of me as if I was his own family."

Edna smiled. "He loved you like a daughter, Sunny. He would have done anything for you."

"He would have done anything for *you*," Sunny said. "It was obvious how devoted to you he was."

"Frank was a wonderful man. He was a loving husband and a wonderful father to our child." Edna looked at Johnny. "We had a daughter, and her name is Beth."

"You mean Moonbeam," Sunny said.

Johnny looked from Edna to Sunny then back to Edna. "You named your daughter, er…*our* daughter Moonbeam?"

Edna laughed. "No, I named her Beth, but she renamed herself Moonbeam. She was a teenager in the seventies, and she took to that hippy-dippy life as if she were custom made for it. She was always the sweetest girl, kind and loving to everyone. She thought being a flower child was the most romantic and wonderful thing in the world. After high school, she and a couple of other long-hairs traveled around the country in this ridiculous VW bus. They'd painted it with stars and flowers and fixed it up inside so it was like a little camper. They ate peanut butter and jelly sandwiches and drove that stupid thing all over the country. She came home after a few years of that and informed us that she was changing her name to Moonbeam and she and her friends had bought some land down in southern Colorado and were going to start a commune."

"Did they?" John asked.

"Oh yes," Edna said. "She may have inherited my sassy spirit, but she's got a stubborn streak in her that's all you."

Maggie laughed out loud. "Oh, sorry. I mean, of course she did, because Edna's not stubborn at all. In fact, I've never met a more flexible person in my life."

Edna gave her a look, ignoring Maggie's usual sarcasm. "Anyway, they bought this big farmhouse and started a garden and set up one of those roadside stands to sell stuff. I don't know all that went on down there. I think they smoked a lot of that wacky weed, and they probably ran around naked in the moonlight. But they seemed to make it work. And it still does. She still lives down there in that big old farmhouse."

"She still lives on the commune?" John asked.

Edna nodded. "Yep. I told you she was stubborn. She came home once in the early eighties to tell us that she had met a man. His name was Cosmic River. I assume he chose that himself, because who in their right mind would pick that name for their child? Well, she brought Cosmic to meet us and to tell us that they were having a baby. We were terrified she was going to try to have that child out in a field of flowers or some such nonsense but Frank convinced her to stay with us until the baby was born."

"Did she?"

Tears filled Edna's eyes, and she nodded. "That was the most wonderful summer. We had our daughter home, and she had the most beautiful baby girl. She named her Zoey Shining Star Allen, and even though I thought that was a ridiculous name, that little girl was our shining star. We had so much fun with a baby in the house."

Her eyes took on a faraway look as if she were lost in the memory. "She and Cosmic stayed with us for almost a year. They took the baby back to the commune but let her spend summers with us. Johnny, she was the most wonderful child and smart as a whip. She was sweet and kind, like her mother.

But in most things, she was the complete opposite of her momma."

Edna gave a little cackle. "In every way that Moon was a free spirit, Zoey was the contrary. Moon would leave things lying all over the house and left a trail of stuff everywhere she went. But Zoey kept all of her toys neat and tidy, and everything had to be organized and in exact order. It drove her mother crazy. Which just tickled me to death."

"You do have a wicked sense of humor," Cassie said. She had collected the dirty plates and napkins and stacked them up in front of her, ready to take to the dishwasher. "And there's nothing wrong with being organized and tidy."

"Of course not," Sunny said, still standing in the kitchen. "Some of us just prefer our clutter, or as I like to call it, controlled chaos." She laughed and pointed to the dishes in front of Cassie. "Bring those over here. I'll help you put them in the dishwasher."

Cassie picked up the plates while Maggie studied John's face. "I can see the resemblance. She looks a little like you, around the eyes. Moonbeam looks a lot like Edna, except she's quite a bit taller, but I can see the resemblance to you in Zoey. She's really a beautiful woman. But she doesn't know it. She's more reserved and kind of quiet until you get to know her. I can't believe she's not married yet."

"You know Zoey? And Beth, er Moonbeam?" John asked.

"Of course. We all do," Maggie said. "Well, not Piper because she just moved in with Cassie this year. But the rest of us have been friends for years. We've met Moon when she's been down for the holidays, and Zoey comes to visit several times a year."

John turned to Edna. "So what happened to this Cosmic River character? Was he a good father? Did he stay in their lives?"

"Oh, yeah, he's still around. He and Moon are still together. They never got married because they don't believe the courts should govern how they feel, blah, blah, blah, and that knowing they can leave anytime makes their relationship work. It all seems like a bunch of hooey to me. But it works for them, and they love each other. He's always been good to Moon and Zoey, so that's all I care about."

"And what happened to Zoey?"

"She grew up. And did the opposite of her mother. She went to college. Got a degree in accounting and became a CPA. She moved to Denver and got an apartment right in the middle of the city. I think she lives above a Starbucks, which drives her mother nuts. She works at Cavelli Commerce, which is some fancy firm downtown run by a couple of Italian brothers. Or she did until a few weeks ago when this whole shenanigan-thing with the money laundering happened."

"Hey, Edna," Sunny said. She stood at the sink looking out the kitchen window. "There's some man in your backyard. I just saw him slip into the shadows by that big lilac tree. Jake's porch light is on, and he just crossed under the light as he slipped into your yard."

John pushed back his chair and moved to the window. "Where? Show me."

The other Page Turners crowded the sink behind them to see out the kitchen window. Edna walked to the kitchen door and flung it open. "Hey, who's out there? I've got a gun, and I'm not afraid to use it."

"Edna, close the door," Maggie said, moving toward her. "It could be the guy who threw the rock."

"Good, I've got a few things I'd like to say to him, starting with he owes me two hundred dollars to replace my window." Edna shouted the last bit into the yard.

Maggie, being quite a bit taller than Edna, reached above her head to close the door. Before she could, a small man wearing a trench coat and a fedora hat slipped out of the dark and into the kitchen.

Havoc raced around the man's feet, barking and nipping at his heels.

Edna pulled out the nearest kitchen drawer, scrambling for a can of Mace. She grabbed a black vial and held it out in front of her. "Stop right there or I'll shoot. And I guarantee this will burn like a mother."

"Chill out, Grandma. It's me." The "man" pulled off his fedora and a spill of blonde hair fell across her shoulders. She tossed the hat onto the kitchen counter, reached down to scoop up the little dog, and cuddled it in her arms. Havoc wiggled with doggy joy, licking her face like they were old friends.

"Lord have mercy," Edna said, clutching her chest. "Zoey, you about gave me a heart attack. What in the hell are you doing here, and why in heaven's name are you dressed like that?"

Zoey held the dog in one arm and shrugged out of the trench coat. Underneath she wore a simple outfit of black yoga pants, a turquoise t-shirt, and cross trainers. "I'm in disguise."

Maggie raised an eyebrow. "That old-man disguise seems to be all the rage these days."

Edna opened her arms and her granddaughter stepped into them, hugging her tightly. Zoey was of average height, standing close to five foot seven, but she seemed tall compared to her tiny grandmother.

"Why do you need a disguise?" Edna asked.

"The press is hounding me like crazy. They've camped out in front of my apartment building and reporters are stationed at every exit. I can't step outside without fifty microphones stuck in my face and camera flashes blinding me."

Zoey looked around the kitchen and nodded at the Page Turners. "Looks like I interrupted book club. Hi, gals."

Maggie waved, and Sunny stepped forward and drew Zoey into a hug. "Hey, Zoey, good to see you. Even if you did scare the crap out of us."

"Hi, honey. You poor thing." Cassie grabbed a hug next then pointed to her niece. "This is my niece, Piper. She's been living with me since this spring and she's the newest member of the Page Turners."

Piper lifted a hand in greeting. "Hey, nice to meet you."

Zoey smiled at Piper then held her hand out to John. "Hi, I'm Zoey Allen, Edna's granddaughter."

Edna watched John's face as he stood before his granddaughter for the first time. His expression was a cross between pride and tenderness. "This is John, he's—"

"An old friend of the family." John finished her sentence, taking Zoey's hand in both of his. "It's an honor to meet you."

"Well, I don't know how much of an honor it is, but it's a pleasure to meet you as well. Did you know my Grandpa Frank, then?"

John nodded. "I did. We grew up together. He was my best friend. I loved your grandfather very much."

"So did I," Edna said, not quite under her breath. She drew a quick glance from John and knew he was wondering if she meant the grandfather Zoey grew up with or the man standing in front of her now.

"So, who is this little guy?" Zoey asked, still holding the dog, who now lay contently in her arms.

"That's Havoc," Edna said. "He's John's dog. They've been staying with me the past few days. And watch out, he lives up to his name."

"He's really taken with you. Havoc's usually a little more wary of strangers," John said. "Unless they have food."

The doorbell rang and the book club members froze. Cassie hurried to the front room and peeked out the window. "It's the police."

Edna opened the door to the basement and waved John over. "Quick, get in here. We'll get rid of them then give you the signal when it's safe to come out."

John hurried down the basement stairs, and Edna closed the door behind him. A hard rap knocked on the front door. "Hold your horses," she hollered.

She opened the front door to see Officer McCarthy standing on the stoop. And he did not look happy. "Hiya, Mac. What's going on? Isn't this a little late for a social visit?"

Mac narrowed his eyes and peered into the room behind Edna. "This is not a social visit. We got a call down at the station from one of your neighbors. They claim they saw a suspicious elderly man sneaking around your back yard and coming in your back door."

"What? One of my neighbors was spying on me? And called the police?" Edna said. "It was probably that ornery old Mr. Ferguson. Nosy old cuss."

"It doesn't matter who called it in," Mac said. "*Did* you have an elderly man sneak through your yard and into your kitchen tonight?"

"That was me." Zoey and the other Page Turners stepped out of the kitchen. Havoc followed close on her heels then sat and looked adoringly up at her.

Edna moved back so Mac could enter the room. "Mac, this is my granddaughter, Zoey Allen."

Mac arched an eyebrow at Zoey. "And may I ask why you were dressed as an elderly man and sneaking around your grandmother's backyard?"

"She was in disguise," Maggie said.

Piper held the trench coat and fedora. "See, these are her clothes."

"She's hiding out from the press," Cassie said.

"She's *that* Zoey Allen," Sunny explained. "The one that's been on the news."

Mac looked Zoey up and down, his expression thoughtful, as if he were recalling the news story in his head. "I read about that. You're the auditor that uncovered the money laundering scheme and is testifying against the CEO of the company? Some Italian company, isn't it? Savelli or Cavelli?"

She nodded. "That's me. It's Cavelli Commerce."

"That's right. So is it true? That you're here because you're hiding out from the press?"

"That, and a few other things. I've been getting some threatening messages about the upcoming trial. Apparently I didn't make any friends by exposing them."

"What are you talking about?" Edna rushed to her granddaughter's side and wrapped an arm around her waist. "You didn't say anything about any threatening messages."

"I haven't really had time. There was one on my cell phone this afternoon, and I tried to just blow it off. Then when I got home tonight, the press was terrible. I barely made it into my apartment building without getting crushed. I had another threatening message on my answering machine, and I kind of freaked out. I knew I needed to get out of there. I threw a few things in a bag and snuck out the back alley in the old-man clothes. This was the safest place I could think of, so I hopped in the car and drove down here."

Edna squeezed her shoulder. "You did the right thing, honey."

"Did you save the messages?" Mac asked, all business. "Can I listen to them?"

"Sure. I have the one on my cell phone with me." She reached down the front of her shirt and pulled her cell phone from her bra. "I think I can remotely get the message off my answering machine at home. If I can remember the pass code."

Maggie watched Mac's eyes widen when Zoey unintentionally flashed him a little cleavage as she dislodged her phone. She shook her head. "She's just like her grandmother. Do all the Allen women consider their bras as a second purse?"

Zoey laughed. "I usually have a pocket. But I did learn that trick from my grandma." She touched a few spots on the phone. "Here, I'll put the message on speaker."

The group crowded closer as a gravelly voice spoke from the phone. "Listen closely, because I'm only gonna say this once. Whatever you think you know about Cavelli Commerce, I'd suggest you forget it. I wouldn't want to see a pretty little thing like you get hurt over a few false accusations."

Cassie shivered. "Creepy."

"Why aren't you freaking out? Hiding under the bed with a gun?" Sunny asked.

"I am freaking out a little. I dressed up like an old man and ran to hide at my grandma's house." Zoey forced a laugh. "But hey, on the plus side, he did say that I was pretty."

Mac pulled a business card from his pocket and passed it to Zoey. "Here's my card. I'd like you to come down to the station tomorrow, and we can get a recording of that message and the other one. We'll see if we can't get some more information on who made the calls."

"Okay."

"Are you sure you're going to be all right here? Would you like me to stay for awhile? Take a look around?" Mac peered into the kitchen.

"That won't be necessary." Edna gripped his elbow and steered him back to the front door. "We've got everything under control here. I won't let anything happen to my granddaughter. I've got a license to carry, ya know."

"Somehow that information does not make me feel any better." Mac opened the front door. "I'll send a patrol car through the neighborhood a couple of times tonight just to be on the safe side, and you can call me if you see anything suspicious or that makes you feel uncomfortable." He looked down at Edna. "I don't suppose you've heard from our friend, John, have you?"

Edna shook her head. "Nope. Not a peep."

"And you'd let me know if you did, of course?"

She bobbed her head up and down. "Oh, of course. You betcha." She pushed the door shut behind him, speaking her last sentence through the crack in the door. "The minute I hear anything, you'll be the first to know."

Zoey waved a hand in front of her face, fanning herself. "Holy hot-man-in-uniform. If all the cops in this town look like him, I'm getting myself arrested tomorrow."

Cassie grinned and wiggled her eyebrows. "And he has a motorcycle."

"Oh my."

"Enough about Officer Hottie," Edna said, striding toward the kitchen. "Somebody needs to let John out of the basement. I'm going to go get my gun."

"How about I call Jake, instead?" Sunny said, already reaching for her phone.

Zoey raised her hand as if asking a question in class. "I'll let John out of the basement, then somebody needs to tell me what's going on with him. Something tells me he's more than just an old friend of the family."

The next morning, Edna woke with the sun. She liked to get up early and putter around the house before her day started. Enjoying a cup of coffee on her back deck while watching the birds, and sometimes her other neighbors, was one of her favorite morning activities. The air was getting cooler in the morning, and she knew fall was on its way, whether she was ready to see the summer end or not.

This morning, before heading straight to the kitchen, she had popped into her bathroom. Taking a few extra minutes, she washed her face, freshened up her hair and swiped a touch of mascara across her light eyelashes.

It wasn't every day that she woke up to a handsome man in her house, and her stomach fluttered a little in anticipation of seeing him. Either that, or it was indigestion from too much dessert last night.

She debated a dab of lipstick but decided against it. *Don't want to look like I'm trying too hard.*

She did wrap herself in the flowing pink satin robe that matched her pajamas. She had a drawer full of nice matching pajama sets—evidently that was the gift of choice for elderly women. Everybody wants you to look nice when they stick you away in a home.

She walked into the kitchen thinking about what ingredients she had on hand to whip up some breakfast, and was surprised to see John standing at the stove, cracking an egg into a bowl.

He was clean-shaven and wore khaki pants and a green golf shirt. Tied around his front was one of her frilly kitchen aprons, and Edna laughed out loud at the sight of him in pink polka dots and ruffles. "Nice apron. Who are you supposed to be? Betty Crocker?"

"I prefer Bernie Crocker, Betty's lesser-known male counterpart." John bowed and fluffed the apron. "I'm not too skilled in the kitchen, but I can make a mean omelet and thought breakfast was the least I could do to pay you back for the trouble I've caused, making you hide out a fugitive and all."

"You didn't make me do anything. And you don't owe me." Edna took a coffee cup from the cupboard. "But I do like omelets, and I appreciate the gesture."

She wiggled her eyebrows at him. "And you look kinda sexy in that apron and wielding a spatula."

A huge grin broke across John's face. "Really?"

"Absolutely. It really lends credence to your bad boy status."

"Ha. I haven't been considered a bad boy in forty years."

"Well, you're the first fugitive I've had cook me breakfast, and I don't have very many 'first' experiences anymore, so there's a lot of pressure riding on the tastiness of this omelet." She loved flirting with him. Loved watching his face light with surprise then turn to a naughty grin.

"What happens if I mess up the eggs—will you call in the cops or just handcuff me?"

"Oh my. You are a little rascal." Edna swatted at him with a dishtowel, but still felt a little heat warm her cheeks. "Is it getting hot in here or is that just the stove? I might have to open a window."

John laughed.

She had missed the sound of that laugh. She'd missed him. His easy manner and how comfortable she felt around him. It had been over half her lifetime since she'd seen him, but it felt like yesterday that they were together, teasing each other just like today.

"Am I interrupting?" Zoey stood in the doorway of the kitchen, wearing a pair of Edna's pajamas with her blonde hair crushed against one side of her head. In her haste, she had forgotten to pack anything to wear to bed. Digging through her pajama drawer, Edna had found a lavender set with cotton capri pants and a soft t-shirt that still had the tags hanging from the sleeve.

With her sleepy eyes and the pastel-colored pajamas, she looked to Edna just like the little girl who used to spend her summer mornings in this very kitchen, a cereal box propped up in front of her at the table. "Heavens no. Come on in. John is making us breakfast."

Edna poured Zoey a cup of coffee, and they sat at the kitchen island, watching John cook the eggs. He plated the omelets and joined them, all the while keeping up a lighthearted conversation. They laughed and talked as they went through a second pot of coffee. Havoc languished in Zoey's lap as she patted his belly and fed him the crust off her toast.

"Oh goodness," Edna said, glancing at the wall clock. "The morning's half over, and I'm still in my pajamas and haven't even got the paper yet. This hiding-out thing is kind of fun."

She opened the front door and was surprised to see the paper on the front stoop of the porch instead of out in the driveway. The days of paperboys riding by on their bicycles and tossing the paper on your porch were gone, replaced by delivery people who drove by with the window down and pitched your paper onto your driveway or yard.

A white sheet of paper was wrapped around the paper, secured with the rubber band. She brought it in and set the newspaper on the table as she unfolded the page.

"So much for hiding out," she said, dropping the white paper on the table. In large block print, someone had scrawled, "I KNOW YOU ARE HERE."

Zoey gasped. "How did they find me?"

"You?" John asked. "I'm sure this note is meant for me." They had given Zoey an abbreviated version of why John was hiding out at Edna's. Basically telling her that he had been wrongly accused of a crime he didn't commit.

"But how could anyone know *either* of us were here?" Zoey asked.

"Where did you leave your car?" John moved to the front window and peered out through the break in the curtains.

"I parked it a few houses down." She joined him at the window and pointed to a blue sedan parked on the street in front of Sunny's house. "That's my car, the blue Ford Taurus. It's not much to look at, but it was affordable, is fairly cheap on gas, and it runs."

John shook his head in disbelief. "I'm driving the exact same car." He smiled down at Zoey. "And for the same reasons. But my car is in the parking lot of that little grocery store three or four blocks from here."

"Then whoever left the note could have easily mistaken my car for yours," Zoey said.

"Or vice versa. That doesn't help us determine who that note was meant for."

"Well, whoever it's meant for, nobody touch it." Edna reached into a kitchen drawer and withdrew a Ziploc bag. "We'll stick it in here and see if the police can get any prints off it."

She picked the note up with a pair of kitchen tongs and dropped it into the baggie, then looked from John to Zoey. "Looks like our peaceful morning is over. Zoey, you and I better go get dressed. I'll call Mac and tell him we're coming down to the station. He wanted to get a recording of those phone messages anyway."

"I'll stay here and clean up," John offered.

Edna raised an eyebrow. "A man that cooks *and* cleans. I think I'm in love." She laughed it off like she was joking, but she knew she truly was still in love with him. It didn't matter how many years had passed or how gray their hair had gotten; her heart still recognized him as the boy she fell in love with.

Forty minutes later, Edna and Zoey walked into the Pleasant Valley Police Station.

Edna had the note in her purse next to her pocket Taser. Zoey was dressed in the same yoga pants and tennis shoes as the night before, but now she had her hair concealed in a ball cap and wore large, dark sunglasses. A baggy quilted jacket of Edna's completed her disguise.

The heavy jacket seemed a little out of place for the summer weather, and the huge round frames of the sunglasses engulfed

Zoey's face. But she told Edna that she didn't care. With the intended recipient of the note still unknown, she would rather look a little silly than be recognized.

Edna approached the counter. "We're here to see Officer McCarthy. He's a personal friend of mine. In fact, I usually just call him Mac."

The desk clerk looked unimpressed. She barely glanced up from her paperwork. "Yeah, we all call him Mac. May I ask what this is in reference to?"

"No, you may not. We are here on official police business. So, if you don't mind, could you get him, please? We've got a bit of an urgent matter."

The clerk picked up the desk phone and punched a few keys. She looked Edna and Zoey up and down, as if appraising the urgency of their matter. "Hey, McCarthy, there's a couple of ladies here to see you. They claim it's urgent police business. One of them claims she's a close, personal friend of yours, even gets to call you Mac." She listened a moment then gave Edna another once-over before answering. "Yep, that's her all right."

She hung up the phone. "He says he'll be right out."

Edna tipped her nose into the air. "Told you so."

Officer McCarthy stepped out of a back office. He spotted Edna and Zoey and made his way across the room to where they stood. "Good morning, Edna. It's always a pleasure to see you." He smiled down at Zoey. "Miss Allen, are you doing all right?"

Zoey smiled, and Edna noted the slight blush to her cheeks. "Yes, I'm good. Thanks."

Edna shook her head in disgust. "You know, Mac, she's usually more articulate than that. That girl's smart as a whip. Graduated top of her class. She's even good at math."

Zoey rolled her eyes, and the slight pink of her cheeks deepened in embarrassment. "Oh, Grandma, stop it. He doesn't care about my math skills. Let's just get on with why we're here."

Mac winked at Zoey. "I don't know about that. I'm usually impressed by a girl's knowledge of algebraic equations."

Zoey laughed. "Okay, I'll quote you some tangents and cosines later."

"I'll look forward to it." He looked down at Edna. "So, what can I do for you? I have a feeling this is about more than recording Zoey's phone messages."

Edna nodded, lowering her voice. "A threatening note was left on my doorstep this morning."

He sighed and rubbed his hand across his shaved head. "Come on, then."

Edna sashayed past the desk clerk, doing her best not to thumb her nose.

Mac led them through the noisy station and into an empty interrogation room. "All right. Let me see the note."

Edna pulled the message from her purse and set it on the table.

Mac picked it up and examined it from all sides. "You did a good job putting it in a baggie. Who else touched it?"

"Just me," Edna said. Thank goodness she had gotten the newspaper and not John. "And the person who wrote it, of course."

"Of course. I'll have somebody take a look at it, see if we can lift any prints from it." He turned to Zoey. "This note could have been meant for either you or Mr. Collins. I'd still like to get a recording of that message you played me yesterday and see if we can't get the other one you mentioned."

Zoey pulled her phone from her bag. "Yeah, sure. This just seems crazy to me. I've never been threatened over anything in my life."

"When it comes to money, people will go to extreme lengths. And it sounds like your testimony is going to cost some guys a lot of money. Have you noticed anything else suspicious? Anyone hanging around that you might not know?"

"How could I tell? There's a huge group of reporters clustered in front of my apartment. I don't know any of them."

Edna gasped. "You think the guy who's threatening her could be posing as a reporter? He could have been right outside your door, Zoey. You might have walked past him a dozen times."

Mac held up his hand. "I'm not saying that. I just want you to be thinking about all the possibilities. Did you tell anyone that you were coming up here to see your grandma? Or have you mentioned that you have relatives in Pleasant Valley?"

Zoey shook her head. "No. Not that I can remember."

Edna narrowed her eyes. "Why? What are you not telling us? You know something, don't you, Mac?"

"I'm not sure if this is related to Zoey or Mr. Collins. Or it could be a random coincidence, but a guy stopped by the station yesterday and was asking a lot of questions."

"I don't believe in coincidences," Edna said.

"Neither do I."

"What kind of questions?"

"Well, they were mostly about you, Edna."

"Me? What could someone want to know about me?"

"I'm not sure. I wasn't here. He talked to Officer Royce. Royce said he was an older guy, claimed he's a retired cop and up here to do a little fishing. He said he always likes to check in with the local station, say hello. All that seemed fine until he brought up your name. Said he had an old friend that lived in town and wondered if we knew where Frank and Edna Allen lived."

"Who was he?" Edna asked. "I don't know any retired cops. Or none that I can think of."

"His name was Ward or Wayne-something. Royce told me about it last night after I got back from the call at your house. He's off for the day, but I'll call him and see if he wrote it down. I assumed it had something to do with John, but now that I think about it, maybe he was trying to ferret out information about Zoey."

"Well, let me know if he comes by again," Edna said. "I'd like to get a look at the guy."

Zoey handed Mac her cell phone and a piece of paper. "Here's my phone and the passcodes to listen to the messages. I really don't need to hear them again."

"I get that. Give me a few minutes. I'm gonna take this over to my tech guy and have him get a recording of these. I'll be back in five." He stared directly at Edna. "Do *not* leave this room. Understood?"

Edna shrugged and held her hands up in an "I surrender" gesture. "Understood. We'll sit right here and be quiet as church mice."

"I'll believe that when I see it," Mac muttered, then pulled the door shut behind him.

Edna turned to Zoey. "He's a good man. And a good cop. He'll do his best to help us figure this out."

"Yeah, he seems nice."

"And handsome too. So tall."

"Grandma."

"What? I'm just saying."

True to his word, Mac was gone less than five minutes. He handed Zoey back her phone. "Let me know if you get any other calls or threats of any kind."

A tinkling ringtone sounded, and Edna pulled her phone from her bag. "Hang on. It's Sunny." She held the phone up to her ear. "Hey Sunny. Listen, honey, we're down at the police station."

She paused, listening, then her face drained of color. "We're with Mac now. We'll be right there."

She hung up the phone and grabbed her bag, herding Zoey and Mac out the door. "Sunny said someone blew up Zoey's car. It was sitting in front of her house, and she heard the explosion. They've called 911 and the fire department is on the way."

Mac quickened his pace, holding the door for the women as they raced outside. "Come on, we'll take the squad car. I can get us there in five minutes."

She was scared for Zoey, but Edna's pulse picked up an extra beat at the thought of getting to ride in the police car. "Can I turn on the siren?"

Four and a half minutes later, the squad car pulled up in front of Edna's house. The street ahead of them was blocked by emergency vehicles. They could see a plume of smoke rising into the air above a blackened shell of a car.

Edna had called shotgun and Zoey sat in the seat behind her. Edna craned her neck to see the car. "Oh my Lord, that could have been you in that car."

Zoey stared at her car in shock. She patted her grandmother's back. "I'm fine, Gram. But why is there an ambulance? Sunny didn't say that anyone got hurt."

Mac opened his door. "They always dispatch the ambulance with the fire engine, just in case. I'll see if I can find out what's going on." He slammed the door and headed toward the fire truck.

"Surely he doesn't think we're just going to wait in the car," Edna said, pushing open the car door. "I need to see if Sunny's okay."

The women hurried through the yard. They spotted Sunny and Jake and headed their way.

"Are you all right, honey?" Edna asked Sunny. "Did anybody get hurt?"

"I'm fine," Sunny said. "No one was hurt except poor Zoey's car." She gave the younger woman a hug. "I was sitting in the living room reading a book when Beau stood up and growled at the front door. Then I heard a whoosh and a pop, and by the time I made it to the window, the car was in flames. I called 911 and saw Jake running for the car with the garden hose trying to put out the fire."

"I wasn't sure whose car it was at first," Jake said. "I thought it was John's, then Sunny told me that Zoey had the same model car. And that she'd parked it in front of her house last night."

Mac strode toward them, a stern look on his face. "Zoey, you need to be inside. If this was aimed at you, the perpetrator could be watching for you to show up or for your reaction."

Zoey scanned the neighborhood. "Little coward."

"This could have been meant for John." Edna slipped her arm through Mac's as they walked across the grass to her house. "You know he drives the same model and color of car as Zoey?"

"Same car, both being threatened. Those two seem to have a lot in common," Mac said, opening the front door of Edna's house and stepping back for her to enter first.

"More than you know," Edna muttered. She stepped into the house and called loudly for the dog. "Havoc, here, boy. We're home. Zoey and I are here with our friend, Mac, the police officer."

Mac looked down at her, the frustration obvious in his expression. "Really? Could you be any more obvious? You do know that I'm a detective, right?"

"I'm sure I have no idea what you mean. I was just saying hello to the dog." She did her best to keep her eyes on Mac and not scan the house for signs of John.

Mac's expression turned serious. "Listen, Edna, I know you think this guy is safe, but you haven't seen him in a long time. He may have changed. He never said why he came to town. Maybe he's in some kind of trouble."

Edna looked at Zoey. "I know why he's here, and it's not to cause any trouble."

"Listen, something happened last night. I was just talking to a buddy of mine, he drives the ambulance. He said they picked up Irma Jean Johnson last night and took her to the hospital. You know she works down at the courthouse. He said someone had broken into her house and beaten her up pretty bad."

The color drained from Edna's face. "Oh no. Of course I know Irma Jean. We play bridge together every month. Why would someone want to hurt her?"

"That's a good question. They broke a couple of her fingers. You don't have to be a detective to know that's a common tactic used to get information."

"What kind of information could Irma Jean possibly have?"

Mac shrugged. "I don't know. She works at the courthouse so she has access to a lot of records. Do you think Mr. Collins could have been looking for information?"

"What do you mean? You think John could have done this?" Edna reached for the edge of the sofa to steady herself.

"Edna, you haven't seen him in many years."

"Mac, I don't care if I haven't seen Johnny in a hundred years, he would never purposely hurt anyone. He hates violence, of any kind. And he would *never* hurt a woman."

"I'm sorry, Edna. I have to look at this objectively and with no emotion involved. A wanted fugitive arrives in town, and Irma Jean gets assaulted. It's my job to establish if they're connected in some way."

"I can assure you there is no connection," Zoey said.

Mac narrowed his eyes. "How would you be able to assure any such thing? You don't even know him." A light dawned in Mac's eyes, and he turned to Edna.

She straightened her shoulders and stood up to her full five foot two. "Well, I know him, and I *can* assure you that last night John Collins was nowhere near Irma Jean Johnson's house."

Mac sighed. "I'm expecting to get the test results back on that gun you gave me any day now. So, for the moment, I'm going to pretend I did not hear that last comment. But if I find out anything, and I mean *anything*, that makes me even the least bit suspicious that this guy could be involved in this or in any way pose a threat to you or Zoey, I will come back and tear this house apart looking for him. You understand?"

Zoey put her arm around her grandmother's shoulder. "Of course. We understand. We know you're just doing your job, and we appreciate it."

"I've got to get back to the station. Do you want to ride back with me or do you want to give me your keys, and I'll have a couple of officers drop your car off later?"

"I'll come with you," Zoey said, pulling the large-framed sunglasses from her bag. She squeezed Edna's shoulder. "Why don't you lie down for a bit, Grandma? Try to get some rest. I'll be back in a half an hour with your car."

Edna nodded and sank onto the sofa. "That's fine, honey. I think I could use a little rest. The keys are in my purse."

Zoey kissed her cheek then dug the car keys out of Edna's bag. "I'll be back soon."

Edna lay back, waiting for them to leave. As soon as the door closed behind them, she popped up from the sofa and hurried into the kitchen. She opened the basement door and saw John sitting on the top step, his head in his hands.

She eased down onto the step beside him. "Did you hear all of that?"

John looked up at her, and she was surprised to see tears shimmering in his blue eyes. "I did. And as much as I appreciate you standing up for me, I'm responsible for that woman being in the hospital."

"What? You couldn't be. You were here all night. Both Zoey and I will vouch for you."

"I don't mean I'm the one who actually hurt her. I could never do that. But I knew her. I just saw her yesterday."

What was he talking about? How could he possibly know her? Was Mac right? Had it been too many years? Could Johnny really have changed that much? She didn't believe it. Couldn't believe that he was different at his very core. "How could you know Irma Jean Johnson? I thought you just got to town a few days ago."

"I did. That's when I met her. At the courthouse. I needed to see the county records. I needed to verify the dates of when you and Frank got married and to see Beth, I mean Moonbeam's, birth certificate. To verify if I could have been her father."

She blew out a breath, thankful that she was right in her assumption of John's character. "So what if you knew her? That doesn't make you responsible for her assault."

"Officer McCarthy is right. She got attacked right after she helped me. There has to be a connection between my visits to the courthouse and her being beaten. It's a small town, and we know someone's been following me. They could have watched me go into the courthouse or seen me talking to her. The rock came through your window before Zoey arrived, so regardless of who these 'messages' are intended for, we are dealing with a dangerous individual. And I can't help feeling like if I hadn't asked her for help, she would still be okay."

Edna took his hand. "You can't blame yourself for this. You went into a courthouse to check out some records. Even if someone was following you, you had no way of knowing they would hurt an innocent woman."

John leaned forward and laid a gentle kiss on the back of Edna's hand. "Thank you. You always know the right thing to say."

The feel of his lips on her hand made her insides go a little soft. She could feel the heat rising in her cheeks. "Well, I have no idea what to say right now." She touched his cheek and looked up into his blue eyes, now devoid of tears. "Johnny Collins. I can't believe you are here. Sitting next to me. Alive.

And I am touching you. You have rendered me completely speechless."

John's face softened, and he squeezed her hand. "You are still so beautiful, Eddy. I look at you and I still see the face of that girl I fell in love with all those years ago." He leaned down and ever so lightly kissed her upturned lips.

An entire colony of butterflies fluttered around Edna's stomach. Twisting and turning. A cross between excitement and terror. She had dreamt of his kisses. Of his touch. Laid awake on hot summer nights reliving the memories of the summer they spent together. He tasted like butter rum lifesavers, and she could smell the woodsy scent of his aftershave.

She felt like she was that young girl again, and she kissed him back. Hard. Kissed him with the memory of their youth on her lips. With the spirit of her twenty-year-old self and the image of his youthful hard body emblazoned in her mind.

She didn't care if her hair had turned white and her veins showed blue through her wrinkled skin. She felt alive and passionate, and she wrapped her arms around his neck and twisted her fingers into his hair.

His arms found their way around her waist, and he pulled her to him. He kissed her mouth, her cheeks, her neck, then laid his forehead against hers, gasping for breath. "Whew. Did you forget I'm an old man? I haven't been kissed like that in a decade. Are you trying to kill me, woman?"

"Old is just a word. You still look pretty good to me." She looked up at him and winked. "And if I were trying to kill you, I would've flashed you my boobs."

John broke into a grin, and he laughed out loud. "You still know how to make me laugh." He pulled her close to him and kissed her once more, lightly on the lips. "You make me feel like a teenager. My heart is racing, and my hands are shaking. I have never stopped loving you, Eddy. Not a single day's gone by that I haven't thought of you."

Edna nodded, her eyes filling with tears. "I have always loved you, Johnny. You took a piece of my heart with you when I thought you died, and I've never been able to fully love another man the way that I loved you. With pure abandon, never thinking about the consequences or that you wouldn't be there to return that love. After you died, I protected my heart and sheltered it so I would never be hurt like that again."

She reached up and brushed his hair from his forehead. "And now here you are. Sitting beside me. Kissing me like a teenager on the basement stairs. Even now, I'm scared to death to even say the words. To tell you that I still love you. Always have and always will."

"Edna, I can't promise that I will always be here. I'm over eighty years old. I could die tonight. But if I do, I want you to know that you have always been the one that holds my heart. And if I live until tomorrow or I live until I'm a hundred, I don't want to spend another day without you. I want to go to bed with you at night and wake up to your sweet face first thing in the morning."

She raised an eyebrow at him. "John Collins, are you suggesting we shack up together? That we live in sin?"

He grinned. "No, of course not. That was my foolish way of asking you to marry me, Edna Allen."

"Holy cow!"

"That's your answer? I was expecting a 'hell no' or maybe an 'absolutely,' but not a 'holy cow'."

"Would you prefer 'divine bovine'?" She giggled. Actually giggled, like a schoolgirl. "I don't even know what to say."

The sound of the front door opening interrupted Edna's response. Zoey's voice could be heard calling into the house. "Hello. Grandma, I'm back. And it's just me."

"We're down here," Edna called. "If I can get up off these stairs, we'll come up." She hauled herself up by the railing and the assistance of John's hand. She stood a few steps higher and turned to him, her face now level with his. "We'll continue this conversation later."

He grinned at her and winked. "Oh, I know we will. Now that I have you back in my life again, I'm not letting you go."

Her face beamed with a radiant smile and her insides melted. She reached up and touched his cheek. "That's a deal."

He turned her toward the kitchen door and gave her a light pat on the fanny. "Good, now let's go see our granddaughter."

19

"I get the feeling there's more to you and Johnny than just being old friends." Zoey handed a dripping plate to Edna, who stood next to her at the kitchen sink.

It was the following afternoon, and Edna, Zoey, and John had just finished lunch. John had left to retrieve his car and move it to Edna's garage. They figured even if the car was in her garage, they couldn't prove that John was with them, and they all felt safer with the car locked up.

Edna took the plate and wiped it dry with a towel. "There are all kinds of old friends."

Zoey turned and gave her an "I'm not an idiot" stare.

"Okay. You're right. Johnny was my first true love. I met him at the same time as your Grandpa Frank, but I fell in love with John. We spent the summer together and had planned to marry. I didn't get together with Frank until after Johnny died."

"Died? You mean that guy we just had lunch with was a ghost?" Zoey had inherited the family trait of sarcasm. She passed Edna the last plate and drained the soapy water.

"We all believed he died. He faked his own death, and we had a funeral for him. Frank had been his best friend and my sole companion, and it was only natural that we would seek solace in each other. One thing led to another, and the next thing you know, we were married."

Zoey put her hand on her hip. "Nothing is *ever* that simple with you. I like John, and I haven't asked many questions about this whole 'harboring a fugitive' thing we've got going on, but now I know there's a love story involved. So spill it. What's really going on here?"

Edna sighed. "I better get us some tea." She fixed two glasses of iced tea, and Zoey followed her into the living room. Edna sank into the couch and recounted the tale of her summer in Coopersville. She told Zoey everything up until Johnny's death, not ready to reveal the true identity of her grandfather yet. She wouldn't do that without John.

"So, he's been in hiding all these years, and he left out of love for you and Frank." Zoey's eyes filled with tears, sentimentality being another Allen trait. "That is so romantic."

"It might be romantic, but it makes me mad as hell."

"Why?"

"Because I missed out on all those years with him. We could have spent our whole lives together. And he made that decision on his own, without even asking me."

Zoey picked up Edna's hand and held it in hers. "Grandma, I hate to sound clichéd, but I really do believe everything happens for a reason. You have had a good life. And Grandpa Frank was a good man. You've always grabbed life by the horns and squeezed every ounce of living out of it. I've never known you to look back with regrets. Plus, you got me out of the deal. That wouldn't have happened if you hadn't married Grandpa and had my mom."

Edna wished she could tell her the truth. Would it be better for her to know the truth now? To give her a chance to get to know John and have a relationship with him or to hold onto the grandfather she grew up with? The one who took her fishing and read her books and taught her how to change a flat tire. The one who gave her his name and always loved her as his own.

Frank was still her grandfather. Johnny's presence would never change that. Zoey was smart and kind. She was one of the most loving persons that Edna had ever known. Could she make Zoey see that John was an additional grandpa instead of a replacement one?

Edna smiled at her granddaughter. "He's asked me to marry him."

Zoey's eyes widened. "Oh my gosh, that's wonderful. What did you say?"

"Holy cow."

Zoey scanned the room. "Holy cow what?"

"No, that's what I said. Holy cow. I haven't given him my answer yet."

"Why not? You were just complaining that you missed out on having a life with him. Well, as far as I can tell, you're still alive. You have a chance to spend the rest of your life with him now."

"First of all, I don't complain." Edna paused, waiting for her granddaughter to challenge her. Zoey just looked at her. When did this little girl grow up into a woman? And when did she get so smart? "You do realize we are both in our eighties? Having a wedding at my age would create quite a ruckus."

"Eighty-schmeighty. And when have you ever shied away from a ruckus?" Zoey cocked her head and regarded her grandmother. "Is there something else going on here that you're not telling me? Is there a reason why you don't want to marry him?"

Yes. There was one big gigantic beating reason. Her heart. She had vowed to never risk loving another man the way that she had loved Johnny Collins. She had spent her entire life guarding herself from ever having that pain again. She loved Frank. She did build a good life with him. But she always protected herself. Never fully trusting him with everything. With the full passion of her heart and soul.

"Don't you still love him?"

Edna nodded, her voice barely above a whisper. "With every fiber of my being."

The back door opened, cutting off any further response from Zoey.

John walked into the kitchen, towing Havoc on a leash. He wore the fedora/trench coat disguise and he tossed the hat on the kitchen table and grinned at Edna. "You look more beautiful than when I left a half hour ago."

Edna waved a hand at him. "Oh stop it, you old coot! Not really. Keep going."

"No, stop, please." Zoey laughed. Havoc had run straight at her, dragging his leash behind him and catapulted himself into her lap. She unhooked the leash and nuzzled into his furry neck, giggling as he licked her ears. "Did you have any trouble getting the car?"

John poured himself a glass of iced tea from the pitcher Edna had left on the table. "Nope. It seemed fine. Right where I left it. And now it's safely locked in your garage." He carried his tea into the living room and sank into the arm chair across from them. "What have you girls been up to? Solved the plight of the world yet?"

"Not yet," Zoey answered. "We're still working on the Northern Hemisphere."

Edna watched John and her granddaughter as they laughed and joked together. It made her heart happy to see them getting along. Heck, it made her happy to see Johnny at all. He looked pretty good for a dead guy. His hair was still thick and his eyes bright. Geez, it sounded like she was describing a dog. A really handsome dog.

The years working on the farm had kept John in good physical shape, and Edna admired the fact that he still seemed so healthy and robust.

Zoey was right. She did have a zest for life, and it seemed like John shared that zeal. He could have shrunk into a hermit-style existence, hiding from the law and turning completely paranoid. But he seemed as if he hadn't let life or his circumstances get him down. He found something he enjoyed and built his life around it. Working outdoors and with animals seemed to have made him happy, and she still loved to hear him laugh.

And now they had the whole afternoon ahead of them. It was great watching them get to know each other. How fun that she got to spend the entire day with two people that she loved like crazy.

Edna clapped her hands together, startling the dog. "Well, what shall we do with our afternoon? We could start a gin rummy tournament, or I can make some popcorn and we can veg out in front of a movie."

Zoey groaned and held her stomach. "I'm still full from that delicious lunch you made. I'm gonna gain ten pounds if I stay here much longer, Gram."

The house phone rang, putting off their decision for a few minutes. John picked up the handset and checked the caller ID. "It's an unknown number. Do you just want to ignore it?"

Edna reached for the phone. "No, I love sales calls. I get a kick out of messing with them. I either string them along for ten minutes to get them back for wasting my time or I tell them about the Bible and try to convince them to follow Jesus. Either way it's fun." She depressed the on button and answered in a cheery voice. "Hello."

Her cheerful greeting died on her lips, and she motioned for something to write on. Zoey grabbed a pen and notepad from the kitchen counter and passed it to her grandmother.

Edna scribbled a quick note as she listened intently to the caller. *It's the retired cop that was asking ?'s at the police station. Has info about W's murder. Wants to meet.*

"Look, sir, I don't even know you. How do I know you're not just trying to get me alone to rape me and steal my money?" Edna huffed in annoyance. "Sir, you can stop laughing now. I don't see what's so amusing about that statement."

She listened for a few more minutes. "All right, but I'm not coming alone. I'm bringing three friends along, and two of them are Smith and Wesson. We'll be there in fifteen minutes."

Edna hung up the phone. "That was the guy Mac told us about. He said his name is Officer Halloran, and he's a retired cop from Kansas. He's been following this case for years and supposedly has information that can clear Johnny's name. He wants me to meet him up the pass at the Waffle Inn on Highway 36."

The town of Pleasant Valley was nestled against a mountain range. Within a few miles of the city, Highway 36 led into the mountains and over a treacherous pass.

"I'm confused. Why does he want to meet you? Why wouldn't he just give the information to the police? Especially if he *is* a policeman." Zoey wrung her hands together, as if she were the elderly woman instead of her grandmother. "Maybe we should call Mac. Or Jake. This feels really fishy to me."

"Of course it's fishy. I don't trust this Officer Halloran, if that's even his real name, for anything. But he knows about the murder, and he mentioned Johnny's name. He's obviously up to something, and we need to see what it is."

"I don't like this," Johnny said. "It feels like a trap or like he is trying to draw us out. Maybe this is the guy that set the car on fire."

"First of all, we don't know if that fire was meant to scare Zoey or you. And if this guy is involved in these threats, that's great. He may think he's drawing us out, but really we'll be luring him in. It's a win-win."

Zoey looked skeptical. "I don't like this either. It sounds dangerous."

Edna rubbed her hands together. "That's what makes it exciting. Plus, I have my gun and a pocket Taser. And if we start to feel like anything is getting too dangerous, I'll call Mac. I promise. First sign of trouble and he's on speed dial." She reached for her purse. "We need to go. I said we'd be there in fifteen minutes and it will take ten just to get up the pass. I've eaten at the Waffle Inn years ago. I know where it is."

John looked at Zoey and shook his head. "It doesn't sound like she's gonna listen to reason. I guess we're going for a drive. We'll take my car."

The phone rang again, and they froze. Was he calling back already? Had he changed his mind?

Edna picked it up and checked the readout. "It's not him. It's the police station. I'd better take it." She pushed the button to answer. "Hello. Oh hi, Mac." She held her hand over the receiver. "It's Mac."

Zoey rolled her eyes.

"I'm here with Zoey, but we were just heading out. We're going to get some waffles." She listened a few minutes more. "Okay, I'll wait here. How soon can you get here?" Pause. "All right, see you soon."

She hung up and swore. "Well, crap! I guess you all will have to go check out the Waffle Inn without me."

"Without you?" John asked. "Why? What does Officer McCarthy want? Why is he coming over here?"

"He said he got the ballistics tests back on the gun used in Weasel's murder, and he has some questions for me."

"Then we should stay and see what he found out. It may be important."

"No. We can't take a chance on missing out on this lead. There's something going on with this guy, and we need to check it out." Edna grabbed one of her jackets and a gardening hat from the front closet. "Zoey can wear these and go with you. They'll disguise her from any press that may be looking for her and hopefully trick this Halloran fellow into thinking she's me. Zoey, you need to have your phone ready. Try to get some pictures of him, or better yet, some video."

Zoey shook her head. "I don't feel very good about this idea, Gram. Maybe we should wait for Officer McCarthy and have him go with us."

"No way. That's half the reason I'm staying—to distract Mac so you all can go check this guy out."

Accepting that they wouldn't convince her, John and Zoey agreed. Zoey put on the disguise, and after a quick hug, she and John left.

Edna paced her kitchen for the ten minutes it took Officer McCarthy to show up on her doorstep. Impatient to hear his news, she had the front door opened by the time he walked up the steps. Ushering him in, she'd already poured him a glass of iced tea and had it sitting on the kitchen table.

With an appreciative nod, he picked up the glass and took a long drink. "Thank you, Ms. Allen. I needed that. It's a warm one out there today."

Edna had a moment of pity for poor Zoey wearing the jacket and hat on a warm day, but was more concerned about the reason for Mac's visit. "Enough with the pleasantries. What's going on? You said something about some tests."

Mac pulled out a kitchen chair, took a seat, and waited to speak until Edna was also seated. "The tests came back on the gun used in Warren Farris' murder. Ballistics proved that it was a match to the murder weapon and the only fingerprints on it were indeed Donna Kaufman's. The prints are arranged in a manner evident of her firing the gun. It's enough evidence to clear John and issue a warrant for Donna."

Edna released a huge sigh. "Praise the Lord! I always knew he was innocent, but now everyone will know. And he won't have to hide anymore."

"On the crazy off chance that you might see him, you can let him know we're dropping the charges against him. It may take a few days for everything to go through, but as far as I'm concerned, he's a free man."

"And what about that wicked Donna? Have you arrested her? Is she even still alive?"

"Yeah, she's alive. But she seems to have disappeared. No one seems to recall having seen her in the last few weeks."

"That's strange. Where does she live? Is she in a home?"

"No, she lives with her son. She's stayed in Coopersville all this time. Eventually got married and raised her son there. We had a little trouble tracking her down because we were looking for Donna Kaufman instead of her married name of Halloran."

Edna almost choked on her tea. "Did you say Halloran?"

"Yeah. Why?"

"Oh my Lord. That's the name of the retired police officer that's been nosing around the station this week." Edna was already grabbing her purse and moving toward the front door. "We need to go. He called here a little while ago and said he had information on Warren Farris' murder. He wanted me to meet him up at the Waffle Inn up on Highway 36. When you called, I said I would stay here, but John and Zoey are already headed up to meet him."

"That waffle place closed last winter. It's nothing but a deserted building now."

Mac and Edna raced for the patrol car. Mac threw the car in gear and sped toward the highway. "Tell me everything you know."

"I just did. I knew something fishy was going on. That this guy was trying to lure us out. But I never imagined it would be Weasel's son. He must be the one who's been threatening John. I wonder if he's even a real police officer."

"Royce said he was legit."

"Donna's dad was the chief of police. It would make sense that her son would follow in his footsteps and join the force. He would have access to all of the evidence and be able to use his resources to track John. If he thought John was responsible for his dad's death, he could've been hunting him for years."

"Most likely his whole adult life." Mac weaved his way through the cars on the street then turned to head up the highway. The steep road twisted and curved up the mountain and he had to slow a little to make the sharp curves.

"I'm going to try to call Zoey and warn her." Edna dug in her purse for her phone. She touched the keypad and put the phone on speaker, trying to stay calm as she waited for Zoey to answer.

The ring seemed deafeningly loud in the car, and Edna cried with relief when Zoey answered the phone with her normal "Hi, Gram" greeting.

"Zoey, I'm so glad that you answered. Are you all right? Is John?"

"Of course. We're actually headed back down the mountain already. We just passed that one house, the one with the big purple barn. This whole thing was a wild goose chase. That Waffle Inn was closed down. The place was deserted and empty. We got out and walked around for a few minutes, but the guy never even showed up."

"That guy was Weasel's son. I'm with Mac; we're headed up the pass to check on you. We think he's the one who's been responsible for these threats."

"The guy who was murdered? It's his son?"

"Yes, and we think he may have been searching for John this whole time."

Zoey's voice took on a note of alarm, and Edna could hear her speaking to someone else. "John, what's wrong? Keep trying them. Gram, there's something wrong with the car. We're coming down the mountain, and the brakes aren't working."

Mac accelerated the car, hugging the curves of the mountain road. He yelled into the phone. "I know where you are. We're only minutes away. Try to find someplace to turn off. And have him try the emergency brake."

"There are no turns. There's only the guardrail and the drop-off. John, he says to try the emergency brake."

"Hold on, Zoey. We're almost to you." Edna scanned the highway ahead of them, looking for the blue sedan.

Edna's heart stopped as she heard her granddaughter's voice cry out in alarm. "Watch out! We're gonna hit it!"

Then the line went dead.

"Hold on, Zoey! I'm going to try the emergency brake." John's heart was racing, and his palms were damp as he clutched the steering wheel.

The car had been steadily gaining speed as they wound their way down the steep mountain road. He scanned the highway for any place to turn off or anything that would slow the car down, but this section of road only had steep drop-offs on either side.

Zoey clung to her seatbelt. "Do it! We have to try something."

John eyed the road and saw no other cars near them. He pulled on the emergency brake lever. At first nothing happened, then the brake caught and the car went into a spin. Bile rose in his throat as the car completed a full 180-degree turn.

He stamped on the brakes, his brain telling him it would do no good, but his body reacted in panic. *Stay calm, John! Think.*

The car completed the spin, now facing up the mountain as it crashed into the guard rail. The force of the impact had the driver's side of the car crumpling into the railing as the tires of the other side lifted off the ground.

The screech of metal on metal was deafening, and John heard Zoey scream as the car rolled over the rail.

He reached out, automatically holding his arm in front of her. His efforts were useless against the force of the crash. Mindless of himself, his only thoughts focused on protecting his granddaughter.

Something on the car caught on the railing, and it stopped before it plunged completely over the side. The car hung upside down. It clung to the railing, teetering precariously.

A hush filled the air after the deafening noise of screeching metal. The only sound in the car was their labored breathing as they clung to the safety of their seatbelts. Zoey hung completely upside down and John was scrunched against the door, his leg bent at an unnatural angle.

Zoey turned her face slightly, her eyes wide in terror. The slightest movement on her part could counterbalance the weight of the car and send them plunging over the edge. "John," she gasped. "Are you okay?"

He looked at her, this beautiful young woman. His granddaughter. A purple knot was forming on the side of her forehead. He could see blood oozing from a long scrape on her forearm, the red color bright against her pale skin. That blood was his. She was his family, and his blood was trickling from her body.

In this moment, he didn't care about himself. He had lived a good life but she still had hers ahead of her. He would gladly sacrifice his body to save her. "Hold on, honey. I'm gonna get you out of here."

His head throbbed. The effort of forming words contributing to the pain. A warm flow of blood crossed his forehead and he lifted his hand to swipe at the liquid before it dripped into his eye. The small movement sent waves of pain through his body. It didn't matter. The only thing he cared about was getting Zoey safely out of this car. "We're okay for the moment. Try not to move. I can see you hit your head. Are you hurt anywhere else?"

"I don't think so. But I'm pretty sure that your leg is broken. At least I've never seen it bent that direction before."

John laughed. A small, dry huff of sound. This girl had inherited her grandmother's sense of humor. And her beauty. His heart filled with the love he felt after spending only a few days with her. She was bright, and funny, and shy. And beautiful.

He would not let her die in this car. "Zoey, listen to me. In a minute, we're going to release your seatbelt and you're going to have to aim your fall towards me. We have to get the majority of the weight on this side of the vehicle so it doesn't topple over the other side."

His body was pressed against the driver's-side door, and he moved his hand gently to the door rest. He felt for the buttons and pushed the one on the left. The glass of the door glided down with a soft hum, and John had to shift slightly to keep his head from falling out the window.

A screech of metal sounded as the car shifted slightly. John froze. The warm summer air filled the car, drying the perspiration on his forehead. "Zoey, this has to be fast. When your seatbelt releases, you need to thrust your body this direction. I want you to crawl across me and out this window."

Zoey's eyes filled with fear. "I'm not crawling across you to escape. Let's just wait. Gram knows we're here. I'm sure Mac has already radioed for help. They'll be here any minute, and we'll both get out."

John steadied his breathing and lowered his voice, taking on an air of authority. "Zoey, we don't have time to wait. Any sudden movement could cause this car to go over. My leg is broken. I am *not* crawling out of this window. And I refuse to let you die."

He slowly reached his hand forward to rest on the seatbelt fastener. "I'm going to count to three, then I'm pushing this button. You move fast. I will help as much as I can. Now, do as I say."

Zoey nodded. A small slight bob of her head. Tears streamed from her eyes and her teeth began to chatter.

She was going into shock. He needed to hurry. "One, two, three!" He hit the button, and her body collapsed against his.

The car shifted, and she screamed in unison with the shriek of metal. Her legs churned as she crawled across him. Pain shot through his leg. Oblivious to his own torture, he used all of his strength to catapult her body across him and out the open window.

Zoey's tennis shoe dug into his rib as she scrambled across his body. He propelled her legs forward and she pulled herself through the window. The car creaked and moaned as it tilted sideways with the weight shift.

Straining against the pain in his muscles, John gave a final push to her legs. He heard her cry out as she hit the pavement below.

With her weight lifted, the car shifted again and tipped further over the side of the cliff. Although bent at an awkward angle, John was still strapped in his seatbelt. Blurs of black haze clouded the edges of his vision as he fought to stay conscious. He heard Zoey at the window and felt her arms reaching in to pull at his seatbelt.

A loud shriek of metal was followed by a terror-filled scream from Zoey, then the car slid sideways. There were no extra pounds to counterbalance the weight. With a final tip, the vehicle fell forward, careening down the side of the mountain.

John slammed into the door with the motion of the vehicle. His body banged against the underside of the dashboard and sharp jolts of pain shot up his broken leg. He screamed in anguish.

The front windshield shattered and chunks of glass rained down on his mangled body. He felt a crash and a jerk against his shoulder. Then the black haze closed in, winning the war on his consciousness, and everything went black.

"Hurry, Mac. Please!" Edna frantically scanned the highway in front of them. The patrol car sped around the corner, then the road opened up, allowing them to see further up the mountain. "There they are!"

A blue Ford swerved down the road toward them. It was still too far away to see the occupants, but Edna knew it had to be John's car. She watched in horror as the car went into a spin, then hit the guardrail and rolled over.

Mac accelerated and grabbed for the patrol car's radio. "Dispatch, this is Officer McCarthy. Car accident has occurred five hundred yards west of mile marker 16 on Highway 36. Blue Ford Taurus just went over the guardrail. Two people inside the vehicle. Dispatch fire and ambulance immediately."

A crackle of the radio preceded the dispatcher's response. "Ten-four. Dispatching emergency team now. Rescue on the way."

"And Rosie, you better send a wrecker. This looks bad."

"You got it, Mac. And I'm including some prayers."

Edna screamed as she saw the car wobble on the railing. It was upside down and seemed to be teetering on the edge of rolling over.

Seconds felt like hours as they drew closer to the accident. Her heart pounded against her chest as she fervently prayed for the safety of John and her granddaughter. "Mac, look. Zoey's climbing out of the window."

She watched Zoey scramble out of the window and fall to the blacktop.

Gravel flew as Mac veered on to the shoulder and skidded to a stop. Edna was out of the car and racing across the road before he had turned off the engine. A horn blared as a car swerved around Edna's petite frame. Oblivious to the traffic, she shouted Zoey's name.

Seeing a break in the cars, Mac sprinted across the highway. He saw Zoey get up and reach into the car window. The screech of metal tore through the air as the car tipped. Edna screamed, and Zoey fell backward as the car toppled over the side of the highway.

"Johnny!" Edna's tortured cry rent the air as the car disappeared over the embankment. She reached her granddaughter and fell to her knees, weeping as she wrapped Zoey in her arms.

Mac raced to the side of the road and peered over the edge. "I can't believe it."

The car was wedged between the embankment and a tall pine tree. It was about twenty feet below the road and completely vertical. Branches of the tree stuck through the shattered windshield.

It looked as if the slightest breeze could dislodge the car and send it plummeting down the mountain. "John! Can you hear me?"

"I can see him," Edna said. She was laying on the road, hanging over the edge, trying to see inside the vehicle. "He's not moving, and his eyes are closed. Please Lord, let him just be unconscious."

Edna scanned the side of the embankment, looking for a way to crawl down to get to the car. Not necessarily for *her* to crawl down, but for Mac. Oh, who was she kidding? If there was a way to save John, she would crawl through cut glass. "Can you get down to the car from over there?"

"No, the bank is too steep. I'm afraid if I start down it, I'll just slide down the cliff."

"There's got to be something we can do," Zoey cried. "He just saved my life. We've got to get him out of there."

The sound of sirens echoed up the highway. Help was on the way. Edna leaned forward, just another inch, and called down to the car. "Johnny. Are you all right?"

John's eyes fluttered open, and Edna cried out in relief. "He's alive. His eyes are open."

Mac called down to the car. "John, I need you to hold perfectly still. The vehicle you're in is wedged between a tree and the embankment. Any sudden movement could dislodge the car. Blink if you can hear me and understand what I'm telling you."

Edna watched, holding her breath, then saw John's eyes close twice in rapid succession. "He blinked! He heard you, Mac."

The noise of the sirens grew louder and an ambulance and a red fire engine rounded the curve. Zoey waved her arms, directing them to pull on to the shoulder of the highway near the ruined guardrail.

Two yellow-coated men jumped down from the truck and hurried toward Mac.

The ambulance had pulled in behind the fire truck, two EMTs inside. A young black paramedic got out and headed directly for Zoey. He flashed her a gorgeous grin. "Looks like you're pretty lucky if you survived a car crash and are out walking around." He gingerly lifted her blood-stained arm. "Why don't you let me take a look at this cut?"

The ambulance driver, a heavy set woman in her late forties, got out and approached the edge of the highway. She peered over the side, keeping her body well back, as if she were afraid of heights. "How the hell did he get down there?"

"That doesn't matter," Mac said, his voice all authority. "What matters is how we're going to get him out." He pointed to the car. "I've been studying how the vehicle is wedged in there, and the slightest movement could knock the car loose. I'm not sure how badly he's hurt, but we need to move quickly."

"I'm sure his leg is broken," Zoey said over her shoulder as the EMT led her to the back of the ambulance to treat her arm. "It's bent at a funny angle. And he has a cut on his head that's bleeding pretty badly. He's still wearing his seatbelt."

"Good. That may be what's holding him in place and kept him still when he was unconscious."

Edna was staring at the fire engine and the long white ladder affixed to its roof. Anyone who knew her would recognize the gleam in her eyes and know that she was formulating a plan. "Hey, Mac. I think I may have an idea."

She called the firemen over and gave them a quick once-over. Both men were in excellent shape, their muscles evident through their open coats. One seemed quite young, in his early twenties, while the other appeared to be in his mid-thirties.

Edna pointed to the ladder on top of the truck. "I saw them do this on television once."

"Ma'am, I appreciate your effort," the thirty-something fireman began. "But we don't have time for any hare-brained ideas you may have seen on TV. Half of that stuff is staged anyway. We have a real rescue we need to take care of here."

A flare of temper shot through Edna. *Who was he calling hare-brained?*

Mac held out an arm between Edna and the fireman. "Listen, I know Ms. Allen. Why don't we at least listen to her idea?"

The fireman rolled his eyes. "Go ahead. You have thirty seconds."

Breathe. This was for Johnny. She could knock this arrogant guy in the head with an oxygen tank later. "I think we could extend the ladder out over the ledge, and if you hooked into a harness, one of you could lower yourself down and pull John up through the window without dislodging the car."

The younger firefighter looked from Edna to the ladder to the ledge, a thoughtful expression on his face. "You know, I think that just might work. I've done quite a bit of rock climbing and rappelling. I think I could drop down from the ladder and pull him up." He winked at Edna and the fire of her temper diminished slightly. "Good idea."

The older fireman grudgingly nodded. "It's worth a shot."

Within a few minutes, they had the truck turned around and the ladder extended across the wide expanse of open air. The top of the pine tree that the car was lodged against almost touched the edge of the ladder.

Mac, Zoey, and Edna stood on the edge of the road. Edna clutched her granddaughter's hand as they prayed for John's safe rescue.

A fresh white bandage was now wrapped around Zoey's forearm. The knot on her head was purple and bruised, but the EMT said he didn't think she had a concussion. She'd let him give her some aspirin for the pain then told him she needed to be with her grandma.

The younger fireman, who introduced himself as Guy, had stripped down to his jeans and a white undershirt. He'd buckled himself into an elaborate safety harness and was crawling across the ladder. He stopped when he was above the driver's-side door.

With his blond hair and muscular physique, Edna couldn't help but be reminded of Johnny in his youth. She realized she never knew him in any stage other than young or old. She never saw his middle years when his blonde hair became sprinkled with gray and fine lines appeared around his eyes and mouth.

She had missed so much of his life. She didn't want to miss another day. Why had she hesitated when he asked her to marry him? Why had she been so stupid? She should have grabbed his hand right then and hauled him down to the courthouse.

The courthouse. Thoughts of Irma Jean filled her mind, and she wondered if this Halloran character could have been responsible for the assault on the clerk. Could he have been so desperate to find the man he assumed killed his father that he would resort to hurting an old woman?

And where was he now? He had to have been the one who cut the brakes on the car. He must have used that meeting as an excuse to get them up the pass then cut the brakes while they had been trying to get into the abandoned Waffle Inn.

How did he know Johnny would come with her? A horrifying thought came to mind of him grabbing her and holding her as ransom to force Johnny out in the open.

A smattering of cars had stopped on the side of the highway to watch the rescue attempt. Several people stood outside of their cars, and a few teenagers had their phones out, taking pictures or video. A couple of men had crossed to the firemen and offered to help, and Mac had enlisted them to stand by in case they needed assistance in the rescue efforts.

Edna inched closer to Mac. She nodded at the cars lined up on the highway and lowered her voice. "Do you think Officer Halloran could be one of these bystanders? He has to be the one responsible for cutting the brake lines. Would he be ballsy enough to be standing in this crowd now, watching?"

Mac scanned the crowd then shook his head. "No. I don't see anybody that looks like he could have been a cop. Royce said he was in his sixties, a bit on the heavy side, tall, and still had some red left in his hair. I don't see anyone fitting that description. But I'll keep my eye out. I'm fairly certain that you're right, and he's to blame for the failed brakes."

A loud groan of metal sounded, and all thoughts of Officer Halloran were forgotten. The sedan shifted a few inches as the fireman's foot touched the roof of the car.

Guy had lowered himself down about eight feet but had misjudged the angle and was too far over the top of the car. He waved at his partner and yelled instructions. "I'm not far enough over. If I drop any more, I'll hit the car. You gotta pull the ladder in a few feet so I don't land on the roof."

The older fireman crawled up into the cab of the fire truck, and the long ladder hummed as it retracted a few feet. The motion of the ladder caused Guy to swing in the harness, and his leg hit the side of the car.

Edna screamed as the collision caused the car to shift again. It dropped several feet, stripping the tree of branches. The air filled with the sound of cracking wood.

A hard jolt and the car wedged to a stop. The fireman worked quickly, lowering himself down to the window. He gingerly reached into the driver's-side open window.

Edna could tell he was speaking soft and low to John, but she couldn't hear the words he was saying. She hoped it was something like, "Hey, I'm Guy, I have the strength of ten men, and if you just hold on, I'm gonna get you the hell out of here."

Fireman Guy leaned his whole body into the window. He must have been trying to release the seatbelt. The car groaned and shifted slightly. Edna raised her hands to cover her mouth. *Please Lord, let him be alright.*

She saw John's arms reach through the window and encircle the fireman's neck. One of his arms was smeared red with blood. She couldn't see his head yet, but she heard his anguished cry as he shifted in the car.

Zoey had said his leg was broken. Tears filled Edna's eyes as she imagined the pain he must be in trying to maneuver his body out of the car.

The fireman's legs dangled in the air, the top half of his body concealed inside the car. Seconds ticked by as Zoey clutched at Edna's hand.

Guy pulled John's torso through the window. Streaks of blood covered his white hair and one side of his face. His head lolled forward, and after that last cry of pain, Edna was relieved that he had fallen unconscious.

The muscles of the young fire fighter strained as he pulled the older man's body free from the confines of the car.

A horrible screech of metal sounded, followed by a loud splintering of wood. The car pitched and with a last groan, released its hold on the tree and crashed to the ground. It hit the mountain floor with a dull thud and rolled twice before it stopped. It rested upside down, the roof smashed flat.

Dangling from the ladder, spinning in the harness, Guy wore a satisfied grin as he held John's slack body in his arms. He let out a triumphant whoop. "I got him! Now pull us in."

The older fireman still sat in the cab. He retracted the ladder and slowly swung it around so Guy and John were dangling over the blacktop of the highway. They were still ten feet or so off the ground, and Guy used one hand to release the carabiner. The rope made a zipping sound as it lowered.

Mac and the EMT were there, waiting to catch John's body. They gingerly reached for him then eased him down and onto the stretcher that the ambulance driver had waiting. Mac helped her to load John into the back of the waiting emergency vehicle.

Edna and Zoey clambered into the back of the ambulance. Edna's tan slacks were torn and covered with black from the highway. Zoey's face was smeared with dirt, and her mascara was smudged under her eyes from crying. Her shirt was stained with blood, already turning brown as it dried in the warm sun.

Mac gave Zoey's leg a reassuring squeeze. "I'll finish things up here then meet you at the hospital."

"Thanks, Mac." Edna picked up John's hand and held it in hers. *Please, Lord, don't let him die.* For the first time since he'd been back, he actually looked old, his normal vigor replaced with the fragility of an elderly man. Still unconscious, his face wore a pale sheen compared to the usual healthy tan of his skin.

The younger paramedic took his vitals and started an IV, all while calling into the hospital with the apparent injuries. "We're bringing down the car crash victim. White elderly male, appears to be in his late seventies or early eighties, broken leg, several lacerations, possible head injury."

Edna continued to pray, the words he spoke about John's injuries forming one big blur in her ears. Looking down at the face that she had loved for over six decades, she prayed for the life of the man that she had thought was already dead.

It was noon the next day, and Edna's head lay across John's chest. Soft snores sounded in the room, a chorus of John, Edna, and Havoc, who lay curled at the foot of the hospital bed next to John's good leg.

Zoey sat curled in a chair in the corner of the room, reading the latest book club novel that she had found earlier in Edna's purse.

The doctor had set the broken bone, and John's leg now rested on top of the sheets, encased in a heavy white cast. He had woken up briefly the night before, just to smile and squeeze Edna's hand, then the pain medication did its work, and he drifted back to sleep.

Except for a few minutes to use the facilities, Edna had not left his side. She'd pulled a chair up to John's bedside and sat steadfastly with him for hours, holding his hand or smoothing his hair.

A large flesh-colored bandage covered the six or seven stitches sewn into his forehead. Edna had soaked a wash cloth in warm water and lovingly rinsed the blood from his hair, combing out the stray flecks that had dried there.

Zoey and the Page Turners had rotated through the hospital room, bringing her fresh clothes, meals, and a few toiletries to wash her face and comb her hair. Sunny knew that Edna never felt quite like herself without a tiny dab of lipstick.

They sat with her, prayed with her, held her hand, and offered the quiet love and comfort that only true friendship provides.

Jake and Sunny had snuck Havoc in the night before. Though most hospitals would frown on a dog in the room, this was a small town, and Edna had gone to high school with the emergency room head nurse. Why she hadn't retired yet was a mystery to Edna, but she was glad the nurse was there and had turned a blind eye when Sunny had brought in Havoc. Even in his medication-induced sleep, Edna believed John could sense the comfort of the little dog.

Mac had shown up to the hospital within thirty minutes after their arrival. He'd stayed most of the night, sleeping on the waiting room couch.

Earlier that morning, he had driven Zoey back to the house and waited while she showered and dressed. They'd picked up donuts and coffees on their way back to the hospital.

Mac appeared to be acting strictly in a friendly manner, but Edna knew that his actions were also based on his official capacity. He was a cop first and foremost.

By his steady presence and the way he kept a watchful eye on their surroundings, Edna could tell he was worried about her and Zoey's safety. Cassie told her another police officer sat in the waiting room while Mac was gone with her granddaughter, more evidence of his concern.

A slight movement caused Edna to stir, and she lifted her head to see John blinking awake. She ran her hand down his arm in a gesture of comfort. "Hey, Johnny."

His eyes scanned the room then found hers. A grin lit his face. "Hey, Eddy. Am I dead?"

"Not this time." She grinned back. "You're in the hospital, but you're okay. You were in an accident with Zoey. Do you remember?"

He struggled to sit up, alarm rising in his voice. "Is she okay?"

Edna gently pushed him back against the bed. "She's fine, John. You saved her life."

Zoey climbed from the chair to stand next to the hospital bed. "I'm here, John."

He turned to her, a look of love evident on his face. "I'm so glad you're okay."

She smiled down at him. "Thanks to you."

"What about the car?"

Edna laughed. "The car is not as okay. Once the fireman pulled you out, it crashed down the side of the mountain."

"Have they found Donna's son? He had to have been the one to cut the brakes."

"No," Zoey said, shaking her head. "They haven't been able to track him down. And Donna seems to be missing too. No one back in Coopersville has seen her in days."

"Interesting that she vanishes right about the same time that you appear," Edna said.

The door to the hospital room burst open, and a woman wearing purple leggings and a rainbow-colored, tie-dyed tunic rushed in. Havoc jumped to his feet and let out a yip.

The woman appeared to be in her early sixties, her blonde hair streaked with white and twisted into a long braid running down her back. She looked wildly around the room, her eyes homing in on Zoey. "Zoey Shining Star, there you are. Thank the heavens you're all right!"

She weaved around the end of the hospital bed and pulled Zoey into a tight embrace. Fussing over her cuts and bandaged arm, the woman kissed Zoey's cheek with tenderness. "There, there, my darling girl. That will make it all better."

The room filled with the smell of lavender and a hint of incense. The woman let go of Zoey and skirted the end of the bed to hug Edna, patting Havoc on the head as she walked by. "Hey, Mama. I got here as soon as I could."

Edna reached up to hug her. "Hello, Moon. You didn't have to come, but I'm mighty glad to see you." Moonbeam must have inherited her father's build. She stood a good six inches taller than Edna and engulfed her mother's petite frame in her arms.

Turning to John, Edna was surprised to see tears welling in his blue eyes. "John Collins, I would like you to meet my daughter, Beth Moonbeam Allen."

His daughter gently touched his hand. "I'm pleased to meet you, Mr. Collins. You can call me Moon."

John swallowed and said, his voice choked with emotion, "The pleasure is mine, Moon. And you can call me John."

"I think I will call you my superhero. Thank you for saving my daughter's life."

John nodded, unable to speak, the emotions of the moment playing over his face.

Sunny and Jake walked into the hospital room, breaking the awkward silence. Sunny's face lit with surprise. "Moon! When did you get here?"

Moon embraced the younger woman, hugging her tightly. "I just got in. Thanks for taking my calls this morning."

Edna looked dumbfounded at her neighbor. "You talked to Moon."

"Only because you wouldn't answer me," her daughter said. "I tried calling you and Zoey both several times last night and couldn't get an answer. I finally tried Sunny this morning, and when she told me what had happened, I threw some stuff in the car and hightailed it up here as fast as I could. I don't know if I even packed any clean underwear."

Her exodus sounded remarkably similar to Zoey's. Like mother, like daughter. Actually, with her hippy-dippy lifestyle, Edna was just glad to hear that Moon even wore underwear.

"Sorry about that," Zoey said. "My phone was in my purse, which is still in the car at the bottom of the cliff. Mac said he would try to find it when the wrecker pulls the car up."

Edna nodded. "I had my phone, but it died sometime last night, and I didn't have a charger with me." She smoothed her daughter's braid. "Sorry to worry you, honey. My thoughts were occupied with John and Zoey and making sure they were okay."

Moon pulled her mother into another quick hug. "That's okay, Mama. I'm just glad you're all okay. I was worried sick."

"Well, as it happens, I'm really glad you are here," Edna said. "This way you can be my maid of honor at the wedding."

Moon's jaw dropped, and she arched her untweezed eyebrows. "Wedding? What wedding? Who the heck are you getting married to?"

Edna turned to John and picked up his hand. "This man right here, if he'll still have me. He asked me a couple of days ago, and I haven't had a chance to answer."

She looked into his eyes, hers filled with every bit of love she could muster for the man who had stolen her heart sixty years before. "Yes, John Collins. I would be honored to marry you and finally be your wife."

John grinned. "It's about time. How soon do you want to get hitched?"

Edna checked her watch. "How does six o'clock grab you?"

"I may have a hard time waiting that long."

Edna laughed. "All right. Make it five, then." She looked at Sunny, who had her hands covering her mouth and fat tears leaking down her face. "Sunny, can you rally the troops and pull a wedding together in four hours?"

"You bet I can!" Sunny threw her arms around Edna in delight. "I'm so happy for you. The Page Turners will make it happen and it will be beautiful." Pulling out her phone, she dialed Cassie's number and grabbed Jake's hand.

Edna heard her excitedly tell Cassie the good news as she led Jake from the room and hurried down the hall.

Moon stood in the same place in the room, an astonished look on her face. "Mother, what is going on? Have you finally lost your mind? Or did you just all of a sudden fall madly in love? I just talked to you last week, and you said nothing about getting married."

"I didn't know I was getting married last week." She motioned to the empty chair in the room. "You better have a seat, and I'll get you up to speed."

Moonbeam moved the paperback and sat down in the chair next to Zoey. She folded one leg under her body and slumped in the seat, a skeptical look on her face.

For the third time in as many days, Edna told the love story of her and John Collins. John drifted off to sleep in the middle of the tale, but woke up again when she got to the part about the murder and John faking his own death.

Moon reached out and touched John's hand, her mother's words appearing to soften her skepticism and touch her sentimental heart. "That must have been so hard on you. I'm sorry for that."

"So, you see," Edna said, "I did not all of a sudden fall madly in love. I have always been madly, deeply, and desperately in love with this man. And my heart feels like it could burst with happiness at the thought of finally being his wife."

Moon arched an eye at her mother. "I'm not used to you showing this kind of depth of emotion."

"I am not used to *having* this kind of depth of emotion. I am actually a little astounded myself at how happy I feel." In fact, her heart was pounding, and she felt a little nauseous. She was either really happy or she needed an antacid.

"Well, I'm happy for you, Gram." Zoey patted Havoc, who had jumped off the bed and into her lap during Edna's story. She turned to John. "I think you got the raw end of the deal, but I'm so glad to see the two of you finally together."

Moon nodded, big silver hoops swinging from her ears. "I'm happy for you too. And any man who would risk his life for my daughter certainly makes the short list of qualifications to marry my mother."

Zoey was still looking at John, as if trying to read his expression. "I feel like I owe you so much, John. But you only met me a few days ago. Why would you risk your life for me?"

John looked at each woman, tenderness evident in his eyes. He gazed questioningly at Edna, who nodded, then he turned his eyes back to Zoey. "I would risk everything I have, everything I am for you. I would die before I let one drop of your blood spill, Zoey. Because the blood running through your veins is also mine. I am your grandfather." He swept his gaze to Moon. "And you, Beth Moonbeam Allen, are my daughter."

Moon sat motionless, a stunned look on her face. She turned to her mother, shock giving way to anger. "Mom? What is he talking about?"

"I'm sorry, honey. I was already pregnant with you when I married Frank. He married me to take care of me and his best friend's child." Edna looked down at her hands.

"And you were just going to keep this from me my entire life? Why haven't you ever told me?"

"There was no reason to. I thought Johnny was dead. And in every other way, Frank was your father."

"Mother, you are over eighty years old." Moon's voice rose in pitch. "You could have died and buried this secret with you. And never even told me. What if we would have had a health problem or been in the hospital and needed to know my true father's health history?"

"Health history? You haven't been to a hospital since you had Zoey. You make your own cold medicine out of dandelions or something."

"That is not the point, Mother, and you know it. This is something I had a right to know."

Edna touched her daughter's arm. "All right, Moon. Settle down. You're right, I should have told you. Can you stop a minute and see it from my side? Johnny was gone. Frank stepped in and took his place, and the only way I knew to repay him was to let you believe he was your real father. He couldn't take Johnny's place in my heart, but he could be a father to you. I could give him that and let him be your dad. I wasn't taking away something from you. I was giving something to him. Can you understand?"

Moon nodded, and a single tear ran down her cheek. "Yes, I guess so. I wouldn't ever want to hurt Dad. I mean Frank."

"Frank Allen is a good man and deserved the title of Dad to you," John said to Moon. "You were raised by the man I loved as deeply as if he were my own brother. I could not have picked a better person to take care of the most important women in my life. I never want to take away from the relationship you had with Frank. I'd just like to be part of your life now. If that's okay with you."

Zoey pushed back her chair and dumped Havoc into her mother's lap. She leaned over John and gingerly hugged him. "Of course you can be part of our lives. You already are part of mine. I have plenty of room in my heart for two grandpas."

Edna's heart filled with pride. Her granddaughter never ceased to astonish her. She had the most precious gift for kindness and acceptance of any situation.

A lone tear trickled down Edna's cheek as she looked at her daughter. "You know you did that, Moon. You gave her that loving spirit, that gentle heart that's big enough to fill a museum. You taught her to be accepting and forgiving. I couldn't be prouder of the both of you."

Moon waved a hand of dismissal at her mother. "Thanks, Mom, but I can't take any of the credit. That girl was born that way. I was just blessed to have her as my daughter." She turned to John, a warm smile on her face. "And I guess now I'm blessed to have a chance to have a father again. Another father. Not every girl gets two."

"I'm feeling pretty blessed myself right now," John said, resting a hand on Zoey's shoulder. "If the good Lord took me today, I would die a happy man."

Edna swatted at the side of the bed. "Heavens to Betsy! John Collins, do not even joke about that. You better not die on me today. We've got a wedding to go to."

Moon smiled at her mother. "Well, you're already old, and he's definitely something new, so I guess I'd better go borrow something blue."

22

Edna stood in the dressing room next to the hospital chapel. The Page Turners had pulled off a miracle and put together a wedding in four hours. Sunny had been in charge of securing the chapel and finding a chaplain. Maggie, the super shopper, was in charge of finding a dress. Cassie and Piper had the duties of food and flowers.

Moon and Zoey had agreed to both stand up with her. They sat in the dressing room in a couple of brocade chairs that looked as if they easily could've been there since the seventies.

Surprised at the little flutter of nerves in her belly, Edna checked her watch once more as they waited for the Page Turners to show up with the dress.

The door burst open, and a flurry of activity blew in. Sunny, Cassie, Maggie, and Piper exploded into the small dressing room, their arms laden with shopping bags and boxes. Purple ribbons streamed from a cardboard box holding a gorgeous bouquet of flowers. Gold and purple ribbons wound through a selection of white roses, multicolored pansies, and shocking purple sprays of lavender.

Edna gasped when she saw the bouquet. "Oh, Cassie, this is beautiful."

"I know how you love pansies, and purple is your favorite color," Cassie said, her bright smile beaming with pleasure. "So I just told the flower shop to combine those two themes, and this is what they came up with."

. "Well, they did a wonderful job," Edna said. "I love it."

Following Cassie's instruction, the book club unloaded the bags and boxes.

Piper was handed a shopping bag full of ribbons and silk flowers and instructed to find Maggie's sons Drew and Dylan and work on decorating the chapel. By the grin on her face, Piper seemed happy to be on a task with Drew, as they had been dating all summer.

Zoey and Sunny were handed a makeup bag, a curling iron, and a bottle of nail polish and put on beauty detail.

"What about the dress?" Edna asked as Zoey pulled a brush through her silvery hair. "I'm dying to see my wedding dress."

Maggie picked up a tan dress bag. "Keep in mind, I had a limited time to shop, and there was no way I was going to find a traditional white flowing wedding dress in two hours."

"That's okay. I'm not a very *traditional* kind of gal. Plus, it's my second wedding, and Lord knows my virgin-ship set sail a long time ago, so white's not the best choice anyway. "

"Yes, I know. I took all of that into consideration, plus the fact that you have a rather exuberant personality, when I was shopping for this dress."

"All right, enough of the fancy vocabulary words, just show me my dress."

Maggie unzipped the bag and pulled out the dress. The gasp of each woman in turn echoed through the room.

The dress was tea-length with a full skirt, made fuller by the layers of tulle poofing from beneath it. The bodice was fitted and held up with one-inch gold sequined straps. A wide strip of glittery gold sequins encircled the waist.

The entire dress was layered in different shades of gold, from matte finish to shiny. A half-jacket of transparent tulle was studded with shiny gold beads.

Every part of the dress sparkled and shimmered like gold mermaid scales. It was a cross between Vegas showgirl and Disney princess and bordered on the absurd.

Edna stood speechless. She blinked. Twice. Then a huge grin crossed her face. "It's perfect! I love it!"

Maggie laughed. "I knew you would."

"Let's try it on. I'm not getting any younger." Edna toed off her tennis shoes and shimmied out of her slacks and blouse.

Maggie pulled the dress off the hanger and held it out for Edna to step into. She pulled the straps up over the older woman's shoulders then helped her with the concealed zipper in the side of the dress.

"Uh oh," Moon said. She pointed at the bodice cups that sat flat and empty. "It looks like you're missing a key ingredient in the bra department. Like the boobs to fill it."

Edna looked down at the hollow cups. "I see what you mean." She glanced around the room at the array of shopping bags and tissue. "Surely we can find something around here to fill 'em up with."

Maggie pawed through the disarray and held up some pink paper tissue from one of the gift bags. "How about this?"

Edna shrugged. "That'll work as well as anything." She took it from Maggie, wadded the thin layers of tissue into two balls, and stuffed them down the bodice of her dress. She puffed out her now much larger chest. "How's this?"

Moon rolled her eyes. "That might be a little too much, Mother."

"Nonsense," Edna said, boosting up her crinkling new chest. "It gives me a little extra flair."

"Mom, you're wearing a dress that looks like Liberace and Celine Dion's closets had a baby. How much more flair do you need?"

Edna huffed. "You can *never* have enough flair."

"I'm glad you said that," Maggie said, holding out a shoe box. "Here are the shoes."

Edna lifted the box and peeled back the tissue inside. She pulled out a pair of sparkling gold strappy sandals. "Oh, Mags, these are wonderful."

Taking the tissue from the shoe box, she crumpled it and added it into her considerable bosom, then stuck her tongue out at her daughter. She plopped onto a chair. "Somebody help me get these on."

Her daughter shook her head, muttering, "Oh, Mother," for the gazillionth time in her life, then knelt before Edna and helped her slide the strappy sandals onto her feet.

Moon pulled Edna to her feet just as a knock sounded on the door. Edna tottered over and opened the door.

John sat in a wheelchair, Havoc riding shotgun on his lap and his casted leg jutting straight out. Mac stood behind him, his hands on the grips of the chair, obviously in charge of "driving."

John stared at Edna, his eyes wide. He wore his charcoal gray suit and a stunned expression. Then his face broke into an ear-splitting grin, and his happiness seemed to radiate off him in waves. "Oh, Eddy, you look magnificent. My dear, I can't wait to make you my wife."

Edna curtsied then twirled in a circle, like a little girl showing off her party dress. "Don't you love it?"

He nodded, the grin permanently affixed to his face. "I do love it. And I love you. I have to ask, though: did the bosom come with the dress or did you have to pay extra for that?"

Edna laughed and boosted up her bodice, giving it a tiny shimmy. "They were free. What do you think? Too much?"

"Nah. Just right." The love he had for Edna shone from his eyes and in the adoring look on his face.

Zoey stood to Edna's side, her hands on her hips. "John, I mean Grandpa, you're not supposed to see the bride before the ceremony."

Edna waved a hand at her granddaughter. "Oh, poo. I've been with him all day."

"I only stopped in because I have a small dilemma," John said. "I was talking to Mac and realized I don't have a ring."

"I can help with that." Moon stepped forward and held up her hands. A variety of rings encircled her fingers. She had silver bands of several widths, some plain silver and some adorned with stones and symbols. She wiggled her fingers. "Take your pick."

Edna peered at the choices on her daughter's fingers and pointed to the one on her pinkie. It was a shiny silver ring with tiny stars and crescent moons encircling the band. "It's perfect. That is the exact right ring for Johnny and me. It signifies we've come full circle, and it's surrounded by our family—our Moonbeam and our Shining Star."

Moon nodded at her mother, tears filling her eyes. A sweet smile crossed her face as she pulled the ring from her pinkie and placed it in her mother's hand. "You're right. It is perfect. I love you, Mom."

She wrapped her arms around her mother's small shoulders and hugged her tight, the tissue paper making a crackling sound between them.

"I want in on that hug." Zoey opened her arms and embraced her mother and grandmother. She laughed then stepped back and wiped the stray tears from her cheeks. "Now I'm going to have to redo my mascara."

Mac handed her a folded white handkerchief. "Here, use this."

Zoey smiled at him. "I'm surprised you're still here. Are you worried about John's safety?"

Mac shook his head. "I'm a little surprised I'm still here too. We haven't found Donna Halloran, or her son, so I *am* concerned about his safety. But I guess I'm also the best man. Or the best man he could find on short notice."

"You helped save my life," John said. "That makes you the best man I know in my book."

"As best man, I need to get you out of here so your bride can finish getting ready." Mac pulled the wheelchair back, maneuvering a three-point turn in the hallway without knocking John's leg into the wall. He held out his hand to Edna. "Do you want me to hold the ring?"

Cassie gasped. "We don't have a flower girl or a ring bearer." She looked around the crowded dressing room as if one might have suddenly appeared. "We don't have any little kids to fill those roles."

Zoey grinned and reached for Havoc. She held the little dog up. "Havoc can be the ring bearer. I'll hook the ring to his collar, and he can prance it up the aisle to you. It will be adorable."

Moon shook her head. "This could only be happening at my mother's wedding. The bride's wearing a dress befitting either the red carpet or a piano-singing lounge act, and she'll be followed by a canine ring bearer. I hope someone hired a juggler and an Elvis impersonator for the reception."

Edna's eyes lit up, and she looked at Sunny. "Did you get Elvis for the reception?"

Sunny burst into laughter. She and Cassie had planned an impromptu barbecue in Sunny's backyard for the reception. "No, but I've still got a few hours. I'll see what I can do."

"I can't wait." John waved at Edna. "See you at the altar."

She blew him a kiss. "I'll be there, with bells on. Actually, with shiny gold sandals on." She stepped to the side so Zoey could shut the door, and the heel of one of the gold shoes sank into the heater vent on the floor of the dressing room.

She raised her foot, and the vent came out of the floor still hooked to her shoe. "Houston, we've got a problem."

"Oh no." Sunny bent down and tried to wiggle Edna's foot. She unhooked the strap and helped Edna step out of the shoe. Wiggling the shoe, she tried to get the little spike heel free of the vent.

"Here, let me try." Maggie took the vent from Sunny and twisted the shoe. A small snap sounded, and the heel broke off in Maggie's hand. "Oops."

Edna shrugged. "That's okay. They were hurting my feet already anyway. I've got bad arches, and that strap was cutting into my bunion." She reached for her tennis shoes. "Besides, my sneakers will be more comfortable."

"Oh, Edna, you can't wear tennis shoes with your wedding dress," Cassie said.

"I'm in my eighties," Edna said. "I can do pretty much whatever I want."

Moon shook her head at Cassie. "Don't worry about it. With that dress, and her tissue-filled bosom, no one's even going to notice her shoes."

"Good point."

Edna plopped down in one of the chairs and slipped her tennis shoes on. "Let's get this show on the road. I've got a wedding to get to."

Thirty minutes later, Edna stood at the door of the chapel, a bouquet of flowers in her hand and a belly full of butterflies. Who would have thought she would be tying the knot as she was getting ready to kick the bucket?

It didn't matter if she had ten more years with Johnny, or ten more hours. She wanted to spend every minute she had with him. Talking with him. Laughing with him. And kissing him.

Especially kissing him. She might be old, but she wasn't dead yet.

Her daughter and granddaughter stood before her, both wearing gorgeous deep purple dresses that Maggie had found for them that afternoon.

Sunny had pulled Zoey's hair into a gorgeous up-do, tendrils of her blonde hair loose and curling along her neck. She'd left one side of her bangs lower to cover the purple knot visible on Zoey's forehead and joked that at least it matched the color of the dress.

Cassie had rebraided Moon's hair into a complicated twist and tucked tiny sprigs of purple baby's breath into the braid. Maggie had purchased some cute black sandals for them, and they both looked gorgeous.

They each held a simple bouquet of white and purple roses, the stems tied together with crisscrossing gold ribbon. Zoey had used some extra gold and purple ribbon to tie a bow to Havoc's collar, the silver ring hanging from the bottom of the bow. She held the little dog, its body visibly shaking in her arms. Who knew if the dog was just excited or if it had to pee?

Edna poked her head around the door to see who was in attendance for her big day.

The list of invited guests was small. The Page Turners, of course. And their families.

Maggie had invited her new boyfriend Jeremy and her sons Drew and Dylan. The boys had come with Maggie to help with the preparations, leaving Jeremy in charge of bringing Mabel, his grandmother.

Mabel, who was one of Edna's closest friends, had invited a man friend, and she needed Jeremy to pick him up from the nursing home on their way over. Their group now took up the first two rows of the tiny chapel.

Mabel's spunk was similar to Edna's, and she wore a large pink hat with a brightly colored floral print dress. Her date, a man named Lon, looked rather plain sitting next to her, wearing a brown suit with the remaining strands of his hair combed across the top of his head.

Jeremy looked dashing and handsome, his expensive dark suit and starched white shirt in contrast to Lon's slightly wrinkled and disheveled outfit. Both of Maggie's sons wore khakis and button-down dress shirts.

Like the older men, their looks also conflicted. Drew looked comfortable and confident, leaning back against the pew. His younger brother Dylan, who to Maggie's dismay must have grown an inch overnight, appeared quite uncomfortable as he pulled at his too-tight collar and shifted in the snug pants that now weren't quite long enough.

Jake wore a dress shirt and khakis as well, but as noticed by all the women he walked by in the hospital, his clothes fit perfectly. The green of his shirt brought out the emerald color of his eyes, and the cut of the fabric outlined his muscular physique. He gave off an air of confidence and contentment, his arm casually resting along the top of the bench.

He had arrived earlier with Sunny, who now sat next to him, nestled against his outstretched arm. The light pink summer dress she chose looked great with her blonde hair, and her face shone with a happy smile and excitement for her friend.

Edna's neighbor and Jake's grandfather Walter had arrived a few minutes earlier with his new bride Helen. They slid into the pew behind Jake and Sunny, and the four of them were the only guests sitting on the groom's side of the church.

Piper had ridden over with Cassie, and the two of them sat behind Maggie's group on the bride's side.

Cassie, surprisingly, was on her own, claiming some poor excuse for Matt having to work and the kids being too busy. Edna couldn't blame a couple of teenagers for not wanting to attend an old lady's wedding, but Matt's absence struck an odd chord with her. She'd have to ask Cassie about that later.

It wasn't a lot of guests, but it was everyone Edna loved. She was so happy to be sharing her day with her friends and her beautiful daughter and granddaughter.

Her heart felt so full of joy, she thought it might burst. She probably should have taken an aspirin, just in case she had a heart attack.

She looked to the front of the chapel, and John stood there. Supported by two crutches, but standing there none-the-less. He looked so handsome in his suit. Edna knew the bright smile on his face was just for her.

Equally handsome was the man standing next to him. It was a good thing Mac was a cop, because he definitely did his dark gray suit justice. By the way her granddaughter was looking at him, Edna knew she wasn't the only one who had noticed.

Surprisingly, Mac stepped away from John and up onto the altar. A keyboard stood on a stand, and Mac walked behind it and began to play. Hmm. Who knew the rough-acting cop was also a musician?

The soft strains of "Love Me Tender" filled the small chapel, and Edna forgot about Mac as she was transported back in time to a small bedroom in a tiny house.

In her mind's eye, she could see a younger Johnny Collins as clear as day. Better yet, she could see the real thing right in front of her. She just had to walk down the aisle to meet him, and she would be in his arms.

She gave her granddaughter a nudge. "Let's get this party started."

Zoey grinned at her grandmother then stepped into the doorway of the chapel. She set Havoc on the ground at her feet.

John gave a low whistle, and the dog happily pranced down the aisle, soaking up the adoration of the wedding guests. Edna hoped she got as many oohs and aahs as the dog did. With the dress she was wearing, she might get more "oh my stars" than aahs of admiration.

Havoc reached John, shook his bottom for approval, then sat directly at the groom's feet.

Zoey was next, followed by her mother. They moved gracefully down the aisle, each with their own style. Zoey's posture erect and her steps small and precise, in contrast to Moon's fluid flow of motion, almost as if she glided on air.

Moonbeam approached John, then tipped up and kissed him on the cheek before taking her place at the front of the chapel. The music changed as Mac played the first notes of the "Bridal Chorus." The guests stood and turned to the rear of the chapel.

Edna stepped into the doorway, the smile on her face felt as bright and sparkly as the sequins on her dress.

Cassie had pinned a small veil in her hair, anchored by an imitation gold and diamond tiara. Holding the lovely bridal bouquet in front of her tissue-enhanced bosom, Edna stood still a moment as she soaked up the love (and astonishment) of her beloved family and friends.

She took a few modest steps forward in traditional style. Then, in pure Edna-style, she flung back her arms and did the cha-cha down the rest, complete with a pirouette when she hit the halfway point of the short aisle.

She made it to John amidst applause and laughter, and she couldn't think of a time she had ever been happier.

However, the chaplain was a bit more on the somber side. His frown of disapproval indicated he was either not a fan of the cha-cha or of tissue-enhanced bosoms. Or both. He cleared his throat and began the ceremony. "Dearly beloved, we are gathered here today…"

The words washed over her as she soaked in the moment. Edna was lost in Johnny's crystal blue eyes. She had looked into replicas of those eyes in her daughter's and granddaughter's faces, but to see them here now, to see her own smile reflected back in them, was pure joy.

The chaplain declared the words of the ceremony, speaking of love and commitment. Every word seeping into Edna's heart as the love she had for Johnny poured off of her in waves.

They pledged their love to each other through the traditional vows. John's voice choked on emotion as he pledged his love, for richer and for poorer, in sickness and in health, for as long as they both shall live. This was his first wedding and it had taken him sixty years to finally be able to tell the woman he loved that he would honor and cherish her for the rest of their days.

"Do you have the ring?" the chaplain asked after they had finished their vows.

John leaned down to pick up the little dog and retrieve the ring. Havoc must have thought this was a new game. He sank to the floor and yipped twice before racing around Edna's legs.

"Havoc, come." John used his most stern voice to no avail. The little dog raced between his legs then up onto the altar, knocking into one of his crutches as he ran by. Mac grabbed John before he lost his balance and toppled over.

Edna's concern wavered between John falling over and Havoc deciding to *water* the altar flowers.

Zoey squatted down, using her sweetest voice to coo to the dog. "Here, boy. That's a good dog. Come here."

The dog ignored her request, obviously enjoying this game of chase. True to his name, he leapt off the altar and raced under the pews. The cries of the guests pinpointed the dog's path as he escaped every set of hands that reached for him.

Having helped John regain his balance, Mac joined in the chase. Blocking one edge of the aisle, he engaged the help of Maggie's sons and directed Drew and Dylan to block the other side.

Dylan jumped to his feet, his enthusiasm an indication that he was happy to have some excitement added to an otherwise somber event. His older brother shooed the dog his way, and he bent down to grab it as it ran by.

A loud rip sounded as the seam of the too-snug pants gave way, and Dylan's khakis split open. He reached back to cover his now visible striped boxers as his brother fell to the floor, collapsing in laughter.

"Dude." All Drew could do was point as he lay on the chapel floor in a fit of giggles. The dog ran over the top of him, causing another round of laughter.

By this time, half of the guests were in the aisle, some trying to help, while others simply contributed to the chaos. Jeremy took off his coat and passed it to Dylan to cover his backside while Maggie fell into hysterical giggles with Drew.

Jake took the other end of the aisle, and he and Mac tried to corral the dog between them. As soon as one man would get close, he would reach down to grab the dog, and it would squirt out from between his hands and run off again, zig-zagging between the many sets of outstretched hands.

Edna looked at John and laughed. "No one will ever be able to say our wedding was boring."

"Very true." John leaned forward and patted his uncasted leg. "Havoc—here, boy."

The dog totally ignored him, having a grand time playing this new game of chase. His tags jingled on his collar as he sprinted around the chapel.

All activity stopped as an ear-splitting whistle ripped through the room. Mabel's new man-friend, Lon, stepped into the aisle. He pulled what appeared to be a half-eaten Polish sausage from the breast pocket of his brown suit. Ripping a piece from the end, he leaned down and waved it at the dog.

Havoc raced to him, gobbling up the piece of meat as Lon lifted him and carried him to the front of the chapel. He deposited the squirming dog into Edna's arms, where Moon quickly untied the bow, releasing the ring into her hand.

John patted Lon on the shoulder. "Quick thinking there, fella. You saved the day."

Lon winked. "No problem. I have a way with animals."

"Havoc is a fan of sausage. What do you have there? Polish?"

"Bratwurst."

Edna snorted. "I appreciate that you captured the dog, but why in the world do you have a bratwurst in your pocket? Especially at my wedding."

Lon shrugged. "Mabel called around noon, and said she needed a date fast. I wasn't about to pass up on a date with that gal, but I didn't want to miss lunch either." He waved the remainder of the sausage in the air. "I wasn't sure how soon you'd be serving cake, so I covered my bases."

Edna nodded. Made sense to her. She'd brought stranger things than bratwurst to a wedding before.

The chaplain cleared his throat. The sausage was probably making him hungry. "If we can continue?"

Lon shuffled back to his seat. Mabel's face beamed with a smile. She patted his leg, obviously proud that her date had saved the day.

Moon passed the ring to John, and Edna passed the dog to Zoey. The chaplain rolled his eyes.

John slid the silver band onto Edna's finger and repeated the minister's words. "With this ring, I thee wed." He looked up at the chaplain. "Can I kiss her now?"

The chaplain raised his hands to the congregation. "I now pronounce you man and wife." He nodded at John. "Yes, you may kiss her now."

A grin broke out on John's face, and he looked into the eyes of his new bride. "I love you, Eddy. You have made me the happiest man on earth." Then he leaned down and kissed her.

23

John took one hand from his crutches and turned the knob of Edna's front door. He pushed the door open then looked down at his new bride. "As much as I want to carry you over the threshold, my dear, you may have to take a rain-check." He tilted his shoulder down. "Unless you want to climb up here, then maybe I can give you a piggyback in."

Edna smiled up at him. "Tempting. But in light of your crutches and your near-death experience, I'll give you a pass." She winked. "You can find a way to make it up to me later."

John grinned. "You got a deal."

Edna held the bridal bouquet in one hand and her purse in the other as she stepped into the house and helped John to maneuver the crutches and his bulky cast through the door.

The others had gone on to Sunny's to set up for the reception, but Edna wanted John to have a few minutes to rest before the festivities began.

"I'm awfully glad we got a chance to see Irma Jean before we left the hospital," Edna said.

They had been checking out of the hospital when Mac had told them that the older woman had woken up. He had already questioned her, and from the description, it was clear that Donna's son had been the one that had assaulted her.

Entering her room, Edna was shocked to see the intense black and purple bruising covering Irma Jean's face where she'd been beaten. Tears blurred her eyes as she rushed to the bedside of her friend. "Oh, Irma Jean, I am so sorry this happened to you."

"It's not your fault." Irma Jean smiled weakly at Edna. "I'm sorry that I told him that John was here and about your daughter."

Edna lightly touched her shoulder. "Don't you give that a second thought. If you hadn't told him, he would have just found out another way."

"Most likely through hurting someone else." John stepped up to the bed, his crutches making it hard to maneuver in the small room.

Irma Jean appraised John through narrowed eyes, the bruising not hiding the sharp intellect visible there. "Hello, Mr. Adams. From what Officer McCarthy tells me, you had your own run-in with the man."

"I did, but I'm fine. I'm awfully sorry I got you involved in this." He leaned forward and gingerly touched her hand. "I feel like it's my fault that you got hurt."

"Don't be ridiculous. Of course it's not your fault. It's the son-of-a-bitch who beat me up's fault. This was his doing, not yours. But I would sure feel better if I knew the police had him in custody."

"Me too," Edna said. "Mac's working on it, though. They've got an APB out on him." She leaned forward as if sharing a secret. "That's an all-points bulletin."

Irma Jean rolled her eyes. "Yes, I know what it is. You're not the only one with a television set, you know."

John laughed. "He's also got an officer stationed outside your door. So you're safe here. He won't get near you again."

Irma Jean assessed Edna's dress, her eyes narrowing at the gold and diamond tiara. "What's with the fancy get-up? The sequins of your dress just about blinded me when you walked in the door."

With a quick wink at John, Edna lifted her enhanced bosom in pride. "We just got married. I am now officially Mrs. John Collins."

Irma Jean smiled. "I'm happy for you." She looked up at John, still standing by the side of her bed. "Both of you."

Now, stepping into her living room, Edna threw her purse on the couch in disgust. "It just makes me so mad that the creep who did this got away. If I find him before Mac does, he'll know what fifty thousand volts of my stun gun feels like pressed up against his nut-sack."

John stood next to the sofa. He laid one of his crutches against the armrest and massaged the sore spot under his arm where the arch of the crutches rubbed against it. "I'd be happy to hold him down for you. I just wish we knew where the bastard was."

"I prefer the term 'fatherless.' It kind of rolls off the tongue and has a less demeaning quality to it." Officer Warren Halloran stepped out of Edna's kitchen and into the living room.

Edna gasped. Warren Jr. looked just as she imagined Weasel would have if he'd had a chance to grow into a man. Even though he had to be in his sixties, this man's hair still held a hint of red, and his face carried a few freckles buried amongst the wrinkles.

He was of average height and build, carrying a few too many pounds around his middle. His face wore the tired and wrinkled look of someone who had spent his life smoking cigarettes, and the telltale burst capillaries of a lifelong drinker.

"Well, in this case, bastard is more fitting." Edna took a step forward, reaching for her purse.

"I wouldn't do that if I were you." Warren Jr. held a pistol aimed at John's head. "Not if you want your groom to make it to his wedding night."

"Settle down now," John said. "Nobody needs to get hurt. What do you want from us?"

A soft whirring sound came from the kitchen, followed by a rhythmic slide then a clunk. The silver wheels of a walker came into sight, followed by a very old woman. She had an oxygen bag strapped over her shoulder and a mean glint in her eye. Not just old-person-crotchety mean, but royally pissed-off mean. "I'll tell you what I want, Johnny Collins. I want my life back. The life you stole from me the night you took Warren and my life savings."

"Donna? Is that you?" John's face held a look of astonishment.

Edna, never one to hold back a thought, blurted out, "Holy crap, woman, you have not aged well. You should have done more water aerobics or something."

Donna held up one hand, her fingers gnarled and bent with arthritis, and extended her crooked middle finger. "Screw you, Edna."

Edna shook her head, unfazed by the insult. "That is one sorry-looking bird. Your finger's so crooked, it's like you're flipping off the neighbors."

Donna waved her gnarled hand at her son. "Just shoot her now, Junior. Just to shut her up."

John waved his hands. "She's teasing you, Donna. No need to get upset. She didn't mean any of that."

"I meant every word of it. That woman looks like she has one foot and most of her body already in the grave," Edna muttered under her breath.

Donna narrowed her eyes at Edna. "I can see your lips moving. If I had better hearing aids, I'm sure I could have heard your nasty comment. But I don't. Because I'm broke. Because your boyfriend took everything away from me. My man and all of my money."

"That wasn't even your money. You stole it from the bank." Edna searched the room for any way to get them out of this situation.

"Yeah, I stole it, so it was mine! Until you took it from me. And left me with nothing." Donna pointed a gnarled finger at John.

"Donna, I'm truly sorry about Weasel, um, I mean Warren." John's voice was calm and steady. "He was my friend, and I loved him. But that money belonged to the bank. To the people of Coopersville. Besides, I don't have it anymore. I replaced what you and I had taken and then gave it all back."

Donna huffed in annoyance and then broke into a coughing fit. The mucus in her lungs giving off a wet, phlegmy sound as she dragged in air for a breath. She adjusted a knob on her oxygen tank, and with a whirr from the tank and a last wheeze, she got herself under control.

Her voice was raspy as she sneered at John. "I was working at the bank the day you left the money in the night drop. That's how I knew you were back and still alive. I tried to find you then, but you must have already slipped out of town again."

"They still let you work at the bank? Even after you robbed it?" Edna asked, incredulously.

"I didn't rob it. As far as the town knew, Johnny was the one who robbed the bank. And then he robbed me. He took everything from me and left me penniless and pregnant."

"But I heard you ended up getting married," Edna said, waving a hand at Warren. "And he must have adopted Junior here if he gave him the name Halloran."

"Oh, I did get married. To a real prince of a man. Butch Halloran was a drunk and a louse." She pointed at Warren, who was still holding the gun on John. "I told my son how you murdered his father and took all of our money. How we never would have ended up with that man if it weren't for you."

Johnny shook his head, his movements slow and even. "Donna, that wasn't my fault. That was just a bad situation. And I'm sorry for my part in it."

"Your part in it?" She hacked again, coughing into her sleeve. "It was *your* fault. Everything was your fault. Warren and I were going to run away. For once in our lives, we had nice things. We were getting out of that town. Away from Coopersville and away from my father. Instead I ended up married to someone just like him. I left one nightmare and entered another. Because of you."

Nightmare?

Edna had known that Donna's dad was strict and overprotective, but that didn't qualify as nightmare material. She could remember that night in the Elks Lodge bathroom when Donna had told her she was pregnant. There'd been real fear in her eyes when she spoke about her dad finding out. Maybe there was more to the story of Donna wanting to get away from her father.

And maybe she would have more sympathy for the woman if her son wasn't holding a gun on them. "Donna, it wasn't Johnny's fault," Edna said. "He didn't shoot Weasel."

"His. Name. Was. Warren." Donna turned her head to stare at Edna, a crazed look in her eyes. "And you weren't even there. You don't know what happened that night. I was. I saw it with my own eyes. I saw Johnny take out a gun and shoot him."

"Sorry. Warren. Regardless of which name you call him, Johnny didn't shoot him. He was his friend. He cared about him. We all did."

Donna's voice dripped pure hatred. "You shut your mouth. Don't you even speak his name. None of this would have even happened if you wouldn't have flaunted yourself at *my* boyfriend. It wasn't enough for you to have Johnny and Frank bending to your every whim. You had to try and take my Warren too. It was probably your idea for Johnny to kill him. So you could take the money for yourselves."

Did she really believe what she was saying? Had the years and age muddled her mind so much that she really believed Johnny had been the one to shoot Warren? Had insanity taken the place of reason, and she'd now accepted this as her reality?

Edna looked to Warren Jr., trying to appeal to his sense of reason. "Look, I'm sorry about your father. He was a good man. But what happened to him was an accident. John did *not* shoot him. And he only ended up with the money by accident. Turning the money back in was the right thing to do. Do you understand that?"

An evil sneer crossed Warren Jr.'s face. "What I understand is my life would have been different if it weren't for the two of you. My mom has spent every day telling me about my dad and how they had money. Plenty of it. And about the life we would have had if it weren't for John Collins. We would've had cars and nice clothes. And Butch freaking Halloran would never have laid a hand on me or my mom. You robbed us of everything."

Okay. So the son was as bat-shit crazy as the mother. Great. They needed a Plan B. "Look, you're a policeman. You took an oath to obey the law. I'm pretty sure there's a rule in the police handbook about being innocent until proven guilty. I think they frown on cops shooting people, innocent or guilty."

"Well, isn't it convenient that I'm no longer a policeman?" His face was ugly and mean as he jeered at her, nothing like the kind face of his father. "I've spent my life being a cop, and I used every resource I had to track down this bastard. To find the man that killed my father so I could finally avenge his death."

"Avenge his death? Who do you think you are? A middle-aged overweight superhero? I'd like to see you get that paunchy gut into a leotard."

Warren swung the gun toward Edna, pointing it at her face. His hand trembled slightly. She could see spittle at the corner of his lips, his mouth drawn into a tight line. A low growl emitted from his throat.

This was her one chance. If she could get him angry enough, she might be able to get him off balance. All she needed was a few seconds to distract him and give herself a chance to get the gun away.

She sank her shoulders, drooping her posture, and injected a frightened tone in her voice. "I'm sorry. Please don't hurt me. I don't have much time anyway. My heart is already weak." She clutched her chest, took a shuddering breath, and fell to the floor.

Warren stepped into the room, dropping his arms as he leaned over her.

As she fell, Edna curled her legs under her. Sensing the man's presence above her, she fluttered her eyes, just enough to gauge his position. She moaned as if in pain, drawing him just a little bit closer.

One small step. There. Salsa dancing and Zumba lessons had kept her elderly body strong and healthy. She shot out her legs, connecting with the end table and slamming it into Warren's legs. The table hit him right under the kneecaps. He bent forward, dropping the gun and clutching at his legs.

Edna scrambled to her feet, grabbing for any weapon she could find. Picking up a scented candle from the coffee table, she flung it at his head. The chunky jar hit him in the face then fell to the carpet with a thud.

Warren reached for his bruised cheek, grunting in pain. Edna flung a vase full of silk flowers at him, the fragile glass breaking against his forehead and scattering flower petals and colored glass marbles all over the floor.

There was nothing left on the coffee table. Cursing herself for cleaning up that day, she frantically searched the room for any other weapon.

Warren was shaking his head, a tiny trail of blood starting down his forehead. He charged at her with the ferocity of an angry bull, a guttural cry in his throat.

John knocked his crutch to the floor, and Edna grabbed it, forcing it into the chest of the charging man. She held the crutch in front of her, the pointy end pushed against his chest as his arms flailed, trying in vain to grab her.

It would have looked comical, if not for the spit flying from his lips as he swore filthy accusations at her. "You stupid little bitch. I'm going to kill you. I'm going to rip your stupid little gray-haired head off."

Edna's eyes were wide, looking for a way out of this mess. Taking in everything, she saw Donna laboriously pushing her silver walker toward where the gun lay on the floor. Out of the corner of her eye, she saw John hobbling on one leg to her rescue, his breathing labored as he dragged the heavy white cast. "Forget about me. John, get the gun!"

Warren's face changed to one of determination. He turned around, letting the crutch fall to the floor, and headed for the gun.

In seconds, Edna was on her knees, scrambling across the floor to where the weapon lay on the carpet.

Anyone looking in the window would have seen a comical race of one semi-old guy competing against three really old people, two crippled and encumbered by their handicaps and one little old lady crawling across the floor.

The feeling inside the room was anything but comical as Edna and John raced against the insanity of a mother-and-son team intent on killing them.

Warren was too fast. He reached the gun, grabbed it and turned it back on Edna.

She froze, lifting her hands in the air in silent surrender. "Okay. No need to do anything hasty." She changed her tone to her best "mom voice," the one she used to negotiate with her child, a mixture of gentle persuasion and unconscious coercion.

"You don't really want to kill us. You don't want the death of two people on your conscience. You're a policeman."

"Ha." His throaty laugh had a demeaning quality to it. But his next words hung in the air, filling Edna with terror. "You think I care about killing you? Do you think you're the first ones I've killed?"

"Warren. You quit running your mouth," Donna said.

"It doesn't matter, Ma. They're gonna be dead in a few minutes anyway." He stared at John. "You killed my father and that made me the man of the house. I've always had to protect my mom. From the time I was old enough to fight, I never let anyone hurt her. It didn't matter if it was her own father or the bastard Butch Halloran she married. It was my job to keep those filthy son-of-a-bitches from touching us."

Us? Edna's speculation that something else was going on with Donna's dad seemed dead on. Was she afraid of him because he had been stern, or had his overprotection been carried out in other ways? And what kind of evil had Warren Jr. resorted to in order to "protect" them?

Donna had moved back home after Johnny's funeral. Edna had always assumed she wanted to be close to her family to have the baby, but maybe there was more to it. And maybe she had seen Butch as a way to escape her father, but he turned out to be just like him. No matter what had happened, these were some seriously screwed-up people. Twisted with a capital T.

Warren sneered at Edna. "The only good thing about being a policeman means I know how to not get caught. And it let me have all the resources I needed to track down John Collins, the man that killed my father. Plus, it gave me access to some good explosives."

Edna gasped. "You're the one that blew up Zoey's car?"

"Yeah, but I thought it was his." Warren waved a hand at Johnny. "At first, it was fun just to scare you. To send a rock sailing through your window and watch you scramble like little ants. Then I got bored and decided it would be more fun to watch your bodies burst into flames. I set the bomb, but those explosives must have been old, and it went off too early."

"So, you had to lure us out of the house in order to cut the brake lines." If Edna could keep him talking, she might be able to come up with another plan to get them out of this mess. Alive.

Warren Jr. laughed. "That was simple. One phone call and you scurried up the pass. I followed your car and watched you idiots get out and walk around that waffle joint. It was easy to cut the brake lines of that old Ford while you were looking in the windows. Then I just waited for your car to crash down the mountain and off the cliff's edge."

The gun shook in Warren's hand as a rage crossed his face. "Except you didn't die. You keep surviving. So now I need to put a couple of bullets in your heads and watch the life drain out of your eyes so I know that you are really dead. Then I will finally have revenge for my father's death."

Watch the life drain out of their eyes? Who was this guy? Norman Bates' cousin? Did he dress up in his mother's clothes to carry out his nefarious acts? Edna needed a new tack. Stern and motherly was obviously not the way to go.

"Killing Johnny will not avenge your father's death," she said. "Because he wasn't the one who shot him. If you wanted to seek revenge on your father's killer, you only had to look across the breakfast table. Your mother is the one that shot Weasel."

A blank look crossed Junior's face. "What the hell are you talking about?"

Edna pointed at Donna. "She's been blaming Johnny all these years, but she's the one that pulled the trigger. I think it was an accident, but *she's* the one who killed him. John's had the gun this whole time, and we turned it over to the police last week. They ran a ballistics test and it was a match to your father's murder, and her fingerprints were the only ones on it."

A low, keening sound had all of them turning toward Donna, who crumpled against her walker, her head bent forward. She clutched her chest as she wept, deep, wailing sounds of anguish. "Warren, I loved you. I didn't mean to hurt you. We were going to run away together. The gun just went off. It was an accident."

She wept against her chest, then drew in a deep, phlegmy breath. Her desperate crying stopped, as if a switch had been turned off.

Raising her head, she appeared to be a different woman, her tear-filled eyes now full of rage and hatred as she turned toward Johnny. She raised a crooked finger and pointed at his chest. "You're trying to trick me. To trap an old woman. I loved Warren. I would never hurt him. *You* shot Warren. You stole our money and our car. It's your fault, John Collins. You did this."

Warren Jr. stared at his mother, confusion clouding his face.

The front door suddenly opened, and Zoey walked in, Havoc in her hands. "Sunny needed some more napkins." She froze, her eyes scanning between her grandmother and the man holding a gun on her.

Time stood still for one agonizingly long second, then all hell broke loose. Edna screamed and dove for the gun. Warren knocked her aside, striking the butt of the gun against her head and knocking her to her knees.

Stars spun in the air as she clutched the side of the sofa. Struggling to stay conscious, she saw John fall forward, desperately attempting to prevent the madman from reaching their granddaughter.

Warren lunged at Zoey, grabbing a handful of her hair and yanking her towards him.

Zoey dropped Havoc, who raced around the room, barking and yipping at Warren.

"Shut that damn dog up!" Donna commanded her son.

With one hard kick, Warren's foot connected with Havoc and sent him sailing across the floor. A yip of pain and a dull thud sounded as the little dog's body connected with the wall then lay limp and lifeless on the floor.

Zoey cried out, in pain from her assailant and for the dog she adored. Warren Jr. had her petite body pulled tight against him, his meaty arm wrapped around her throat. She stood on her tiptoes, trying to keep her head above his arm and her airway open.

Edna turned her gaze to John, a silent look of understanding passing between them that they would do whatever it took to keep their granddaughter safe.

John lay on the floor, trapped by the heavy, cumbersome cast. Edna knew he would do what he could, but for now, he was basically useless. If anybody was going to save Zoey, it would have to be her. She wasn't a superhero, but Wonder Woman had nothing on a pissed-off grandma whose baby was in trouble.

Edna held up her hands in surrender to Warren. "Look, we don't want anyone to get hurt. Just tell us what you want."

"We want you to pay for what you did to my Warren." Donna spat the words out, venom in each syllable.

"And we want the money." Warren glanced at his mother. "Right, Mom? Remember, we want the money?"

Donna slowly bobbed her head up and down, her eyes glazed. "Yes. And we want the money. The money that you stole from us."

"Okay. How much do you want?" Edna slowly reached for her purse. It lay on the sofa next to her bridal bouquet, reminding her that less than an hour ago, she had felt the happiest of her life. "I can write you a check."

"What the hell am I going to do with a check? We want the cash." Warren's voice rose to a fevered pitch. His desperation was showing in the ragged breaths he took in and the wildness on the edge of his eyes.

Edna fought a wave of nausea, sure that she had a concussion, but desperate to get them out of this situation. She spoke slowly with a calming voice. "Look, Warren. I don't have that kind of cash here at the house, but I have fifty thousand dollars in my checking account. I'll write you a check for all of it, and you can take it to the bank right now and cash it. You can even leave your mom here with a gun on us if you want. I promise the check is good. It's the only way I can get you the money."

She watched him mulling over his options as she slowly reached for her handbag. Pulling it toward her, she gently eased her hand inside.

Warren yanked on Zoey's hair. "Does your granny really have fifty grand in the bank?"

Zoey's eyes were wide with fear. She nodded. "Yes. I'm sure she does. My grandfather left her a lot of money."

Donna cackled, letting loose another phlegm-riddled cough. "I'll just bet he did. I always knew Frank would do well. That's who I should have gone after. Not this piece of white trash who would never amount to anything."

How dare she call John white trash when her murderous son was holding a gun to a young woman's head. Edna wanted to rip her oxygen tank off her shoulder and shove it down her wrinkled old neck.

Deep breath. Focus. She needed to stay calm. She would only have one chance. "What's it gonna be? I'm not getting any younger. Do you want the check or not?"

Warren looked at his mother. "Can you keep them here until I get back? I don't know how else to get the money. And I don't want to go through all this just to go home empty-handed."

Donna sneered at her son. "Of course I can keep them here, but I can't promise that I won't shoot Edna before you get back. Especially if she keeps running off her stupid mouth."

Warren nodded at Edna. "Write the check."

Edna looked at her granddaughter, silently conveying a message with her eyes. "Zoey, do you remember that game that we used to play in the backyard when you were little? We'd get all the neighborhood kids together, and you could play that game for hours."

Zoey looked confused, then a light dawned in her eyes. A steely look of determination crossed her face, and she nodded at her grandmother.

Edna raised her purse, her hand still inside. She stared into the eyes of the man holding her granddaughter, his arm now slack against her throat. "Now!"

Zoey dropped to her knees, slipping from Warren's grasp.

A loud bang! A flash of light!

The bottom half of Edna's handbag exploded with gunfire and a red stain blossomed on Warren's chest.

Zoey was on her knees, scrambling toward her grandfather.

Donna screamed her son's name then crumpled to the floor—either in a faint, or she'd had a stroke. Edna didn't care. Let the old bat stroke out.

Warren clutched his chest, a look of confusion on his face. He raised his arm again, pointing the gun directly at Edna. He squeezed the trigger.

Bam! Another shot rang out.

Warren's arm flung back, the gun dropping from his hand.

Edna turned, her purse still in her hands, but she hadn't fired a shot.

Instead, she'd been saved by their best man. Standing in the kitchen doorway, his gun drawn, and looking handsome as ever, stood Officer McCarthy. He swept into the room, securing his gun and slapping handcuffs on Warren.

"Well, Mac, it's about time you got here." Edna dropped her purse and fell to her knees next to Johnny. He had pulled himself to where Havoc's body lay and drawn the little dog into his lap. "Is he hurt?"

The dog opened his eyes and shook his head. His tail gave a few weak wags, and he licked John's hand. "I don't think so. It must have just knocked him out when he hit the wall."

"I have a friend who's a vet. We'll have him come over and check him out." She tenderly touched John's cheek. "How about you? Are you okay?"

John nodded. "My pride's hurt more than anything else. I was trying to save you and instead, I had to lie on the floor and let you save me."

Edna picked up his hand and held it to her lips. "I'll let you save me the next time a maniac tries to kill us."

"It's a deal." John turned to his granddaughter, who still knelt by his side. "Are you all right?"

"I'm fine," Zoey said, grinning at Edna. "Thanks to my crazy grandmother who carries a gun in her purse."

"What was all that nonsense about playing a game in the backyard?" John asked. "I knew it had to be code for something, but I didn't get it."

Zoey laughed. "My favorite game as a kid was Duck, Duck, Goose. Gram would call over all the kids in the neighborhood to play with me. I knew what game she meant, and when she said 'now,' I was pretty sure she didn't want me to 'goose.'"

"You always were my smartest grandchild."

"I'm your *only* grandchild."

Edna affectionately pulled on a lock of her hair. "See how smart you are."

"I wish somebody would have been smart enough to call me," Mac said, shaking his head. "What the hell happened here?"

The sound of sirens could be heard in the distance, and Donna began to stir. Mac stepped around Edna and hooked on a set of handcuffs, connecting Donna's wrist to her walker.

He reached down and helped John to his feet, guiding him over to a spot on the sofa. "I've called an ambulance. We can have somebody check on you when they get here."

John waved him away. "I'm fine. They need to check on Eddy. She took a pretty hard hit to the noggin."

Mac reached over and lifted Edna's curly bangs.

Zoey gasped at the purple bruise surrounding the big knot on her grandmother's forehead. "Oh, Gram."

Edna pushed Mac's hand away. "Don't worry about me. I'm fine. But how did you know to come in when you did?"

"I got a call about Zoey's threatening text message, and I wanted to tell her about it. I went to Sunny's first, thinking she would be there setting up for the reception. They said they hadn't seen her in a while, but thought she'd come over here. I walked up to the door and saw Halloran through the window with a gun at Zoey's head. I snuck around the back and slipped in through the kitchen door. I just waited for the best time to take a shot." He flashed a grin at Edna. "But you and your purse beat me to it."

"What can I say? My purse is a good shot."

The ambulance pulled into the driveway, followed by two police cars. It seemed the whole Pleasant Valley police force showed up when shots were fired.

Mac opened the front door, and the room was flooded with paramedics and police officers. The Page Turners were right on their heels, and Sunny, Cassie, Maggie, and Piper rushed into the crowded living room and ran straight to Edna's side.

"Are you all right?" Sunny asked, pulling Edna into a hug.

Maggie looked around the room. "What the hell happened in here?"

The paramedics were assessing Donna, and they waited while one of the police officers unlocked the handcuffs connecting her to the walker.

Warren Jr. was cussing as they loaded him onto a stretcher and wheeled him from the room. A large red stain covered the carpet where he had fallen.

Cassie made a face at the blood-soaked rug. "You're going to have a heck of a time getting that stain out. Do you want me to start pre-treating it now?"

Edna waved her hand in dismissal. "Don't bother. I needed new carpet anyway."

Zoey grinned at her grandmother. "I guess you can afford it with all that money you've got stashed at the bank. Do you really have fifty thousand dollars just sitting in a checking account?"

"Heck no. I'm lucky if that account has *fifty* dollars in it."

"You were bluffing?" John asked. "Are you crazy, woman? What if he would have taken that check to the bank?"

"That was the idea. For one thing, it would have gotten the lunatic out of here, and if the three of us couldn't have overpowered one old lady with a walker and nursing pneumonia, then we deserved to be shot. Besides, this is a small town and everyone at the bank knows me. If he would have shown up wanting to cash a check from me for fifty grand, it would have raised all sorts of red flags and hopefully someone would have called in the police."

"That's an awful lot of presumptions on your part," John said.

"Well, it was all I had, and I didn't see anybody else coming up with a plan. And really, I just needed an excuse to get into my purse. I knew I had a gun in there, and I was ready to use it if I could just get a chance."

Edna watched through the open front door as the paramedics led Donna from the room and loaded her into the ambulance with her son. "I feel sorry for her. Nursing that grudge all these years. You should have seen her. I think she really had herself convinced that John was the one who shot Weasel, and not her."

She looked around the room at her friends and her new husband and clapped her hands together. "Well, now that they've taken the trash out, I think we've got a party to get to."

24

"You never told us what happened with the threatening messages on Zoey's phone," Edna said to Mac. She sat on the sofa in Sunny's living room, her hand resting on John's good leg as he sat beside her, his casted leg propped up on the coffee table.

It had been two hours since the ambulance had taken Donna and her son away, and the barbecue/wedding reception was winding to a close. Only a few guests remained. The book club, along with Moon, Zoey, and Mac now sat in her living room eating the wedding cake.

Jake, Jeremy, and Maggie's sons were cleaning up after the party and restoring the backyard.

Zoey sat on the floor, a worn-out Havoc snoozing in her lap. Edna's vet friend had stopped by to check on the dog. But by the time he arrived, Havoc had eaten half a hotdog and a watermelon rind, and was chasing a squirrel around Sunny's backyard.

The vet gave him a quick check-up, declared that the dog didn't seem any worse for wear, and left instructions to call him if they noticed anything unusual. Sunny sent him home with a big piece of wedding cake for his trouble.

Havoc raised his eyes, following the motion of Zoey's cake-filled fork as she lifted it to her mouth to take a bite. "Oh yeah, do you know who sent them?"

Mac nodded. "The Denver police picked up one of the Cavelli brothers and he had the phone on him. He admitted to leaving the messages, but claimed he was just trying to scare you." Mac balanced a plate full of cake on one knee and a purple cup of iced tea on the other. "The Denver PD is trying to get him on bigger charges, so they're using the harassment charge to hold him for a bit."

Mac took another bite of cake. "That's not the only thing my guys found out. We called the Coopersville PD back in Kansas and had them take a look at the house where Donna and her son live. They found the remains of Butch Halloran frozen solid in a freezer in the basement."

"What?" Zoey said, her shoulders shaking in an involuntary shudder. "Those people are crazy."

"Yes, they are. But they're not going to be bothering anyone else for a long time."

"That makes me feel a little better. I hope the press doesn't find out about my involvement in this case as well, or I'll never be able to return to my apartment."

"What a mess," Edna said to Zoey. "You're welcome to stay here as long as you like. In fact, it would be great if you stuck around a couple of days to watch my house and the dog while John and I sneak off for a quick honeymoon."

"Honeymoon?" Maggie asked. "Where are you going? Niagara Falls? You do realize he can barely walk, and you probably have a concussion? You're not going to be able to do a lot of sightseeing."

Edna looked at John and gave him a quick eye-brow wiggle. "Who said anything about sightseeing? This man's face is the only sight I want to see." She turned to Maggie and winked. "Besides, who said anything about leaving the room? There's still plenty of zippety left in this old doo-dah."

Maggie wrinkled her nose in disgust. "Ew. Don't ever say that again. I think I just threw up in my mouth."

Zoey laughed. "I'd be glad to stay at your house and keep an eye on Havoc. I'm not ready to head back to Denver yet."

"I can check in on you," Mac said. "I mean, if you want, just to make sure you're okay."

A hint of blush colored Zoey's cheeks as she smiled at the handsome police officer. "I'd like that."

Cassie threw a last handful of plates in the trash and wiped down the counters. "I still can't believe you're married."

"Me either." Piper was curled into the recliner, working on her second piece of cake. "But I'm happy for you."

"I am too," Sunny said, dropping onto the loveseat across from Edna and John. "Does it feel strange to have him here after all this time?"

"And after thinking he was dead?" Cassie asked.

"Yes," Edna replied, picking up John's hand and holding it in hers. "To both of those things. It is strange. And wonderful, at the same time. I was in shock when I first saw him, but so happy. And everything was so crazy right after he got here. It wasn't until later, I think when I was sitting in the hospital waiting for him to wake up, that I also realized how angry I was at him."

"Angry?" Moon asked. "What for?"

Edna sighed. "For everything. For the hurt he caused me by faking his own death. By not trusting me enough to tell me sooner that he was still alive. For not taking me with him when he left. And even now, when he came back and made me fall in love with him again I was angry that I finally let my heart feel again, and then he was going to die and leave me once more."

John lifted their joined hands to his lips and laid a kiss on her fingers. "I'm sorry, Eddy. I know that I hurt you."

"You did hurt me," Edna said, tears building in her eyes. "And I had to face that hurt and *choose* to forgive you. Life is full of choices and we're all human. We make good choices and bad ones, and we can either choose to hold on to the pain and mistakes of yesterday or let go of the past and focus on the joy of today. Having you back in my life brings me great joy. Life is too short to waste by dwelling on the past when the present holds so much happiness."

She turned to the Page Turners and looked at each in turn. To Sunny and Maggie and Cassie and Piper. "I've lived a long life, and I've made my share of mistakes, but what I've learned is that keeping your heart sealed off only causes it to suffocate and shrivel up like a raisin. You've got to put yourself out there. Fall in love and give your heart freely. That's what will bring you true happiness. Loving and being loved.

"Time is misleading. All we ever have is the now. We can't go back and relive the past, and though we can hope for a future, there's no guarantee of one. So we just go. We live today, and we go back to normal."

Sunny laughed. "As normal as the Page Turners can be."

Edna nodded, enjoying the role of sage advice-giver. "You're right. Normal is just a setting on the dryer. Instead, we choose to be happy. We live our lives. We do what we need to do. Piper needs to get enrolled in school. Cassie can go back to clipping coupons and entering contests. Sunny can finish summer break and fondle Jake's muscles. And Maggie can do whatever that thing is that she and her nerdy boyfriend do on the computer."

Maggie laughed. "And what about you, Edna? You've never been normal a day in your life. What will you go back to doing?"

Edna grinned as if she were the cat that had just eaten the canary. "I tried normal. It was boring. A few weeks ago, I was having a normal Monday morning, then a ghost showed up on my doorstep and love walked back into my life. This Monday, I'm forgetting normal and I'm going for spectacular."

She winked at her new husband. "And I can't wait to see what happens on Tuesday."

The End

MAKE SURE TO CHECK OUT ALL THE ADVENTURES OF THE PAGE TURNERS BOOK CLUB:

Another Saturday Night and I Ain't Got No Body
Book 1 of the Page Turners Series
On Amazon: http://amzn.com/B00AQPJ924
On Amazon UK: http://www.amazon.co.uk/dp/B00AQPJ924

Easy Like Sunday Mourning
Book 2 of the Page Turners Series
On Amazon: http://amzn.com/B00HUTZLG2
On Amazon UK: http://www.amazon.co.uk/dp/B00HUTZLG2

Be the first to find out when the newest Page Turners Novel is releasing and hear all the latest news and updates happening with the Page Turners book club by signing up for the newsletter at:
Jenniemarts.com

If you enjoyed this book, please consider leaving a review!

ACKNOWLEDGEMENTS

First and foremost, I must always thank my husband, Todd. For believing in me, for supporting me, and for loving me through it all.

My family means everything to me and I thank my sons, Tyler and Nick for their support of my writing career.

A special thanks goes out to my mom, Lee Cumba, for her invaluable support of this book. Thanks Mom, for listening to hours of plot lines and working through countless ideas of how to make this story better.

I have an amazing group of proofreaders and beta-readers, who will drop everything and read my books as soon as I call. Each has their own skills and they find commas, legal issues, plot holes, and logistical impossibilities. My books benefit greatly from their keen eyes, support, advice and grammar knowledge. Thanks to Carla Albers, Lee Cumba, Julie Feuerbach, Terry Gregson, Linda Kay, Jean Slane, and Joelle Whinnery.

A special shout-out goes to my critique partner, Robin Nolet. Her help and critiques were invaluable. Thanks Robin, for being fast, efficient, and full of great ideas.

I am blessed to be surrounded by an awesome group of writers who continuously offer guidance, support and critique help. I would be lost without the friendship and support of Michelle Major, Lana Williams, Annie MacFarlane, the Colorado Indie Authors and the Mason Jar Indies.

Big thanks goes out to Arran McNicol of Editing 720 for his mad editing skills.

I cannot say enough about the Killion Group and their amazing work with my covers and marketing material. My thanks goes out to Kim Killion and Jennifer Jakes for your fast and efficient work. I value your creativity, your advice and most of all, your friendship.

My biggest thanks goes out to my readers! Thanks for loving my stories and my characters and for asking for Edna's book. I am making each of you an honorary member of the Page Turners Book Club! And I can't wait to share the next Page Turners novel with you.

ABOUT THE AUTHOR

Jennie Marts loves to make readers laugh as she weaves stories filled with love, friendship and intrigue. Jennie writes for Entangled Publishing and she's the Kindle Bestselling author of the Page Turners series, which includes the romantic comedies: **Another Saturday Night and I Ain't Got No Body, Easy Like Sunday Mourning** and **Just Another Maniac Monday.** Reviewers call her books "laugh out loud" funny and full of great characters that are "endearing and relatable."

She writes from the mountains of Colorado where she lives with her husband, two sons, a golden retriever named Cooper and a new Sheltie puppy named Maggie. Jennie enjoys being a member of (RWA) Romance Writers of America, The Colorado Indies, and Pikes Peak Writers.

Jennie is addicted to Diet Coke and adores Cheetos. She loves playing volleyball and believes you can't have too many books, shoes or friends.

Jennie loves to hear from readers. Follow her on Facebook at Jennie Marts Books , or Twitter at @JennieMarts.

Visit her at www.jenniemarts.com and subscribe to her newsletter for the latest on new releases and to find out the current happenings with the Pleasant Valley Page Turners.

JUST ANOTHER MANIAC MONDAY

Printed in Great Britain
by Amazon